THABITI M. ANYABWILE

Foreword by MARK A. NOLL

THE DECLINE OF AFRICAN AMERICAN THEOLOGY

From Biblical Faith
to Cultural Captivity

IVP Academic

An imprint of InterVarsity Press
Downers Grove, Illinois

InterVarsity Press
P.O. Box 1400, Downers Grove, IL 60515-1426
World Wide Web: www.ivpress.com
E-mail: email@ivpress.com

Design: Cindy Kiple
Images: pastor and child: Sinden Collier/Getty Images
black and white print: Library of Congress Prints and Photographs Division

ISBN 978-0-8308-2827-2

Printed in the United States of America ∞

Library of Congress Cataloging-in-Publication Data

Anyabwile, Thabiti M., 1970-
  The decline of African American theology: from biblical faith to cultural captivity / Thabiti M. Anyabwile.
    p. cm.
  Includes bibliographical references and index.
  ISBN-13: 978-0-8308-2827-2 (pbk.: alk. paper)
  1. Black theology. 2. African Americans—Religion—History. 3. United States—Church history. I. Title.
  BT82.7.A592007
  230.089'96073—dc22

                                                                    2007031445

P 21 20 19 18 17 16 15 14 13 12 11 10 9 8 7
Y 25 24 23 22 21 20 19 18 17 16 15

For Christ Jesus who purchased me with his own blood.

To the saints of African American heritage—gifts to the entire Body of Christ.

To the women in my life: Kristie, Afiya, Eden, Frances and Joyce.

To my son: Titus Ezekiel.

Contents

Foreword

It is remarkable that, to my knowledge, there has never been a book that attempts what Thabiti Anyabwile's *The Decline of African American Theology* attempts. For historical purposes, the book makes an unusually valuable contribution with its full account of the course of African American Christian thought. Theologically, it makes another signal contribution with its critique of the general development of that thought. For both historical and theological reasons, this is a very important volume.

As a survey of historical theology, it offers an expert, well-contextualized, and very nicely organized survey of a truly important topic. Its treatment of six areas of doctrine is as clear as the doctrines are important. For some of the individuals treated here, more extensive material is available elsewhere, but I do not think that anyone has *put together* such a serious reading of so many sources, and done it so well. For a few of the figures (especially Jupiter Hammon and, surprisingly, the notable nineteenth-century Bishop Daniel Alexander Payne), what Rev. Anyabwile provides is some of the best exposition of these figures available. To be sure, there might be some omissions that could be filled in if this were to be a life's work of 1,000 pages (for example, there is nothing on the pioneering Reformed Baptist, David George). A full roster of other worthies—Daniel Coker, Richard Allen, David Walker, Henry Highland Garnett, Henry McNeal Turner, and Martin Luther King Jr.—are mentioned only in passing. But for a book of reasonable size, the coverage is very broad. Especially the treatments of Jupiter Hammon, Lemuel Haynes, Bishop Payne, William Seymour, Marcus Garvey, Howard Thurman, James Cone, and T. D. Jakes are outstanding. To see such figures considered together makes for a superb contribution to the historical understanding of African American theology throughout the whole of American history.

How Rev. Anyabwile himself interprets the theological history he narrates so well will not please all readers, since he makes that interpretation from his position as a firm Reformed theologian of the old Puritan school. Yet since the book clearly differentiates between historical exposition and theological critique, the perspective of the author does not prevent readers of any sort from benefiting from the whole. Indeed, Rev. Anyabwile's interpretation of this history makes an important theological contribution of its own and should be the right kind of challenge for all readers. The firmly Reformed will much appreciate it; those that lean in that direction (like myself), or that lean against it, will be encouraged to think more carefully about normative theological judgments; while those who strongly oppose such a Reformed view (like strong Arminians, strong modernists, strong liberationists, strong health-and-wealthists) might be quite irritated. This result is not a problem. In fact, because the book is written from a well-defined angle, it actually gives readers purchase for understanding the historical survey and reacting to Rev. Anyabwile's judgments.

Along the way, one of the most interesting of many provocative matters is to see how the paranormal and the theological coincided in African American history. In a word, it is remarkable that dreams, visions, and disembodied voices often communicated to more-or-less illiterate audiences (often kept illiterate by the malice of masters) a picture of the Christian faith that was very close to what Bible-believing readers and careful theologians also held. Of many such insights on individual thinkers and topics, this book is full. Because I have already learned so much from its pages, I am delighted to recommend it wholeheartedly to others.

Mark A. Noll
Francis A. McAnaney Professor of History
University of Notre Dame

Acknowledgments

I am greatly indebted to a number of people who offered great guidance, encouragement, time and support to this project.

I have found a virtuous woman, and quite amazingly she has condescended to be my wife! Without the grace of God shown in large measure to me through my wife, this book would not be finished. Chief among those that I must acknowledge is my beloved Kristie. Sweetie, "I see you in my eyes."

If any man should be blessed by God in this life to appropriately use the term "friend," he will have met with the kind of people who leave lasting, formative and positive impressions upon his life. He will have encountered tangible expressions of God's love. The completion of this project is owed to God having placed in my life such "friends."

Many thanks are owed to Mark Dever, pastor of Capitol Hill Baptist Church in Washington, D.C., a friend and colaborer in the gospel. Mark challenged me to work on this project in earnest and provided faithful spiritual care to me during the years of work on this book. He is a faithful shepherd and a dear brother.

Mark Dever also introduced me to Mark Noll, who took time during a busy sabbatical to comment on some early outlines for the chapters of this book. In addition to the praise I and the Christian world owe God for the voluminous and edifying works of Mark Noll, I am incredibly grateful for his encouragement and support on this project. And I am thankful for what I pray is the start of a lasting friendship as well.

Any man with the privilege of calling C. J. Mahaney a "friend" is a man blessed of God indeed. I've learned more about godliness, service, love of family and church from C. J. Mahaney than perhaps anyone. And God placed it in C. J.'s heart to cultivate "evidences of grace" in my life and this project. I am thankful to the Father for C. J.

At the completion of this project, two churches stand out as great models of Christian family, love and support in the body of Christ. Members of Capitol Hill Baptist Church and First Baptist Church of Grand Cayman have prayed for this work, read many drafts, commented, edited and in most every way imaginable made this a better book. I praise God for his body in both places and I thank him for the way both families have impacted and shaped my life.

Special thanks are owed to Joel Scandrett at InterVarsity Press who worked so faithfully and patiently to bring this book to completion.

Then there is the crew of men who stir me on to love and good deeds. They are many and they are loved. I thank and praise God for Rickey Armstrong, J. R. Scott, Ken Jones Jr., Anthony Carter, Sherrard Burns, Michael Leach, Peter Rochelle, the elders at First Baptist Church and Capitol Hill Baptist Church, Derrick Scott, Randy Scott, and Louis Love for their faithful labors and their friendships in Christ.

Figures

Introduction

The church is perhaps the most studied organism in history and the social sciences. This general statement is no less true for the African American church. Over the years, many scholars have probed the origins, functions and activities of the African American church. For the most part, these authors and their studies have been concerned with locating the African American church in particular historical contexts and discerning its contribution to black social and civic life.

While the works of W. E. B. DuBois, E. Franklin Frazier, C. Eric Lincoln, and others have been particularly well received and useful for understanding the church in historical and sociological terms, the seminal work of these writers and others has stopped well short of tracing the *theological* understandings and contributions of African Americans and the African American church. In other words, what should be studied as the most central characteristic of the church—its theology—has been for the most part neglected by scholarly research and writing. The thing that makes the church the church—its understanding of God's nature, work and interaction with man—has not received sufficient attention as either a subject unto itself or as a motivating factor in more plentiful historical and sociological studies. As James Cone insists, "A community that does not analyze its existence theologically is a community that does not care what it says or does. It is a community with no identity."[1]

The present work is an attempt to contribute to much-needed theological reflection both *inside* the African American context and *between* African American and other ethnic communities. By "theology," I generally mean the

---

[1]James H. Cone, *A Black Theology of Liberation, Twentieth Anniversary Edition* (Maryknoll, N.Y.: Orbis, 1986), pp. 8-9.

study and knowledge of God. Moreover, this book is concerned with *Christian* theology in the African American context rather than the broader topic of African American religion, so it takes the Bible as the authoritative and normative source for theology. The term *theology* is applied to academic discourse (e.g., systematic theologies), applied or practical works (e.g., sermons and lectures), and to what might be called Christian folk thought (e.g., slave songs and testimonies). To be certain, varying levels of specificity and elasticity of concepts are found in these repositories of African American Christian theology. Nonetheless, the academic, practical and folk productions reveal much about how African Americans think about, experience and explain the nature and ways of God in the world. From them a more robust picture emerges for consideration. Here, then, "theology" is what is believed, taught and confessed in various forms by African Americans.[2]

The presentation of a coherent study of the theological reflections and contributions of African Americans and the African American church must take advantage of and set in dialogue various sources. A survey of African American theology is immediately confronted by either the absence of African Americans *doing* theology or the relative lack of source material from the earliest periods. In contrast to the development of the white European and American churches from the 1500-1900s, the African American church was not primarily engaged in the production of written intellectual theology *per se*. For much of this period, African Americans were either barred from the academies of theology or legally prohibited from acquiring an education of any sort. In addition, many of those who escaped the educational and physical oppression of slavery in the U.S. chose very different educational and career paths. Consequently, the early African American church is largely without a cadre of technical, writing theologians; thus an easy approach to surveying African American theology via a review of such writings is not available for the

[2]Here, I'm following the framework advanced by Jaroslav Pelikan in his magisterial five-volume history of Christian doctrine, *The Christian Tradition: A History of the Development of Doctrine* (Chicago: University of Chicago Press, 1971-1991), pp. 1-10. Pelikan identifies what is "believed" as the doctrines present in devotion, spirituality and worship; what is "taught" as the content of the word of God extracted by exegesis and communicated through proclamation and instruction; and what is "confessed" as the testimony of the church in polemics, apologetics, creed and dogma. This corresponds roughly to the professional writings of academic theology; the sermons and teachings of Christian leaders; and the songs, poetry and other literary work of African Americans in this present volume.

earliest period of that history. One is left to extract from other sources a summary of the beliefs expressed in narrative, testimony and song.

But despite the absence of academic theologians, one should not conclude that African Americans were either uneducated theologically or completely inactive in theological reflection. In the African American experience, the persons most likely "doing" theology were preachers and civic leaders as opposed to the academically trained theologians of the "white church." While European and American theologians contended with intellectual threats to Christian theology, African Americans developed their theological understandings in the crucible of the slave experience. Early African American Christian theology was birthed and grew up in the context of American chattel slavery and the Colonial experience. Consequently, one has to look not in the academy but in sermons, slave narratives, political speeches and popular writings for traces of the early beliefs of African Americans since the 1700s. In these sources one can trace a set of theological ideas and convictions arguably as important and influential in lived experience than more precise, academic statements. These sources vary in depth, intention and representativeness, but are collectively a good collage of African American beliefs. And when set in "dialogue" with later academic theologians, great potential for tracing a story emerges—a story not necessarily of cause and effect, but of vision and revision based to some degree on the historical and social settings in which African Americans found themselves.

Premise. The present work attempts to trace the development of African American theology from its earliest manifestations in the slave narratives, slave songs, sermons and popular writings from the 1700s to current reflections and contributions. The white evangelical church of the 1700s is largely credited with giving birth to the African American church in the plantation south. Missionaries and evangelists associated with Baptist and Methodist churches were the first to make successful inroads into the religious lives of African Americans. Contrary to what might be supposed given the prohibition of education, reading and writing among slaves, early black Christians evidenced a rather sophisticated and clear theological corpus of thought. This clarity of early theological insight produced perhaps the most authentic expression of Christianity in American history, forming the basis for the African American church's engagement in both the propagation of the gospel and social justice activism.

However, over time, especially following emancipation from slavery through the Civil Rights era, the theological basis for the church's activist character was gradually lost and replaced with a secular foundation. The church became less critical theologically and increasingly more concerned with social, political and educational agendas. Disentangled from its evangelical and Reformed theological upbringing, the church became motivated by a quest for justice for justice's sake rather than by the call and mandate of God as expressed in more biblical understandings of Christianity. Secularization overtook the African American church, along with its "white" counterpart.

As secularization took root, the predominant framework for understanding the African American church shifted from theology to sociology and was influenced by the work of W. E. B. DuBois, E. Franklin Frazier, and others. With an emphasis on a sociological framework for studying the church, the African American church came to be understood primarily as a social institution and self-help organization with a vague spiritual dimension, rather than as a spiritual organism born of God's activity in the world. This is not to imply that the church has not always played a major role in educational, social and political agendas, but to point out the loss of a God-centered understanding of why such pursuits were appropriate for the church.

As a consequence of theological drift and erosion, the black church now stands in danger of losing its relevance and power to effectively address *both* the spiritual needs of its communicants *and* the social and political aspirations of its community. In effect, cultural concerns captured the church and supplanted the biblical faithfulness that once characterized it. It has lost the law and the gospel, and stands in danger of lapsing into spiritual rigor mortis. The present work is undertaken as a reminder to the church of its rich theological past and as a call for the church to reclaim its effectiveness by returning to a proper theocentric view of itself and the world.

Method. Were the theological contributions of several African American theologians and church leaders abundant and codified according to the traditional themes of Christian theology, especially from 1700-1900, one might simply review the work of these leading thinkers. However, for much of African American church history an easily identifiable corpus is not readily available, making the work of historical theology more difficult.

An undertaking of this type requires a method that is one part historical and one part literary review. Mark Noll has outlined the history and important shifts in American Protestant evangelical Christianity and identified five periods: the Revolutionary era, evangelicalism, and second Great Awakening (1750-1800); the rise of "evangelical America" and American denominationalism (1800-1865); the decline of Protestant America (1865-1920); the emergence of Modernism and Liberalism (1920-1960); and the Civil Rights era and Postmodernism (1960-present). These periods of American and church history provide an important backdrop for understanding the interaction of African American theology with the ideas of other segments of Christianity and philosophy.[3]

The present work adopts a historical framework that roughly aligns the timelines of the African American experience with Protestant, evangelical Christianity in America and Europe. I have opted for this framework (1) as a method for displaying the convergence and departure of these two Christian traditions and (2) as a method for locating important literary works and thinkers in the context of broader church history. Each chapter is organized into five periods:[4]

Early Slavery Era Through Abolition Era (1600-1865)

Reconstruction, "Jim Crow" Segregation, Great Migration and the "New Negro" Movement (1865-1929)

Depression and World War II (1930-1949)

Civil Rights Era (1950-1979)

End of Century, Postmodern Era (1980-present)

Significant shifts in the treatment, freedom and mobility of African Americans characterize each period of African American history. For each era, the major theological contributions of key African American thinkers, preachers and writers are examined for their representativeness of, and impact on, the trajectory of the black church's theology. One key criterion for selecting persons for inclusion was the availability of a body of written material to survey.

---

[3]Mark A. Noll, *A History of Christianity in the United States and Canada* (Grand Rapids: Eerdmans, 1992).
[4]Adapted from Milton C. Sernett, *African American Religious History: A Documentary Witness* (Durham, N.C.: Duke University Press, 1999), pp. 482-87.

The volume attempts to present these thinkers and leaders "in their own words," so written materials were essential. This selection criterion produced some lamentable omissions. For example, Richard Allen is arguably one of the most important figures in African American Christian history. Yet, he receives only passing treatment because not much of his theological and sermon material remains. But on the whole, the figures included not only left source material but also exerted significant influence on their peers and subsequent generations.

I attempt to maintain some continuity of themes (doctrines) across each time period by examining the contributions of key thinkers to the doctrines of revelation, God, man, Jesus Christ, salvation and the Holy Spirit through each era of African American history. The evolution of the church's doctrinal understanding of these themes is examined with particular emphasis on points of convergence and divergence from historical orthodox Christian theology.[5] Orthodox Christian theology, a Reformed theology in particular, serves as the baseline for judging the strength of African American beliefs for two reasons. First, the earliest generation of African American writers generally held to a broadly Reformed perspective as a result of their early contact with Calvinistic Baptist and Anglican missionaries and because this theology shaped the wider Colonial and American society at the hands of New England Puritans. Second, the Reformed understanding, especially the Reformed doctrines of revelation, God and salvation, best represent the biblical teaching on these subjects. So, for historical and theological reasons the Reformed heritage of African Americans is used as the starting point for tracking the decline in African American ideas about God.

A Reformed starting point and bias notwithstanding, an attempt is made to let the writers speak for themselves by resisting the temptation to impose an interpretation on the authors' words. Too much of the work that focuses on the theological perspectives of slave testimonies, for example, superimposes meanings and conclusions not clearly present in the original texts. To the best

---

[5]By "historical orthodox Christian theology" I refer to that body of teaching generally accepted by Christians throughout church history and generally reflected in the great ecumenical creeds and confessions of the church before the great split of Roman and Eastern Orthodox churches. I also refer to the recovery of biblical truth achieved during the Protestant Reformation of the 1500s and 1600s which placed emphasis on the authority and sufficiency of Scripture in matters of faith and conduct and "justification by grace alone through faith alone in Christ alone for the glory of God alone."

of my ability, I have let authorial intent govern the presentation of included perspectives. I have tried to first make clear what an author intends to say in a given work and only after doing so to then evaluate the contribution and impact of that work on the strength or weakness of theology in African American Christianity. Without doubt, I have done this imperfectly and only ask the reader to charge any errors to my head and not to my heart.

The emphasis throughout the book is not on a detailed social, political or ecclesial history, but on the theological ideas themselves. So, the chapters are organized according to the typical heads of a systematic theology. Some readers will want more historical detail. For them, I've attempted to call attention to general references that may be helpful. The choice to organize the chapters by the theological headings leads to some repetition, but I pray any redundancy is outweighed by the potential of learning from the writers and sources as they're set in "dialogue" over these major theological issues. Moreover, I pray that the organization of the book helps shift the focus and conversation in the church to theology itself and to some extent away from history.

Each chapter concludes with a reflection on the slide from orthodoxy to cultural captivity occurring over the three hundred years of African American Christianity and an assessment of the impacts that slide made on the black church. Some consider African American theology to have been without critique for most of its history.[6] Certainly there will be many who disagree with some of the critiques offered. Perhaps the concluding comments in each chapter will provide some stimulus for the beginning or expansion of critique and discussion across various traditions.

My hope and prayer is that this work might contribute to a reformation among African American churches, where sound theology is recovered and once again given prominence in our understanding of church history and in our contemporary practice. African Americans are a people who care deeply about history. I pray that this volume contributes significantly to our understanding of this rich theological heritage while providing critical insights for reassessment and careful appropriation of biblical truth. And most impor-

---

[6]For example, see Ken Jones, "The History of the Black Church," Carl F. H. Henry Forum Lecture delivered October 26, 2003, at the Capitol Hill Baptist Church in Washington, D.C. Available at <www.capitolhillbaptist.org>.

tantly, I pray that this small volume would in some measure bring glory to God the Father and his beloved Son Jesus Christ, who loved the world in such a way as to shed his own blood for the redemption of our souls.

Soli Deo Gloria.

1

"I Once Was Blind, but Now I See"

The Doctrine of Revelation
in the African American Experience

But can mortal man behold him? The eagle veils his eyes
before he can gaze upon the unclouded sun.
Who then can gaze upon the visage of that God
whose shadow illumines the sun, and who covers
himself with light, as with a garment?
Nevertheless the pure in heart shall see God.
They shall see him in all his works of nature, providence, and grace.
They see him alike in the minute insect, and huge elephant;
in the sagacious mocking bird and the stupid ostrich.
They see him sprinkling the earth with flowers,
and gilding the firmament with stars!
They see him walking with Shadrack, Meshack, and Abednego,
in the fiery furnace, and sitting with Daniel in the lion's den.
They see him while a babe in the manger, and a man
quelling the raging sea amid the howling storm!
They see him amid the lightnings and thunders of Sinai,
and amid the tears, the groans, and the blood of Calvary!

BISHOP DANIEL ALEXANDER PAYNE

GENERAL INTRODUCTION AND CONTEXT

How does one know God? How can his divine will be apprehended and followed? Is it possible to truly know something of the character of the divine Creator? Can we know God in any way other than through sacred writings and traditions?

These questions are not new, neither were they new at the dawning of African American religious history. Every people and culture in human history struggled to find satisfactory answers to this epistemological problem—how does one know? And more specifically, how does one know *God?*

General revelation: God revealed in nature and conscience. Historically, Protestant Christianity resolved the problem of knowing, particularly knowing God, by considering two sources: general and special revelation. The doctrine of general revelation held that God left his imprimatur on the design of the universe and in the conscience and moral laws of humanity. So, the psalmist proclaimed that "the heavens declare the glory of God" (Ps 19:1), and the apostle Paul asserted, "since the creation of the world God's invisible qualities—his eternal power and divine nature—have been clearly seen, being understood from what has been made" (Rom 1:20). According to the doctrine of general revelation, the Creator communicated something of his person and divine will through the created order, including the conscience and moral laws ingrained in the individual and human society. With application of reason, then, the natural order reveals God in a real and true sense.

However, Christian theologians through the ages taught that while general revelation was enough to apprehend God in some sense, to know that he exists, humanity needed another form of revelation to better comprehend God's specific attributes and will. For example, Jonathan Edwards (1703-1758), opposing the Enlightenment's emphasis on human reason, illustrated the limits of human reason by pointing to the inability of one person to know the unexpressed thoughts of another. "We find that the things of men cannot be known by other men any further than they reveal or declare them." The same must be true, Edwards reasoned, of God. "So says the apostle it is with the things of God that we are told in the gospel. They are things that concern God himself, his secret counsels and sovereign will, and things in himself which he alone can be supposed to see and be conscious to immediately. And therefore, our reason will not help us to see them any further than God's Spirit is pleased to reveal."[1] Edwards argued that to make reason the final arbiter of divine truth was to subordinate God's rule and make the fallacious claim that fallen human reason was a better guide in spiritual things. Reason had an important role in determining whether Scripture was divine in origin and infallible in content; however, once that was established Edwards argued that "modesty and humility and reverence to God require that we allow that God is better able to declare to us what is agreeable to that perfection than we are to declare to him or ourselves. Reason tells us that God is just, but God is better able to tell what acts are agreeable to that justice than we are."[2]

The typical view expressed by Edwards and others in the early Colonial era held sway through much of the country's history. For example, Princeton theologian Archibald Alexander (1772-1851), refuting rationalist tendencies coming from Unitarians of his day, concluded, "we must unequivocally deny to reason the high office of deciding at her bar what doctrines of Scripture are to be received and what not" and "insist that all opinions, pretensions, experiences, and practices must be judged by the standard of the Word of God."[3] The Princeton theologians, from Alexander to B. B. Warfield (1851-1921), exalted the supremacy of divine revelation over human reason and natural revelation well into the 1900s.

Special revelation: God revealed most clearly in Scripture and in Jesus Christ. The doctrine of special revelation answered the church's need for more particular or specific information regarding the character and plans of God, his commands for his people, and the way of salvation. The Bible, in both the Old and the New Testaments, contained this special revelation of God. It, the church held, recorded God's work in history to redeem and save a covenant people for himself. The pages of Scripture unveiled the attributes of God—his wisdom, omnipotence, holiness, mercy, love, supremacy, sovereignty, justice, etc.—in sufficient clarity for human beings to know and relate to him with ac-

---

[1] Jonathan Edwards, "Ministers to Preach Not Their Own Wisdom but the Word of God," (May 7, 1740), in *The Salvation of Souls: Nine Previously Unpublished Sermons on the Call of Ministry and the Gospel by Jonathan Edwards*, ed. Richard A. Bailey and Gregory A. Wills (Wheaton, Ill.: Crossway, 2002), p. 115.

[2] Ibid., p. 127.

[3] Archibald Alexander, *A Sermon Delivered at the Opening of the General Assembly of the Presbyterian Church in the United States, May 1808*, as excerpted in Mark Noll, *The Princeton Theology, 1812-1921: Scripture, Science and Theological Method from Archibald Alexander to Benjamin Warfield* (Grand Rapids: Baker Academic, 2001), pp. 53-54.

curacy and for their eternal redemption. In the Bible, one observed God revealing himself in and through the history of his people. In the Bible, prophets and apostles spoke and wrote the very oracles of God as they heard "the word of the Lord" coming to them, interacted with angelic messengers, or received visions directly from God.

And ultimately, Jesus Christ embodied all the truth of divine revelation, and was himself the message of God to fallen humanity. Where general revelation provided an awareness of the existence of God as demonstrated by his creation, special revelation particularized who this God was in his triune character, what his intentions were vis-à-vis humanity and history, and how God and humanity could be joined in meaningful relationship. The pages of Scripture contained this message and provided the one sure means of knowing the person and mind of God. In these pages, God disclosed himself and crossed the epistemological chasm between his infinite existence and humanity's finite reason.

The principal representatives of the main Protestant churches in the American colonies brought with them these formulations of general and special revelation, doctrines that served generations of Christians before them. This way of knowing—via Scripture and general revelation—provided the foundation for the ordering of society in matters religious, political, scientific, economic and social. Owing to a theological consensus forged over a nearly two-hundred-year period by Reformation thinkers and European churchmen, the American colonies began their experiment "under the Puritan canopy,"[4] which subscribed to this two-source view of revelation.

The African American church and its doctrine of revelation first emerged and developed in the shelter of this canopy, but it also fed on input from other sources. Eugene Genovese observed, "Afro-American religion arose from a conjuncture of many streams—African, European, classic Judeo-Christian, and Amerindian—but pre-eminently it emerged as a Christian faith both black and American."[5] How these "streams" shaped the African American doctrine of revelation is the subject of this chapter.

[4]Mark Noll, *America's God: From Jonathan Edwards to Abraham Lincoln* (New York: Oxford University Press, 2002), see chapters 2 and 3.
[5]Eugene Genovese, *Roll, Jordan, Roll: The World the Slaves Made* (New York: Vintage Books, 1976), p. 209.

EARLY SLAVERY ERA THROUGH ABOLITION ERA (1600-1865)

African American Christians in the northern colonies stood as heirs of the Puritan and evangelical tradition of divine revelation. The orthodox consensus regarding special and general revelation reigned from the founding of African American literature in the works of Jupiter Hammon to the end of slavery in the essays of Bishop Daniel A. Payne.

Jupiter Hammon: A characteristic orthodox view of the Bible and its authority. Jupiter Hammon (1711-1806?), for example, expressed a cogent and characteristically orthodox view of the Bible and its authority. Hammon, at the age of forty-nine, became the first African American to publish a work of literature. A slave his entire life, Jupiter Hammon worked as a clerk and bookkeeper for the wealthy slave trading Lloyd family of Long Island, New York. Young Hammon probably benefited from Anglican missionary educational efforts established in the Oyster Bay area of Long Island. In addition, through the Lloyd family's economic and cultural ties to Boston, Hartford, New York and London, Hammon had access to literature and works of theology.[6]

"A devout evangelical Christian, Hammon had been converted during the earliest stirrings of the Great Awakening."[7] His Christian convictions likely received reinforcements under the Quaker ministrations of William Burling (1678-1743) of Long Island and abolitionist John Woolman (1720-1772) who visited Oyster Bay on at least three occasions. The Quakers of Oyster Bay and Philadelphia published Hammon's *Address to the Negroes in the State of New York* with a posthumous acknowledgment of close association with Hammon. Sondra O'Neale observes that "as a writer [Hammon] used Christianity and its foundation of biblical language, allusion, and imagery to mount a public assault against slavery. He left four poems, two essays, and a sermon, however that offering includes the first, and most comprehensive statement of black theology as well as the earliest antislavery protests by a black writer in all of American literature." And yet, as O'Neale concludes, "Hammon's dual commitment to Christianity and freedom has been either undervalued or ignored."[8] To recover a historical understanding of African American theology,

---

[6]Sondra O'Neale, *Jupiter Hammon and the Biblical Beginnings of African-American Literature* (Metuchen, N.J.: American Library Association, 1993), pp. 1-39.
[7]Ibid., p. 1.
[8]Ibid.

then, the pattern of ignoring or undervaluing Jupiter Hammon must be reversed.

In *An Address to the Negroes in the State of New York*, Hammon wrote:

> The Bible is the word of God and tells you what you must do to please God; it tells you how you may escape misery and be happy forever. If you see most people neglect the Bible, and many that can read never look into it, let it not harden you and make you think lightly of it and that it is a book of no worth. All those who are really good love the Bible and meditate on it day and night. In the Bible, God has told us everything it is necessary we should know in order to be happy here and hereafter. The Bible is the mind and will of God to men.[9]

Hammon's contention that "the Bible is the word of God and everything in it is true" indicated his subscription to the orthodox view of inspiration and infallibility. The words of Scripture were, according to the orthodox view, literally God-breathed or inspired (2 Tim 3:16). And given that they originated with an omniscient God, they were also without error in all that they recorded. Accordingly, Hammon urged his hearers to devote themselves to learning to read so that they may "study it day and night."[10] Hammon's views were characteristic of most African American Christians of the period. This view of the Bible as special revelation held sway among African American Christians during the antebellum period and would remain largely unchallenged until African Americans gained access to the liberal schools of theology that emerged in the late 1800s and prospered through the mid-1900s.

Daniel Alexander Payne. Daniel Alexander Payne (1811-1893) was born February 24, 1811, to London and Martha Payne, free blacks in Charleston, South Carolina, during the height of slavery. Immediately following his birth, the elder Paynes dedicated their son to the work of the Lord; however, neither Payne would live to see their hopes fulfilled. London Payne died when Daniel was just over four years old, and Martha followed her husband in death just five years later. Raised by his grandmother, Daniel became a voracious student, devouring every subject of learning he could find. Between the ages of eight and fifteen, young Daniel received educational instruction from the Minor's

---

[9]Jupiter Hammon, *Address to the Negroes in the State of New York*, in Sondra O'Neale, *Jupiter Hammon and the Biblical Beginnings of African-American Literature*, pp. 237-38.
[10]Ibid., p. 239.

Moralist Society and a popular Charleston schoolmaster named Thomas S. Bonneau. While employed as an apprentice to local shoe and carpentry merchants, Daniel taught himself Greek, Latin and Hebrew. By age nineteen, Daniel Alexander Payne opened and operated a school for both slave and free Africans in South Carolina until the South Carolina General Assembly forced the closure of the school in 1835.[11]

Sleepless, loaded with disappointment, failing in prayer and doubting the existence and justice of God, Payne closed the school on March 31, 1835, and shortly thereafter moved north from South Carolina to New York. While in New York, Payne received encouragement to further education and training at the Lutheran Theological Seminary in Gettysburg, Pennsylvania, where he received a Protestant theological education. In June of 1837, after initially resisting any call into full-time Christian ministry, Daniel Alexander Payne was licensed by the Lutheran Church and fully ordained about two years later by the Synod at Fordsboro, New York. He was a little over twenty-six years old.[12]

In the winter of 1841, he joined the African Methodist Episcopal (AME) Church and by 1843 the AME church received him into full connection. Payne made his most significant contributions to the Christian church during his time as a pastor and later a bishop of the AME church. In particular, Payne's tireless efforts to reform the character and educational quality of the African American pastorate earned him the moniker "Apostle of Education to the Negro as well as the Apostle to Educators in the A.M.E. Church."[13]

Payne's view of the Bible. Bishop Payne's view of the Bible corresponded with that of Jupiter Hammon and evangelical America. In his most famous address, *Welcome to the Ransomed*, given on the occasion of the District of Columbia's emancipation of slaves, Payne exhorted his hearers to "rest not until you have learned to read the Bible."[14] His estimation of the Scriptures resonated with that of most African Americans during the time. Quoting Psalm 19:7-10, he concluded that the judgments, statutes and laws of the Bible,

---

[11]Daniel Alexander Payne, *Recollections of Seventy Years* (Nashville: AME Sunday School Union, 1888), pp. 11-40.

[12]Ibid.

[13]Benjamin F. Lee, "The Centenary of Daniel Alexander Payne, Fourth Bishop of the African Methodist Episcopal Church," *Church Review* 28, no. 1 (July 1911): 423-29.

[14]Daniel Alexander Payne, *Welcome to the Ransomed, or, Duties of the Colored Inhabitants of the District of Columbia* (Baltimore: Bull & Tuttle, 1862), p. 7.

"Yield uniform, implicit obedience to their teachings. They will purify your hearts and make them the abodes of the Ever-Blessed Trinity."[15] According to Payne, apart from obeying divine law, the recently freed slaves could not hope to obey human law. In his autobiography, Payne explained the relationship between Scripture, on the one hand, and moral, religious, civil and political ideas on the other. He displayed something of his high view of Scripture's authority and inerrancy as he argued, "an individual man or woman must never follow conviction in regard to moral, religious, civil and political questions *until they are first tested by the unerring word of God.*" The Bible was to be the exclusive source and the norm for personal conviction and conscience. Payne continued:

> If a conviction infringes upon the written word of God, or in any manner conflicts with that word, the conviction is not to be followed. It is our duty to abandon it. Moreover, I will add that light on a doubtful conviction is not to be sought for in the conscience, but in the Bible. The conscience, like the conviction, may be blind, erroneous, misled, or perverted; therefore it is not always a safe guide. The only safe guide for a man or woman, young or old, rich or poor, learned or unlearned, priest or people is the Bible, the whole Bible, nothing but the Bible.[16]

As a Bishop in the AME Church, Payne required responsive reading of the Bible in every local church's public meeting, believing that "the colored race, who had been oppressed for centuries through ignorance and superstition,

might become intelligent, Christian, and powerful through the enlightening and sanctifying influences of the word of God."[17] Following the Bishop's leadership, efforts were made to encourage education in the Scriptures for both men and women and to use such knowledge as the basis for reform and self-improvement among the masses of African Americans.

Bishop Daniel Alexander Payne

Payne's view of natural revelation. However, Payne's doctrine of revelation did not

---

[15]Ibid., p. 8.
[16]Payne, *Recollections of Seventy Years*, pp. 233-34.
[17]Ibid., p. 253.

end with a high view of Scripture. Near the twilight of American slavery, evidence of an understanding of natural or general revelation emerged in the writings of African Americans. Among them was Bishop Payne who, in a brief article in the *Repository of American Religion and Literature*, credited creation with revealing the incommunicable attributes of God. He wrote:

> God has condescended to so adapt the intellect of man to the universe, and the universe to his intellect, that by the proper use of the former, and the contemplation of the latter, he may know as much of the Almighty as it is possible to know. The architect is known by his designs, and the skill with which he executes them; the spirit of inspiration saith, even a child is known by his doings, and hence it is also written, that the heavens declare the glory of God and the firmament showeth his handiwork. And again the invisible things of him from the creation of the world, are clearly seen, being understood by the things that are made, even his eternal power and God-head.[18]

In the creation, according to Payne, God condescended or lowered himself to the level of man's ability in order to communicate "as much of the Almighty as it is possible to know." Appealing to biblical texts like Romans 1:20, Payne concluded that if people would simply apply their minds to the study of the universe, which is suitably fashioned to fit their intellectual abilities, they may come to understand the character, eternality and power of God. For Payne, the idea that God speaks and can be heard in and through the created universe was unassailable. "We maintain the position that in a universe whose proportions are as just as they are stupendous; whose forms are as beautiful as they are varied; whose parts and whose movements harmonize with mathematical precision—there is the utterance of an infallible voice, declaring that God is infinite in wisdom, omnipotent in power, and unbounded in goodness."[19]

In Payne's thought, not only the incommunicable attributes of God were revealed in the physical universe, but the moral laws of God, which "demonstrate the moral perfections of his being," also were codified into the structure of the universe.[20] Payne opined, "The heart of the legislator is always seen in the laws he enacts; if he be just, his laws will be just and equitable; if he be a tyrant, his laws will be unjust and tyrannical. So, also, the just and holy laws

---

[18]Daniel Alexander Payne, "God," *Repository of American Religion and Literature* (January 1859): 2.
[19]Ibid., p. 3
[20]Ibid.

we have just been contemplating demonstrate the character of the heart of that God whom we love and obey."[21]

This moral law, good in essence because God himself is omnibenevolent, applied itself universally and indiscriminately, favoring no persons. According to Payne, "Gabriel, at the right hand of the Eternal, and the meanest slave of Virginia, are placed alike under its glorious and fearful sanctions."[22] One's station in life provided no escape from the just consequences and rewards of the moral lawgiver. In the natural moral law, then, writers like Payne found both a revelation of God's character and a theological weapon for attacking moral injustices perpetrated against Africans, especially slavery. Payne argued that the purpose of God's moral law was "the government of moral agents,"[23] and the existence of this moral law was plainly seen in the nature of relationships and creation.

History as revelation. In his semi-centennial address delivered at Allen Temple AME Church in Cincinnati, Ohio, Payne put forth a three-fold view of revelation. He discussed the revelatory role of both nature and Scripture, but added that God was also manifested in history. Payne argued that God showed himself to his creation through the history of races, nations, governments and "that kind of personal history which we call Biography." The greatness of God, according to Payne, exhibited itself in the origin, growth, decline and demise of nation states, and the exaltation and humbling of despots like Nebuchadnezzar, righteous and humble men like Daniel, and the punishment of crime in the lives of men like King David. Payne saw in history "evidences of (God's) inflexible justice and beneficent providence, as well as his unquestionable sovereignty."[24] While Payne did not further develop this aspect of his doctrine of revelation, he nonetheless foreshadowed later theologians like James Cone (1938-) who consider the history of African Americans a significant source for formulating theological positions. Unfortunately, Cone and others would invert the priority that Payne assigned to the three sources of revelation by minimizing the authority and denying the inerrancy of Scripture

---

[21]Ibid., pp. 3-4.
[22]Ibid.
[23]Ibid.
[24]Payne, "Semi-Centennial Sermon: The Divinely Approved Workman, or the Ministry for Allen Temple During the Next Fifty Years," in *Bishop Daniel Alexander Payne: Sermons and Addresses, 1853-1891*, Charles Killian (New York: Arno Press, 1972), pp. 79-80.

and by exalting the importance of history and culture.

Revelation in slave theology. As historian Mark Noll makes clear, Puritan influences were greatest in New England. And while the Puritans exerted some influence over the entirety of civil, social and political life in the colonies, antebellum southern theology resisted the impress of New England, providing its own theological distinctives.[25] The distinctiveness of southern theology was particularly evident among enslaved African Americans. Perhaps nowhere was the distinctiveness of African American theology more on display than in their doctrine or understanding of divine revelation. While the New England doctrines of general and special revelation, which were largely propositional and cognitive in character, provided a compatible framework for southern theological reflection, the advent of slave conversions gave the African American doctrine of revelation a more immediate, experiential and even emotional flavor. This distinction between white cognitive emphases in the doctrine of revelation and black emphases on subjective and immediate experience may help explain why the two traditions have traveled along mostly separate trajectories in the development of their theology.

Visions, voices and signs. Slaves in the American south most frequently wrote of God revealing himself through visions and voices. While they held the Bible in high regard, they by no means limited the revelation of God to either the Scriptures or to natural law as their New England counterparts had. In the folk theology of slaves, the doctrine of revelation was expanded to include direct, unmediated communion of man and God through visions and voices.

The belief that God was able to and frequently did reveal himself through voices and visions, if not normative by slave standards, was at least normal. The collection of conversion testimonies and short biographies assembled by Clifton Johnson in *God Struck Me Dead* are an invaluable recording of slave theological thought, at least among slaves alive during the twilight of the institution. Many of these slave conversion testimonies featured vision- and voice-based revelations, with the recipient recording very little surprise or disbelief at the prospect of hearing or seeing God through dreams or visions. The pervasiveness of God's spoken revelation was demonstrated in his willingness

---

[25]Noll, *America's God*, p. 33.

to even speak to children as young as eight years old.[26] One interviewee summed up the "normalcy" of hearing from God by saying, "I know that God talks to His people because He talks to me and has been talking to me ever since I was a boy."[27]

In this person's view, the exceptional aspect of God revealing himself through speech is not *that* he speaks with his people—of that the person was sure. Rather, the exceptional feature was that the voice and vision were "spiritual," perhaps occurring in a manner and a dimension other than typical human communication but no less real. "He doesn't talk as we talk but He talks to us and *we hear with the spiritual ear and see through the spiritual eye.*"[28] The slave believed that visions and dreams were "inner" experiences. While the voice of God was unquestionably "audible," it was not identical to the physical vibrations that produce regular sound. For example, one person describing his call to preach recalled, "He told me one morning in a voice as clear as mine but which seemed to be the inside of me."[29] Another commentator, waxing more theological, explained both the normalcy of God speaking to his people and the process through which God's spoken revelation could be received by human beings:

> The soul is the medium between God and man. God speaks to us through our conscience and the reasoning is so loud that we seem to hear a voice. But if God gave us the power of speech, can He not talk? If a soul calls on God, having [no] other earthly hope, will God not reveal himself to such a one?[30]

Where Bishop Payne understood the intellectual faculties of man as particularly suitable for apprehending God in the created physical universe, this former slave regarded the human conscience and soul as specifically designed for communication with God. The force of his rhetorical questions indicate that neither the ability of God to speak nor the fact that he does speak surprised the African slave, even if there was at times uncertainty about whether

---

[26]See, for example, "I Came to Myself Shouting," p. 30; "Fly Open for My Bride," p. 32 (8 year old child); "I Am as Old as God," p. 37 (13 year old child); and "To Hell with a Prayer in My Mouth," p. 41(12 year old child) in Clifton H. Johnson, ed., *God Struck Me Dead: Religious Conversion Experiences and Autobiographies of Ex-Slaves* (Cleveland: United Church Press, 1969).

[27]Johnson, *God Struck Me Dead*, p. 16.

[28]Ibid., emphasis added.

[29]Ibid., p. 14.

[30]Ibid., p. 2.

the voice in question was the reasoning conscience of man or the actual *vox Dei* from heaven.

In addition to the spoken word of God, some slaves also held that God revealed himself through signs. William Adams, a former slave, understood the revelation of God as an ability some Africans had to discern these signs. Adams relayed the following account of his ability:

> How I larnt sich? Well, I's done larn it. It come to me. When the Lawd gives sich power to a person, it jus' comes to 'em. It am forty years ago now when I's fust fully realize' dat I has de power. However, I's allus int'rested in de workin's of de signs. When I's a little pickaninny, my mammy and uther folks used to talk about de signs. I hears dem talk about what happens to folks 'cause a spell was put on 'em. De old folks in dem days knows more about de signs dat de Lawd uses to reveal His laws dan de folks today. It am also true of the cullud folks in Africa, dey native land. Some of de folks laugh at dey beliefs and says it am superstition, but it am knowin' how de Lawd reveals His laws.[31]

For Adams, comprehending the revelation of God was connected to knowledge of precisely how God reveals himself through natural and supernatural signs. Ostensibly, those who knew God's ways in revelation were capable of receiving information from and about God that others, whether more modern Africans or those who derided "superstition," were not. And against the charge of superstition, William Adams responded:

> There am lots of folks, and educated ones, too, what says we-uns believes in superstition. Well, it's 'cause dey don't understand. 'Member de Lawd, in some of His ways, can be mysterious. De Bible says so. There am some things de Lawd wants all folks to know, some things jus' de chosen few to know, and some things no one should know. Now, jus' 'cause you don't know 'bout some of de Lawd's laws, 'taint superstition if some other person understands and believes in sich.[32]

In Adams's view, and perhaps the view of many Christian slaves, the revelation of God through signs, visions and voices was not only directly given, but at times *sovereignly* given to a "chosen few to know." How and who was chosen was left to the mysterious ways of God.

Slaves' view of Scripture. While the African enslaved in the south held to a

---

[31]James Mellon, ed., *Bullwhip Days: The Slaves Remember* (New York: Grove Press, 1988), pp. 73-74.
[32]Ibid., p. 73.

INTERIOR OF THE CHURCH, FROM THE WESTERN WING.
THE FIRST AFRICAN CHURCH, RICHMOND, VIRGINIA.—[Drawn by W. L. Sheppard.]

1874 sketch of the interior of the First African Church, Richmond, VA

view of divine revelation more expansive than that promulgated by their orthodox peers in the North, they did not disparage the sacred Scriptures. The
Bible was almost universally held in high regard. Southern African Christians
accepted that the Bible was indeed the word of God, even if they were suspi-
cious about its misuse in the hands of some slaveholders and whites that
wielded it in support of the chattel institution. John Jea's (1773-?) testimony
is instructive in this regard:

> After our master had been treating us in this cruel manner [severe floggings,
> sometimes unto death], we were obliged to thank him for the punishment he
> had been inflicting on us, quoting that Scripture which saith, "Bless the rod, and
> him that hath appointed it." But, though he was a professor of religion, he forgot
> that passage which saith "God is love, and whoso dwelleth in love dwelleth in
> God, and God in him." And, again, we are commanded to love our enemies; but
> it appeared evident that his wretched heart was hardened.[33]

---

[33]John Jea, *The Life, History, and Unparalleled Sufferings of John Jea, The African Preacher, Compiled and
Written by Himself,* in *Pioneers of the Black Atlantic: Five Slave Narratives from the Enlightenment,
1772-1815,* ed. Henry Louise Gates Jr. and William L. Andrews (Washington, D.C.: Counterpoint,
1998), pp. 369-70.

Despite his owner's hypocrisy and savagery, Jea's references to the Bible indicated both his savvy in responding against his owners by using their own instrument of oppression and his recognition that the Scriptures held the true words of God. He described his longing to hear God's word despite his owner's opposition:

> Such was my desire of being instructed in the way of salvation, that *I wept at all times I possibly could, to hear the word of God, and seek instruction for my soul;* while my master still continued to flog me, hoping to deter me from going; but all to no purpose, for I was determined, by the grace of God, to seek the Lord with all my heart, and with all my mind, and with all my strength, in spirit and in truth, *as you read in the Holy Bible.*[34]

Rather than denounce the Bible as fraudulent along with its white adherents, the slaves recognized that learning to read the Bible and to possess its contents for themselves was real spiritual power, whose potency was made all the more alluring by efforts to prohibit its access. So, slaves vowed to learn to read before they died so that they could read the Bible. They took advantage of every clandestine opportunity to secure lessons from favorable masters or their children, often risking legally sanctioned retribution, severe beatings and death.

By the end of slavery's reign in America, African American doctrines of revelation were beginning to widen and make room for sources of revelation other than the Scriptures, including God continuing to reveal himself through supernatural means and interventions. This expansion of the doctrine of revelation would weaken the centrality of the Scriptures in the practice and thought of African American Christianity.

RECONSTRUCTION, "JIM CROW" SEGREGATION, THE GREAT MIGRATION AND THE "NEW NEGRO" MOVEMENT (1865-1929)

With both sides claiming biblical support for their cause, the Civil War actually weakened public attention to and confidence in the Scriptures. The war sufficiently undermined interpretive processes that otherwise would have checked biblical interpretations hostile to a general Christian framework, unleashing several developments and attacks that threatened historically ortho-

---

[34]Ibid., p. 379, emphasis added.

dox views of revelation and biblical hermeneutics. Intellectual attacks against Christianity arose within the new universities of the era. German "higher criticism" made its way to the country; and meanwhile, modernism reasserted the role of reason in epistemological matters, initiating a "figurative" hermeneutics for understanding biblical texts. In addition, the Social Gospel Movement popularized by Walter Rauschenbusch (1861-1918) and Washington Gladden (1836-1918) influenced some African Americans interested in social concerns.[35] These movements, associated as they were with liberal theology, introduced significant doctrinal debates and changes in the American Christian communities, including that of African American Christianity.

After the Civil War, there arose initially among Methodist congregations a renewed emphasis on personal sanctification and religious zeal known as the Holiness movement. One writer described early adherents of the Holiness movement as persons who "were fundamentalists, acknowledged the role of the Holy Spirit in the believer's life, were revivalistic, and were puritanical in their rejection of tobacco, alcohol, the theater, and cosmetics."[36] Spreading from Methodists between North Carolina, New York and Missouri to Baptist and independent congregations in Michigan, South Carolina and the Mid-South, the early Holiness movement provided fertile soil for the Pentecostal movement inaugurated by the Azusa Street revival of 1906-1908.[37] Under the preaching and leadership of William J. Seymour (1870-1922) at Azusa Street mission, "the actual Pentecostal movement originated in a revival among black Americans" and "has been called a contribution from the black community to the white one."[38]

William Seymour and revelatory tongues of Pentecost. With regard to the Bible, Holiness-Pentecostal leaders like William Seymour and Bishop Charles H. Mason (1866-1961), founder of the largest African American Pentecostal denomination, the Church of God in Christ, held a firmly evan-

---

[35]Noll, *History of Christianity in the United States and Canada*, pp. 306-7, 333, 374.
[36]George E. Simpson, "Black Pentecostalism in the United States," in *Native American Religion and Black Protestantism*, ed. Martin E. Marty, *Modern American Protestantism and Its World*, vol. 9 (New York: K. G. Saur, 1993), p. 143.
[37]David D. Daniels, "Charles Harison Mason: The Interracial Impulse of Early Pentecostalism," in *Portraits of a Generation: Early Pentecostal Leaders*, ed. James R. Goff Jr. and Grant Wacker (Fayetteville: University of Arkansas Press, 2002), pp. 255-70.
[38]Simpson, "Black Pentecostalism in the United States," pp. 142, 145.

gelical view. Nearly all Pentecostal denominations were founded with a belief in the inspiration and infallibility of the Scripture and the authority of Scripture over faith, conduct and reason.[39] Seymour wrote emphatically, "We stand on Bible truth without compromise," and he understood that unity in Christianity could only be achieved through faithful adherence to the Scriptures. "We recognize every man that honors the blood of Jesus Christ to be our brother, regardless of denomination, creed, or doctrine. But we are not willing to accept any errors, it matters not how charming and sweet they may seem to be. If they do not tally with the Word of God, we reject them."[40] In addition, the Bible was the standard against which to judge the appropriateness of Christian conduct. "We are measuring everything by the Word, every experience must measure up with the Bible. Some say that is going too far, but if we have lived too close to the Word, we will settle that with the Lord when we meet Him in the air."[41] Elements of a regulative principle regarding spiritual gifts were also found in Seymour's writings. For example, he proclaimed, "We do not read anything in the Word about writing in unknown languages, so we do not encourage that in our meetings. Let us measure everything by the Word, that all fanaticism may be kept out of the work."[42] The Bible in Pentecostalism was always to be its own interpreter by "comparing Scripture with Scripture so that there be no confusion and no deceptive spirit or wrong teaching."[43] With respect to the Scriptures, Seymour and other pioneers of American Pentecostalism stood, in part, as heirs to evangelical and orthodox views of the generations that preceded them.

However, the doctrine of revelation in Pentecostal circles did not end with their view of the Bible. Like generations of African Americans on southern plantations before him, Seymour believed that God's revelatory activity continued in history, especially in visions, prophecy and the miraculous gift of speaking in tongues.

Claims to such visions were common during the Pentecostal revival of Azusa Street. One writer published in the *Apostolic Faith*, the main communi-

---

[39]Ibid., p. 144; Ithiel C. Clemmons, *Bishop C. H. Mason and the Roots of the Church of God in Christ, Centennial Edition* (Bakersfield, Calif.: Pneuma Life Publishing, 1996).
[40]William Seymour, "Pentecost with Signs Following," *Apostolic Faith* 4 (December 1906): 1.
[41]William Seymour, "In the Last Days," *Apostolic Faith* 9 (June-September 1907): 1.
[42]William Seymour, "Everywhere Preaching the Word," *Apostolic Faith* 10 (September 1907): 1.
[43]William Seymour, "To the Married," *Apostolic Faith* 12 (January 1908): 3.

cations organ of the Azusa Street movement, wrote of a vision given to her by the Lord to explain the Spirit's work in sanctification:

> Several years ago, when I was very hungry, seeking God in all His fullness, I shut myself away in my closet one day, and the Lord gave me a wonderful revelation. As I was kneeling before my Maker, beseeching Him to show me all He expected me to be, right before my eyes I saw this wonderful vision. There appeared a man with a large, long, knotty, but straight log. The man had an axe. Did you ever see anybody score timber? He was scoring the log, and it seemed to me the axe went clear to the bit. And every time he scored, it hurt me. He scored it on four sides and then took the broad axe and whacked off the knots. Then he took a line and he made it pretty smooth. Then he raised it in the air, and taking a great plane, turned to me and said: "This is the plane of the Holy Ghost," and he ran the plane up and down, till I could see the image of the man perfectly reflected in the face of the log, as in a mirror. He did this to all four sides. Then turning to me, he said: "Thou art all fair, my love; there is no spot in thee."[44]

Mrs. Hall explained that the vision indicated God's desire to "take all the bumps, all the barnacles off" believers until they "reflect the image of the Master."

In another edition of the *Apostolic Faith*, the publishers reported the account of "a sister" who received a vision regarding a call to preach:

> Two days ago the power of God came over me and He said, "Whatsoever ye ask in my name believing, ye shall receive." I said, "Give wisdom to speak to the people." Immediately I was in a great hall with tables spread all about, and the Lord was the waiter, and I saw His beautiful, smiling face. He spoke to me and said, "I have called my friends and they did not come, therefore go out and ask everyone you find to come to the wedding." As I looked around to see something beautiful, the scene changed and I was in a hospital and saw poor creatures dying, looking like skeletons. I thought my call was to the hospital and telephoned to know when it was open for visitors, but the Lord revealed to me that it meant all those who are sick in their souls.[45]

Other accounts frequently appeared in the pages of the *Apostolic Faith*, where Seymour published them as evidence of the fulfillment of biblical

---

[44]Anna Hall, "The Polishing Process," *Apostolic Faith* 2 (October 1906): 3.
[45]"Vision and Message," *Apostolic Faith* 3 (November 1906): 1.

prophecies and a continuation of the events recorded in the New Testament book of Acts. Citing trances and visions in Acts, writers in the *Apostolic Faith* wondered how anyone could doubt that Pentecost had come.[46]

Revelation and speaking in tongues. Tongues, too, were seen as revelatory activity of the Holy Spirit. According to a testimony written by a Bro. H. M. Allen of Los Angeles, "I find everything the Holy Ghost speaks to me in the unknown tongues is of profound report. He has not given me liberty to tell all He has shown me in the unknown tongues, but they are the most important things that can possibly take our attention, things that are speedily coming on the whole earth."[47] Apparently, tongues were a medium for prophetic messages—even though they were not always immediately understood by the speaker or appropriately shared with wider audiences.

At other times, messages given through speaking in tongues confirmed the authenticity of disputed portions of Scripture. If Scripture were the final judge of all things, including things revealed by supernatural gifts as Seymour demanded, supernatural gifts were at times pressed into service to vouchsafe the veracity of the Scriptures. In answer to a dispute among some Holiness adherents regarding the acceptance of Mark 16:15-18, one writer concluded:

We feel sure that these are the words of Jesus. The writer herself, being a great admirer of Bro. Godbey, was for some time influenced by his views in regard to the last words of our Lord as given (in Mark 16:15ff). But since being in these Holy Ghost meetings, and *hearing these same words given again and again by the Spirit in unknown tongues and interpreted, all doubt has been swept away in regard to them.*[48]

The Azusa Street emphasis on spiritual gifts caused some to err in either practice or content. Early errors cropped up, warranting the attention of Seymour and the *Apostolic Faith.* For example, this correction was printed in the November 1906 edition just below the vision quoted above:

In our last issue, there was a prophecy by Sister Mary Golmond of an earthquake coming to Los Angeles. She stated that the Lord had not showed the time, but that it would NOT come on Sunday. The word "not" was accidentally omitted.[49]

[46]"In a Divine Trance," *Apostolic Faith* 8 (April 1907): 3.
[47]"When the Holy Ghost Speaks," *Apostolic Faith* 2 (October 1906): 2.
[48]"Shall We Reject Jesus' Last Words?" *Apostolic Faith* 2 (October 1906): 3. Emphasis added.
[49]"A Correction," *Apostolic Faith* 3 (November 1906): 3.

In the October 1906 edition, a Lucy Farrow reported that, "There is a band of saints that do not read the Bible like saints. They say the Bible is for unbelievers so they do not read it at all."[50] Some in the Pentecostal movement apparently adopted the habit of *writing* in unknown tongues—a "gift" nowhere documented in the New Testament Scriptures. The first mention of this "gift" appeared without comment in the first edition of the *Apostolic Faith* in a one-sentence update of Pentecostal outpourings—"The Lord has given the gift of writing in unknown languages."[51] Throughout the revival, Seymour and others fought the charge of fanaticism and emotionalism from without and religious excesses from within. So, by the September 1907 edition of the paper, Seymour felt compelled to write, "We do not read anything in the Word about writing in unknown languages, so we do not encourage that in our meetings. Let us measure everything by the Word, that all fanaticism may be kept out of the work."[52] Despite his protests against excesses, the movement's emphasis on supernatural gifts continued to be seen by critics as an inevitable contradiction of Scripture's final authority and sufficiency.

When viewed from the vantage point of African folk and traditional religion, with its acceptance of visions and voices as forms of direct communication with God, Pentecostalism might not be seen as a radical departure from black religious and spiritual practice. One might conclude that the innovation of Pentecostalism was its attempt to define and defend *from Scripture* a practice that already existed. Such an interpretation has merit. However, assuming the high view of Scripture as the unique source of special revelation that characterized African Americans up to the late 1800s, the Pentecostal movement represented a serious departure from the reigning Reformed consensus of previous generations.

DEPRESSION AND WORLD WAR II (1930-1949)

For most of the years following Emancipation through the Second World War, the African American view of revelation remained essentially unchanged. Over this period, reliance on visions and dreams receded as more people learned to read and gained access to the Scriptures. And while some lamented a decline

---

[50]"The Work in Virginia," *Apostolic Faith* 3 (November 1906): 3.
[51]*Apostolic Faith* 1 (September 1906): 1.
[52]William Seymour, "Everywhere Preaching the Word," *Apostolic Faith* 10 (September 1907): 1.

in the recognition of the Bible's authority in the lives of African Americans,[53] the Bible continued to hold a high place in black spiritual life. In many regards, the rise of the Ku Klux Klan, "Jim Crow" segregation, and violent assaults on the lives of African Americans forced greater reliance on sacred Scripture and the God revealed therein. Armed resistance was not a viable option available to African Americans, consequently "fight or flight" took on the form of spiritual resistance or migration to northern cities. In many cases, African Americans both resisted spiritually and fled the south as the rapid rise of black Baptist and Pentecostal churches in northern cities suggests.[54]

Not until the rise of German higher criticism and liberal theological convictions in the latter half of the 1800s did the orthodox consensus of evangelical Protestant Christianity begin to give way. Inheriting the Enlightenment's rejection of external authority, the depravity of man and the need for external revelation, liberal theology attacked the very foundations of the long-standing orthodox consensus, leaving many disillusioned and skeptical about the existence of absolute truth, particularly in religious matters. With the collapse of orthodox views of revelation and the abandonment of objective truth came the erection of a liberal view of revelation that placed emphasis on rationalism as the method for obtaining truth and proposed an optimistic view of human reason such that subjective human experience and personal encounters with God became the modes of divine revelation.[55]

The fountainhead of the emergent liberal school of theology was Friedrich Schleiermacher (1768-1834), who defined religion as "the feeling of dependence we have for God" and sought to defend the Christian faith from rationalism and traditionalism by "placing the authority of Christianity in the inner self."[56] While Schleiermacher's attempt at a radical subjective view of revelation

---

[53]Consider, for example, the comments of Hester Hunter: "It been de rule to follow what de Bible say do, in dat day en' time. En' now, it seem like de rule must be, do like you see de other fellow is doin'." In Mellon, *Bullwhip Days*, p. 190.

[54]For a review of Ku Klux Klan violence and various community and government responses to it during Reconstruction, See Eric Foner, *Reconstruction: America's Unfinished Revolution, 1863-1877* (New York: Harper & Row, 1988), pp. 88-102, 119-23, 425-44; and James N. Gregory, *The Southern Diaspora: How the Great Migrations of Black and White Southerners Transformed America* (Chapel Hill: University of North Carolina Press, 2005), pp. 197-226.

[55]Robert Saucey, *Scripture: Its Power, Authority, and Relevance* (Nashville: Word Publishing, 2001), pp. 26-31.

[56]John D. Hannah, *Our Legacy: The History of Christian Doctrine* (Colorado Springs: NavPress, 2001), pp. 60-61.

and authority ultimately failed, liberal theology nevertheless found a cozy resting place in late 1800s America and vied for the dominant Christian interpretation through the mid-1900s.[57] During its heyday between 1930 and 1960, liberal theological inquiry and method made inroads into the African American church by welcoming aspiring African American churchmen into liberally-inclined academic institutions, as notable conservative seminaries and divinity schools gripped by racist prejudice shut their doors to black applicants. It was in this social and academic context that Howard Thurman contributed to the devolution of African American theology and the doctrine of revelation.

Howard Thurman: Revelation and mysticism. In the history of theology in the African American church, Howard Thurman (1900-1981) stands as perhaps the most innovative theological thinker. While his enslaved forebears held that revelation through visions and voices possessed an inner dimension, it was Thurman who successfully supplanted orthodox eighteenth- and nineteenth-century commitments to the authority and sufficiency of Scripture with a person-centered and mystical doctrine of revelation and authority. In doing so, Thurman became the wellspring of a theologically liberal view of revelation, and consequently, of theological liberalism in the African American church.

The impetuses for leaving behind earlier doctrines of revelation were probably evident as early as Thurman's youth. Growing up, Thurman's privately religious mother, while not vocal about her Christian beliefs, nevertheless greatly impressed Thurman with her sturdy faith and fervency in prayer.[58] Her example likely planted the seeds for what Thurman later regarded as the private dimensions of religious experience. In his autobiography, *With Head and Heart,* Thurman also recalled schoolyard disputes and divisions over baptism between local Baptist and Methodist school children.[59] Thurman's learned proclivity toward privatized individual faith, combined with these schoolyard divisions, left him with a disdain for sectarian practices that divided people rather than uniting them. For Thurman, creedal formulations and concern for orthodoxy were the main culprits in this division. In his opinion, religion had

---

[57]Ibid., p. 62.
[58]Howard Thurman, *With Head and Heart: The Autobiography of Howard Thurman* (Orlando: Harcourt Brace, 1979), p. 16.
[59]Ibid., p. 10.

become too "identified with sectarianism, and its essence so distorted by it" that Thurman felt compelled to devote his entire self to furthering "the one-ness of the human quest."[60]

Academically, Thurman found guidance and mentorship from George Cross, a professor of systematic theology at Rochester Theological Seminary in Rochester, New York. Cross steeped Thurman in the broader liberal under-standings of the day, and encouraged his young student to "trust and value the insights of his own personality, such that it serves as the interpreter of religion that provides new meanings and directions for the faith."[61] In other words, personal thoughts, experiences and insights, frequently referred to as "Person-ality" in Thurman's writings, replaced the Bible as the authoritative standard for interpreting and judging religious truth. Cross's emphasis on personality aligned well with Thurman's nascent inclination toward a more privatized, less doctrinal basis for religious experience.

Later, while a professor and dean of Marsh Chapel at Boston University, Thurman's view of revelation crystallized and found clear expression in his classroom lectures on the spiritual life and spiritual disciplines. He regarded "the life of the spirit and the meaning of religious experience [as] *intensely per-sonal. It communicated itself in certain worship settings . . . but it was not the sort of thing that one talked about.* One spoke out of it, and one undertook to live out of it, and react out of it, but to make it literal and regularly accessible . . . would be difficult indeed."[62] It was through the personality and through religious experience (direct encounters with God) that revelation primarily took place. Thurman believed God revealed himself in nature and in the reli-gious texts of all religions.[63] However, the filter of individual personality was necessary for understanding any revelation no matter its source. Here, Thur-man's view of revelation followed the theological Personalism of Edgar Shef-field Brightman (1884-1953) and Brightman's teacher Borden Parker Bowne (1847-1910), whose "influence on many generations of students at the Boston University School of Theology . . . contributed decisively to liberalizing the

---

[60]Ibid., p. 199.
[61]Luther E. Smith, *Howard Thurman: The Mystic as Prophet* (Richmond, Ind.: Friends United Press, 1991), pp. 27-28.
[62]Thurman, *With Head and Heart*, p. 177, emphasis added.
[63]Ibid., pp. 7, 265.

leadership of the Methodist Church"[64] and influenced prominent Southern Baptist E. Y. Mullins (1860-1928).

This philosophical orientation led Thurman to a number of conclusions regarding the sources and nature of revelation that stood in marked contrast to the orthodox view of the Bible that preceded him. For instance, Thurman insisted that other religions and religious texts were also true. Thurman's goal was not to demonstrate the truthfulness of Christianity and the falsehood of all other religious forms, but to seek the "essence" of Christianity, and therein, all religions. While he held that Christianity was the highest expression of truth, he mounted no apologetic stance to defend that claim. Instead, he fell back on a formulation that for him held more unifying potential—"what is true in any religion is in the religion because it is true, it is not true because it is in the religion."[65] By contrast, Jupiter Hammon, Lemuel Haynes (1753-1833), Richard Allen (1760-1831) and Daniel A. Payne could hardly be imagined supporting such a view.

Not surprisingly, Thurman's doctrine of revelation led him to a low view of the Bible and of Jesus as well. One biographer summarized Thurman's view of the Bible as "a collection of books which reveals the drama of God making covenant with a people (Israel), and the prophetic interpretation of the meaning of this relationship given through the teachings and person of Jesus. Jesus and the Bible, according to Thurman, are *not the final source of authority for religion*. They are *a* particular way to the authority."[66]

Regarded in historic Christianity as the authoritative, unique and specific revelation of God, the Bible and Jesus became insufficient instruments and intermediaries to an intensely personal and privatized authority in Thurman's theology. Thurman held that Jesus was *an* example, "the example which inspires"; and, Jesus "exercises a moral and spiritual influence," even revealing how personality is perfected and how life should be lived. But nowhere in Thurman's writings does Jesus appear as *the* revelation of God to be worshiped and imitated.[67] Accordingly, Thurman believed that "the church should not

---

[64]John H. Lavely, "Personalism," in *The Encyclopedia of Philosophy, Volume 6*, ed. Paul Edwards (New York: Macmillan, 1967), pp. 107-10.
[65]Thurman, *With Head and Heart*, p. 144.
[66]Smith, *Howard Thurman*, p. 86, emphasis added.
[67]Ibid., pp. 67, 71-72.

limit its sources of religious insight to Jesus and the Bible. Other religions' faith claims, materials from the arts, and any discovery which opens a door to knowing God are useful to Christian nurture."[68]

Through his work as educator, preacher and pastor, Howard Thurman delivered the mood and thought of liberal theology to the African American church. Hailed by *Life Magazine* in 1953 as one the twelve most influential religious leaders of his era and *Ebony Magazine* in 1954 as one of the ten greatest Negro preachers in the United States, he influenced a generation of African American churchmen, pastors and preachers.[69] His view of revelation was essentially subjective, rejecting the authority of externally revealed texts and centering on the person's experience as the primary conduit for receiving revelation of God. Scripture was regarded as a useful guide in Thurman's opinion, but not authoritative or regulative in any sense. The Bible was a framework, a grid through which an individual read her or his experience. And insofar as the Bible and a denominational allegiance was only a framework, they were to be jettisoned when the individual eclipsed them in her or his understanding of religious experience. Thurman's theology may be regarded as the head of a consciously liberal stream of African American Christian theology.

CIVIL RIGHTS ERA (1950-1979)

The Civil Rights era was a period of explosive change and conflict in the United States. Civic upheaval and protest ruptured the country's longstanding racial caste system known as segregation. The nonviolent protests typified by Martin Luther King Jr. (1929-1968) disturbed the slumbering conscience of a society drowsy with racial indifference and intolerance. And on the heels of nonviolent civil protest came the politically radical wake up call of Black Power, which demanded the liberation of black peoples "by any means necessary." The Black Power advocates of the 1960s, including Malcolm X (1925-1965) and the Nation of Islam, Stokely Carmichael (1941-1998) and the Student Nonviolent Coordinating Committee, Black Panthers like Eldridge Cleaver (1935-1998) and Huey P. Newton (1942-1989), cultural nationalists Amiri Baraka (b. 1934) and Maulana Karenga (b. 1941), and

---

[68]Ibid., p. 87.
[69]Ibid., p. 192.

others, called black Americans to reject the oppressive structures, culture and worldviews of white America and to embrace a self-defining blackness as a beautiful and legitimate expression of black life.

During this period, with the burning force of an inner-city race riot, Black Theology erupted onto the theological scene. Black Theology demanded a radical reformulation of theological questions and insights that would mirror the call for Black Power heard in the streets of America's cities. The fuse that lit this explosion was James Cone's *Black Theology and Black Power*. Cone endeavored to bring to theological discourse "a special attitude permeated with black consciousness."[70] In a sense, Cone's theological speculations began at the same place where Howard Thurman's reflections began: both men were prompted by a concern for whether or not Christianity had anything to say about the condition of suffering and oppression experienced by African Americans and other oppressed people. While Thurman ultimately opted for a mystical, individualistic set of responses to that driving question, Cone centered his theological ideas on the group experience of blacks during the segregated period of the Black Power movement.

James Cone, Black Theology, and the doctrine of revelation. James Cone grew up during the 1940s and early 1950s—the age of Jim Crow—in the "Cotton Belt" or "colored" section of Bearden, Arkansas, a rural town of 1,200 residents. Acquainted with the prejudice and racial caste of the era and region, Cone "encountered Jesus through rousing sermons, fervent prayers, spirited gospel songs, and the passionate testimonies of the people" at Macedonia AME Church in Bearden. The faith he acquired at Macedonia provided "a powerful antidote against the belief that blacks were less than whites." Young Cone struggled with a series of inadequacies and contradictions he encountered in Bearden—white churches claiming to love the Lord and to welcome all people while simultaneously practicing segregation; spiritually resilient black churches that nonetheless repressed intellectual exploration. As a recently graduated teacher of systematic theology, Cone found Christian inspiration in the activist theology of Martin Luther King Jr. and a renewed appreciation of his blackness in the critique of Malcolm X (1925-1965) and the Black Power movement he spawned. In 1967, following the Detroit riots, the

---

[70]James H. Cone, *Black Theology and Black Power* (New York: Orbis, 1989), p. 32.

dual influences of King and Malcolm coalesced in Cone's *Black Theology and Black Power*, an attempt to apply critical theological reflection to the struggle for racial freedom among black people in America.[71]

Concerned as he was with the political, economic and social condition of African Americans during the 1960s, Cone offered a decidedly different view of divine revelation than that held by the generations of preachers and theologians before him. Rejecting the previous orthodox view that divine revelation consisted of God revealing himself nature and Scripture, Cone insisted that God's self-disclosure must be found only in the person of Jesus Christ and that Jesus can only be found *in the context of liberation.*[72] Cone asserted that revelation "meant a manifestation of God in human history," where God meets humanity in the concrete human situation, "not as an idea or concept that is self-evidently true" and certainly not in the limiting and inadequate formulation of "revelation as the word of God, witnessed in Scripture and defined by the creeds and dogmas of Western Christianity."[73]

Cone presupposed an inseparable connection between the doctrine of revelation and the act of liberation. He wrote:

> To know God is to know God's work of liberation in behalf of the oppressed. God's revelation means liberation, an emancipation from death-dealing political, economic, and social structures of society. This is the essence of biblical revelation.
>
> There is no revelation of God without a condition of oppression which develops into a situation of liberation. Revelation is only for the oppressed of the land. God comes to those who have been enslaved and abused and declares total identification with their situation, disclosing to them the rightness of their emancipation on their own terms.[74]

"In a word," Cone argued, "God's revelation means liberation—nothing more, nothing less."[75] This notion of revelation as liberation belonged uniquely to the oppressed of a society and included the benefit of God's unadulterated af-

[71]James H. Cone, *Risks of Faith: The Emergence of A Black Theology of Liberation, 1968-1998* (Boston: Beacon Press, 1999), pp. ix-xxvi.
[72]James H. Cone, *A Black Theology of Liberation: Twentieth Anniversary Edition* (Maryknoll, N.Y.: Orbis, 1986), pp. 42-44.
[73]Ibid.
[74]Ibid., pp. 45-46.
[75]Ibid., p. 46.

filiation with that people in their struggle. The definition and purpose of revelation was to explain how God, Jesus and Christianity were relevant to the struggles and hopes of African Americans and to provide what Cone labeled an "epistemological justification of the claims of a community about ontological reality."[76]

Indeed, Cone's Black Theology held that *blackness* was his ultimate reality and the controlling principle and experience in any Christian doctrine of revelation. Blackness, Cone theorized, had "very little to do with skin color"; rather it was the concrete identification of an individual with the needs, means and aims of the oppressed striving for freedom.[77] To be "black," then, was to take the side of the oppressed against the injustice they faced. To think of blackness in Black Theology was to think about an "ultimate reality" that superintended meaning, values and revelation in a way never understood in previous generations.[78] Cone wrote that there was "no 'abstract' revelation, independent of human experiences, to which theologians can appeal for evidence of what they say about the gospel."[79] He proffered an "anthropocentric point of departure for theology," and, more specifically, a point of departure that featured at its center the *black* man as representative *oppressed* man.

Cone's hermeneutical approach and the doctrine of revelation. Not surprisingly, Cone's hermeneutical approach to theology resulted in both a significantly lowered view of special revelation and a drastically amended understanding of general revelation. Cone posited six related sources for constructing a Black Theology of liberation, including: black experience, black history, black culture, revelation (by which Cone meant God's liberating action in space-time history in the person of Jesus Christ who sides with the black oppressed), Scripture and tradition. Cone construed the sources as "interdependent" and, more or less, equally important, but argued that "revelation is [not] comprehensible from a black theological perspective without a prior understanding of the concrete manifestation of revelation in the black community as seen in the black experience, black history, and black culture."[80] So practically speaking,

---

[76]Ibid, p. 42.
[77]Cone, *Black Theology and Black Power*, p. 151.
[78]Ibid., pp. 32-33.
[79]Cone, *Black Theology of Liberation*, p. xix.
[80]Ibid., p. 29.

the black community's experience, history and culture controlled any understanding of Jesus, Scripture and tradition and were the medium through which revelation was to be understood. The theologian's task was to bring the concerns and perspectives of a community to the Scriptures, holding in tension the concerns of the biblical and the contemporary community. The theologian was to do this by creating

> a theological norm in harmony with the black condition and biblical revelation. On the one hand, the norm must not be a private norm of an individual theologian but must arise from the black community itself. This means that there can be no norm for the black community that does not take seriously its reality in the world and what that means in a white racist society. Theology cannot be indifferent to the importance of blackness by making some kind of existential leap beyond blackness to an undefined universalism. It must take seriously the questions which arise from black existence and not even try to answer white questions, questions coming from the lips of those who know oppressed existence only through abstract reflections.[81]

Cone's understanding of what black history, experience and culture entailed was an extremely narrow conception. He viewed black experience in singular terms—"a life of humiliation and suffering" and an existence "where babies are tortured, women are raped, and men are shot" in a system of white racism.[82] Cone seemed unable to imagine a view of blackness not bound by extreme suffering. This framework effectively limited Scripture and tradition—two of the three sources of historical orthodox theology—to instrumental roles in service to political interests of the community. And, by demanding that the norms for theological inquiry must be based in group interests and group questions, Cone's doctrine of revelation consigned the more individualistic questions of salvation and personal communion with God to nonexistence.

View of the Bible. Where individual personality in the theology of Howard Thurman rendered Scripture a "useful guide" for individual spiritual exploration, it was the collective experience of oppression and the struggle for freedom that subjugated the Bible in the theological framework of James Cone. Black Theology reduced the Bible—once believed to be God's special revela-

---

[81]Ibid., p. 36.
[82]Cone, *Black Theology of Liberation*, pp. 23-24.

tion of himself—to "a *guide* for checking the contemporary interpretation of God's revelation, making certain that our interpretation is consistent with the biblical witness"; it disregarded any claims to infallibility and inspiration. "God was not the author of the Bible, nor were its writers mere secretaries."[83] Here, Cone aligned himself with the neo-orthodox views of Scripture and revelation, and, by mischaracterizing orthodox views of inspiration as reducing the writers of Scripture to "mere secretaries," set himself against the earlier positions of predecessors like Lemuel Haynes, Jupiter Hammon, Daniel Alexander Payne, and even revolutionary preachers admired by Cone like Nat Turner (1800-1831) and Denmark Vessey (?-1822).

Cone's Black Theology judged debates over infallibility irrelevant and touted an instrumental view of Scripture that deemed the sole criteria of "whether it [Scripture] can serve as a weapon against oppressors" as supremely important. This was true of Cone's view of tradition as well. "Literalism" enabled the justification of "all kinds of political oppression in the name of God and country" and obscured the essential meaning of the biblical text and true biblical inspiration—in Cone's view, black liberation. He concluded, "Black theology is concerned only with the tradition of Christianity that is usable in the black liberation struggle." Real inspiration consisted of the encounter between community and the resurrected Jesus who calls the oppressed to "risk everything for earthly freedom."[84] With the advent of Black Theology, Scripture was vanquished from its once vaulted place as the special voice of God ruling and interpreting matters of faith and conduct and reduced to the handmaiden of liberation ethics. Perhaps Cone stated his position most clearly in the preface to his later work, *God of the Oppressed*:

> I still regard the Bible as an important source of my theological reflections, but not the starting point. The black experience and the Bible together in dialectical tension serve as my point of departure today and yesterday. The order is significant. *I am black first—and everything else comes after that.* This means that I read the Bible through the lens of a black tradition of struggle and not as the objective

[83]Ibid., p. 31, emphasis added. Cone also observed a distinction between the black view of infallibility and reliability of Scripture. Without contending for the infallibility of Scripture, black people trusted in the reliability of Scripture in revealing Jesus Christ. This, Cone concluded, was the basis for the sustained authority of the Bible in the black experience. See James H. Cone, *God of the Oppressed* (Maryknoll, N.Y.: Orbis, 1997), p. 102.
[84]Cone, *Black Theology of Liberation*, pp. 31-33, 35.

Word of God. The Bible therefore is one witness to God's empowering presence in human affairs, along with other important testimonies.[85]

View of general revelation. Previous generations of theologians wrestled with the question of whether or not any true and accurate knowledge of God could be discerned from sources other than the Bible. Cone regarded the question as irrelevant and simultaneously called theologians to discern God's presence and self-disclosure in contemporary problems related to human affairs. During the Black Power movement, the major human drama requiring the reflection of theologians was the fight for freedom among African Americans, where the innate desire for autonomy was fully displayed. Cone defined the concept of general revelation as "a sense of the presence of God, a feeling of awe . . . that makes [human beings] creatures who always rebel against domestication."[86] He wrote:

> According to black theology, the idea of general revelation is primarily applicable to oppressed peoples. To the extent that we are creatures who rebel against ungodly treatment, God's self-revelation is granted. All human acts against alienative powers of enslavement are acts of God. We do not need to read the Bible to know that human enslavement is ungodly, and that slaves will do everything possible to break their chains. God has created all persons in such a way that none will cooperate contentedly in their own oppression. We are not creatures who can be domesticated. In this sense, whether all persons know what some Christians call special revelation, they nevertheless know God—that is, it is their identity with the divine that makes all slaves rebel against their masters.[87]

The oppressed community's impulse toward liberation unveiled God as liberator and friend of the oppressed. Cone summarized black theology's view of general revelation as that revelation given to all persons indicating that "human oppression is contradictory to the idea of the holy, and every blow for liberation is the work of God. God will not be without a witness."[88]

However, this same general revelation of God as liberator simultaneously uncovered the sinfulness of oppression and the oppressor. General revelation, then, pardoned and affirmed the oppressed and condemned the oppressor, an

---

[85]Cone, *God of the Oppressed*, p. xi.
[86]Cone, *Black Theology of Liberation*, p. 58.
[87]Ibid., p. 50.
[88]Ibid., p. 51.

application of moral law diametrically opposed to Bishop Payne's assertion one hundred years earlier that the moral law of God was no respecter of persons being applied equally and evenly to *both* slave and slaveholder. The multifaceted character of God articulated by Daniel A. Payne vanished from view in James Cone's doctrine of general revelation.

END OF CENTURY, POSTMODERN ERA (1980-PRESENT)

The turbulence and tumult of the Civil Rights and Black Power eras gave way to the individualistic concerns of the 1970s and 1980s. The generation of "me, myself and I" replaced the "power to the people" generation. As people dropped social concerns and became more solipsistic, and as material prosperity flowed over the country, so the theological interests of Christianity shifted to more therapeutic and postmodern questions.

Reemergence of charismatic gifts: Word of knowledge, word of prophecy. In the wake of Black Theology and liberal subjective views of revelation, the modern Charismatic movement arose. The Charismatic movement, typified by popular televangelists like Frederick K. C. Price (1932-) and Creflo A. Dollar Jr. (1962-), had its origins in the Holiness and Pentecostal efforts between the 1870s and early 1900s. Many envisioned themselves as the "third wave" of a divine act of God to restore the apostolic church—beginning with Pentecost in Jerusalem, succeeded by the Holiness and Pentecostal experiences, and culminating in the modern Charismatic reforms. In 1943, the Pentecostal forbearers of the Charismatics broke away from their socially more militant fundamentalist siblings and found a measure of mainstream acceptance in the National Association of Evangelicals. By 1975, the movement once viewed as crude fundamentalism or backward Pentecostalism came of age and found a respectable corner office in most major denominations—including Roman Catholicism.[89]

The Charismatic era ushered in the nadir of African American views on the doctrine of revelation. This deep low-point is characterized by an ambivalence not known in previous generations who were either committed to defending the orthodox perspective or wholly committed to undermining it. The charis-

---

[89]Vinson Synan, "Theological Boundaries: The Arminian Tradition," in *The Evangelicals: What They Believe, Who They Are, Where They Are Changing,* ed. David F. Wells and John D. Woodbridge (Grand Rapids: Baker, 1977), pp. 38-57.

matic generation lapsed into a muddled confusion of both poles.

On the one hand, proponents of the movement teach an "evangelical" view of divine revelation. Most, like their Pentecostal predecessors, would identify the Bible as the divine "Word of God." Many would subscribe to some understanding of the Bible as authoritative for faith and conduct. For example, the websites for the two leaders mentioned earlier, Price and Dollar, include a brief statement of faith affirming the inspiration of Scripture. Price also acknowledges the Bible to be the "authoritative Word of God."[90]

On the other hand, at least as a natural result of their practices, many Charismatic believers do not hold the Scriptures to be *sufficient* for all matters of faith and conduct. No reference to the sufficiency of Scripture is mentioned in any of the four statements offered by Dollar and Price. In the view of many "word of faith" Charismatic leaders, God is believed to be "doing a new thing" among his people, and the traditions and doctrines of previous Christians are often treated with disdain.

While the ambivalence created by Charismatic thinkers is distinct from the commitments of both the conservative orthodox and the liberal heterodox schools that preceded it, the uncertainty is nonetheless the logical consequence of previous generations' efforts at reformulating or attacking the doctrine of revelation. For example, though the early Pentecostals saw tongues as an evidence of Spirit baptism—a soteriological perspective and not primarily a revelatory emphasis—they nevertheless opened the door to the Charismatic promotion of all spiritual gifts, including those affecting the doctrine of revelation. The innovation introduced by Charismatic reforms expanded the doctrine of revelation to include direct revelations through the gifts of prophecy and words of knowledge.

The African American versions of these doctrines rested, historically, upon two pillars—the early African slave's belief in direct communication from God through visions and voices, and the Holiness-Pentecostal declaration that

---

[90]The statement of faith for Creflo Dollar Ministries and World Changers International Church reads, "we believe . . . the Bible was written and inspired by God." The statement of faith for Fred Price's Ever Increasing Faith Ministries reads, "We believe the Bible to be the inspired and only infallible authoritative Word of God"; and the doctrinal statement for his Fellowship of Inner-City Word of Faith Ministries includes, "All scripture is given by inspiration of God." Downloaded from <www.worldchangers.org>, <www.creflodollarministries.org>, <www.ficwfm.org> and <www.faith dome.org> on September 3, 2004.

tongues and other gifts were for the modern church. Both of these earlier
theological perspectives provided fertile ground for the reception of teachings
stressing ongoing divine revelation from God to his people.

Creflo Dollar provides an example of belief in continuing revelation
through prophecy. Interested readers may access a listing of his prophecies at
his ministry website.[91] Dollar is to be commended for putting his prophecies
in writing by date and making them available to the public. In doing so, he
makes himself somewhat accountable for his utterances and sayings.

However, a reading of these prophecies reveals Dollar's belief in continued
revelation by God and an underlying deemphasis on the authority of Scripture. The website opens with the following definition of prophecy: *"Prophecy
is a divinely inspired Word from the Lord spoken through a man or woman of
God."* The site continues, "Prophecy is an exciting part of God's plan for getting things done in the earth and the words He speaks come to pass in the lives
of those who hear *and* release their faith for the manifestation."[92] This definition of prophecy emphasizes continuing inspiration from the Lord and what
might be called a functional or pragmatic role of prophecy, "getting things
done in the earth." But unlike biblical prophecy, where God "makes known the
end from the beginning" (Is 46:10) and brings to pass whatever he wills, Dollar emphasizes that this "divinely inspired Word from the Lord" requires a "release [of] faith for the manifestation" or fulfillment of the prophecy.

For example, in a prophecy called "The Great Release," Dollar states:

> "Now you are about to enter into a phase of great release for all of the pressure and
> trials that this day will hold. For My Word is at hand, and it is on the line, and it
> will stand. But through you I'll show My master plan to this generation of this
> land. So today, is a day of turning points in your way—to move from that which
> has caused you to sway.
>
> "Now rejoice and be exceedingly glad, for all of your enemies will be had. And
> I will wash your troubles away. But now know that this day will not be like others.
> And this time that you have gathered will push your trials further. Now prepare
> yourself in praise this day, for I will surely show you My way—a way that will lead
> you into a place—a place ordained for this very day.

---

[91]Dollar's prophecies are available online at <http://interactive.creflodollarministries.org/bible/
prophecies.asp>. Accessed July 31, 2007.
[92]Ibid. Emphasis in original.

"So again, I say unto you, rejoice with all your might. Rejoice and begin to praise Me! And begin to praise Me, and I'll show up and set you free! So I am about to sit on you now, and when I am done, you won't have to wonder how, for the wisdom that I'll impart will be used to benefit you. And after you understand this day, you're going to know I'm going to bring you through," saith the Spirit of God![93]

Note that Dollar claims that the Spirit of God is speaking this message and his other prophecies. He contends that this is direct revelation from God, revelation of a "master plan" to be shown through Dollar's hearers.

In another prophecy, Dollar indicates that the plan of God involves the United States as a special country and foretells a time where many will turn from sin and be born again:

And as you seek Me and as you pray unto Me, then you allow Me to show you, and then you'll begin to see that I have not forsaken this land. I will not move from this country for it is in My plan. But now I must ask that you yield yourselves to Me; for there are many things in this day and time that I'd like for you to see. For I'll begin to show you and you'll speak it out loud and men will begin to tremble. And they'll cease in all of the foul.

The things that are foul in this place, that I have ordained as My land of grace, I'm about to turn around this day through you. Open your eyes and see and know. For these are the days where you'll cause the enemy to tremble. Because of what I'll show you and what you'll see, others will be born again and their peace will be sound and strong, and ready for these last days. And you'll find that it will become easy to persuade others to go this way.[94]

On the whole, the catalog of prophecies provided by Dollar at his ministry website contain general promises of blessing and prosperity. The prophecies allude to a coming time of progress and prosperity and sometimes to a period of widespread revival, evangelistic activity and conversion. For example, a prophecy called "A Great Revival" contends:

A great revival amongst My church I will begin. For many have known Me, accepted Me, pray to Me and call Me Lord. I love thee more and more. So forget

---

[93]Prophecy delivered by Dr. Creflo A. Dollar on May 20, 2007, 11:00 a.m. at World Changers Church International, Atlanta, Ga.

[94]Prophecy delivered by Dr. Creflo A. Dollar on April 29, 2007, at 7:30 p.m., World Changers Church International, Atlanta, Ga. Emphasis in the original.

not this night and send all your worries and concerns to flight. For I can speak to you words that will direct you, lead you and guide you. If you would call upon Me in praise and great joy, submit unto Me, come with humble hearts and walk in child-like faith, I'll cause these days, hours, minutes and seconds, I'll call this time to be more glorious and awesome. And I'll give you joy that you can't express. For these are My days when I will increase in My power, in My manifestation in these last precious hours. For My Son will return and no man knows the day or the hour, *but I will reveal to My prophets and like in other times they'll know and you will.* So, prepare yourselves. Look up and expect for these days will be great times of victory. Don't focus on the judgment that's outside the cloud. Focus on My Word and I will cause rough areas in your life to be mild.[95]

But note that these prophecies sometimes go well beyond general statements regarding a period of blessing. In the prophecy above, Dollar maintains, under a claim of the Spirit of God's inspiration, that prophets and the church in these times will know even the time for the return of the Son. In effect, this prophecy supplants the Lord's teaching that no angel or man—not even Jesus himself—would know the day or hour of his return.[96] In contradicting the very words of Jesus, Dollar's "prophecy" and "revelation" force an unpleasant recognition—either the "prophet" speaks falsely things God has not said,[97] or he is indeed a prophet and at least some portion of the Scripture can be said to be in error or abrogated. This view of revelation, along with many of its entailments, departs significantly from the historical understanding of African Americans up to the early Holiness-Pentecostal movement.

SUMMARIZING THE DECLINE

This chapter began with a brief look at the orthodox consensus that defined the doctrine of revelation at the advent of African American Christianity. That doctrine held a two-source view of revelation, with general revelation submitting to the superiority of the infallible, inspired special revelation of the Bible. Over the course of two and a half centuries, African American theology fell from the high view of revelation found in men like Jupiter Hammon to the nadir of ambiguity found today. As the generations from Thurman to Cone

---

[95] Prophecy delivered by Dr. Creflo A. Dollar on April 27, 2005, 7:00 p.m., College Park, Ga.
[96] See, for example, Mt 24:36 and Lk 12:40.
[97] See, for example, Deut 13:1-4; 18:21-22; and Jer 28:9.

hacked away at the pillars of the previous orthodoxy, the epistemological certainty once accompanying that orthodoxy collapsed without support.

From Jupiter Hammon to James Cone to contemporary word-of-faith leaders, the story of the doctrine of revelation in the African American church has been one of widening and weakening the earlier evangelical tradition. The earliest African American Christian forbearers were people who held to a high view of Scripture as God's special revelation and an orthodox view of general revelation. One found that position in the Reformed theologies of occasional preachers and poets like Hammon, long-time pastors like Lemuel Haynes, and in the reverence for the Bible held among the most oppressed and uneducated Christian slave. With the notable exception of the enslaved African's belief that God revealed himself through visions, voices and dreams—a belief not inconsistent with the biblical record[98]—African American Christians and the independent black church *before* Emancipation constituted, by most measures, a church with a view of divine revelation in sync with the longer 1800-year history of Christianity.

However, after Emancipation, the Azusa Street revival and the consequent rise of Pentecostalism prompted a significant redefinition of the doctrine of revelation in some African American communities. Azusa Street initiated and Pentecostalism codified the view that God was still pouring out supernatural gifts like tongues and prophecy on the church. The Holiness-Pentecostal emphasis on supernatural gifts, and Seymour's assumption that God was restoring the true apostolic church through the Azusa Street movement, opened the door for challenging the previous consensus that the Bible was a closed canon, a challenge that eventually contributed to the questioning of the final authority and sufficiency of the Scriptures as the only definitive and reliable inspired message of God. The Pentecostal movement ushered in the present-day Charismatic movement, which finally converted the earlier movement's attention to spiritual gifts into an expanded doctrine of revelation that included revela-

---

[98]See, for example, the visions of and voices recorded in several conversion stories in the New Testament book of Acts, including Paul's conversion (Acts 9:1-18), Peter's vision and visit to the Gentile Cornelius's house (Acts 10), and Paul's call to minister in Corinth (Acts 18:9-11). For a good contemporary treatment of the compatibility between orthodox Christian belief and the continuation of visions, prophecy, etc., see Wayne A. Grudem, *Systematic Theology* (Grand Rapids: Zondervan, 1995). For a cessationist response to Grudem, see O. Palmer Robertson, *The Final Word: A Biblical Response to the Case for Tongues and Prophecy Today* (Edinburgh: Banner of Truth, 2004).

tory gifts like prophecy and words of knowledge.

At the same time that some communities were widening their understanding of revelation, theological liberalism launched an intense assault on the nature of the Bible and on its suitability as an epistemological foundation. Previous views of inspiration and infallibility were rejected outright and replaced with mystical quests for the "essence of Christianity," the historical Jesus, and for liberation theologies. For many, earlier Christian claims that the Bible possessed objective, exclusive truth were either untenable or irrelevant.

For some, the doctrine of revelation required no serious defense or study. That God revealed himself could be assumed,[99] and how God made himself known might be as varied as how each individual person learns best.[100] But if the doctrine of revelation is as inconsequential as some in the post-Emancipation African American church and academy seem to have treated it, how then can anyone know with certainty who God is and what God has said? And what effect does such a porous perspective have on the church and individuals?

The doctrine of revelation affects every sphere of Christian thought and conduct. To illustrate this point, consider three profound results that followed the widening doctrine of revelation and the weakening view of Scripture.

First, the Bible continued to be revered but no longer trusted as sufficient for all matters of faith and conduct in the African American church. If new revelations were possible, and if previous understandings of the Bible were wrong as liberal theology claimed, then the Bible could no longer speak to the needs of contemporary society and no longer possessed a relevant message. Consequently, many churches revered the Bible but never read it and certainly never used it to guide the details of daily church and personal life. And with the Bible deemed insufficient (whether explicitly or implicitly through indifference), fads and wrong ideas about how to govern itself preyed upon the vulnerable church while sometimes radical, sometimes subtle hermeneutical approaches undermined any objective authority possessed by the Bible. Individual Christians and entire congregations became susceptible to non-

---

[99]James Cone assumes, for example, that Jesus is the revelation of God and that Jesus is found revealing himself in the struggle of black people for complete liberation. Cone merely asserts this view without offering any real justification or defense for why such a view is desirable or necessary.

[100]This seems to be the practical conclusion of Howard Thurman's view of revelation, as dependent as it was on his view of personality and the importance of individual spiritual encounters.

biblical and anti-biblical worldviews, philosophies and moralities. With the insufficiency of Scripture established in practice, even taught explicitly in some cases, who could oppose the entrance of heretical ideas and claims? Without an objective standard or rule against which teachers were judged, disputes over doctrine seemed to many a wearisome exercise in futility with no possible solution and no obvious benefits. As Bruce Fields observed, "Experience, apart from the transcendent revelation embodied in Scripture and practiced in the community yielded to Scripture, cannot itself be evaluated. It simply rules in the interpretive role just as those with the loudest voices or most persuasive rhetoric may gain the position of defining what genuine life should look like in a given community."[101]

Second, the African American church finds itself without a standard or rule against which to judge "new" revelations. If the Bible is no longer the clearest or most complete revelation of the mind of God, then the random, often contradictory, and failed "prophecies" and "divine utterances" of many preachers cannot be checked. Adherents, in order to maintain membership in the church community and to find another source of authority, vest the preacher or "prophet" with a kind of authority once reserved for the Scriptures. So rather than find the truth in the sacred pages, the whimsy, insight, and charisma of a beloved pastor or leader become the final arbiters of divine truth, such that some African American Christians are now as likely to say they believe certain things about God "because my pastor said so" as they are likely to say "because the Scriptures teach it." Where the early church members searched the Scripture to test the veracity of the apostles' teachings (Acts 17:10-11), the present-day church offers only passive inspection, often accepting a church leader's opinion as a satisfactory basis for defining core belief and conduct.

Third, this widened and weakened doctrine of revelation resulted in weaker, less biblical preaching. Increasingly, the kind of expository preaching modeled by Haynes gave way to the use of the Bible as a prop or convenience for sermons and speeches filled with the speaker's commentary on contemporary issues. Uncovering the meaning of a passage of Scripture and applying it to one's hearers fell out of fashion and political sermons emptied of biblical

---

[101]Bruce L. Fields, *Introducing Black Theology: Three Crucial Questions for the Evangelical Church* (Grand Rapids: Baker Academic, 2001), p. 73.

theology took center stage. The very notion of a "good preacher" morphed from the faithful communication of God's word (even where knowledge of Scripture was extremely meager, as in the case of many slave preachers) to the witty, politically relevant social commentary. To be sure, African American preachers since the abolitionist movement spoke against the political concerns of their day. What was new by the Civil Rights era was the absence or radical refashioning of gospel priorities. The weakened doctrine of revelation undermined faithfulness to Scripture and the counsel of God declared in its pages. Most tragic of all, the preaching of the gospel vanished from many church pulpits, with faithful attendees in many churches never coming to know the wonderful God that makes himself known in the pages of holy writ. After all, how can one know God unless he reliably reveals himself?

2

"A Father to the Fatherless"

The African American Doctrine of God

Did I believe that [slavery] would always continue,

and that man to the end of time would be permitted with

impunity to usurp the same authority over his fellows,

I would disallow any allegiance or obligation I was under to my fellow creatures,

or any submission that I owed to the laws of my country;

I would deny the superintending power of divine Providence in the affairs of this life;

I would ridicule the religion of the Saviour of the World, and treat as the

worst of men the ministers of the everlasting gospel;

I would consider my bible as a book of false and delusive fables,

and commit it to the flame; Nay, I would still go further:

I would at once confess myself an atheist, and deny the existence of a holy God.

NATHANIEL PAUL (1793-1839)

Sometimes it seemed as though some wild beast had plunged his fangs into my heart,

and was squeezing out its life-blood. I began to question the existence of the

Almighty and to say, if indeed there is a God, does he deal justly? Is he a just God?

Is he a holy Being? If so, why does he permit a handful of dying men thus to oppress us?

Why does he permit them to hinder me from teaching these children, when nature,

reason and Revelation commanded me to teach them?

DANIEL ALEXANDER PAYNE (1811-1893)

GENERAL INTRODUCTION AND CONTEXT

The brutal reality of chattel slavery forced the African slave into a radically new physical, social, emotional and spiritual existence. No longer were the freedoms of mobility, culture, celebrations and worship openly available to the enslaved. And, while many resisted social and physical restrictions by "stealing away" to practice and preserve cultural traditions, the heavy hand of slavery eventually prodded a reconsideration of long-held beliefs. Spiritually, slaves reexamined their doctrines of the Person and power of God. Some continued the practice of traditional African religions or Creole mixtures for as long as possible. A few adhered to Islam. But a significant number came to practice Christianity, sometimes as a matter of coercion, other times as a matter of conscience, and almost certainly blended with African elements and practices.[1]

During the Colonial and Revolutionary eras, Reformed theology dominated in most parts of the developing republic and significant numbers of African Americans accepted traditional orthodox formulations of the doctrine of God. Tertullian (c. 160-c. 225) developed the terminology of *trinitas* or Trinity, *persona* or Persons, and "substance" in order to define the early church's theology. The Councils of Nicaea (A.D. 325) and Constantinople (A.D. 381) affirmed the early conception of God as triune in nature and established the doctrinal position that reigns in orthodox Christianity to the present.[2]

In keeping with this Christian heritage, early African American writers and preachers assumed the triune nature of God. Moreover, God's holiness, righteousness, justice and benevolence were held nearly without question, being clearly understood from the Bible.

However, traditional doctrinal perspectives posed serious problems for enslaved and marginalized Africans who were immediately confronted with the question of God's righteousness in light of the evils of slavery. A wooden acceptance of traditional conclusions would not suffice; Christian ideas about God needed to be applied and exercised in the context of their life circumstances. How could the righteousness of God be maintained as a central belief

---

[1] Good treatments of the introduction of African slaves to Christianity are available in Albert J. Raboteau, *Slave Religion: The "Invisible Institution" in the Antebellum South* (New York: Oxford University Press, 1978) and Eugene D. Genovese, *Roll, Jordan, Roll: The World the Slaves Made* (New York: Vintage, 1976), pp. 161-284.

[2] John D. Hannah, *Our Legacy: The History of Christian Doctrine* (Colorado Springs: NavPress, 2001), pp. 78-79.

among the enslaved? Neither was this dilemma completely resolved with the abolition of slavery. New evils like Lynch Laws and Jim Crow emerged to challenge belief in the inherent goodness of God. Legalized segregation, political disenfranchisement and economic deprivation continued to plague African Americans through each successive period of history. So much so, that for some African American theologians, theodicy became the defining issue in understanding the nature and character of God.

This chapter explores African American conceptions of God with particular emphasis on how they reconciled the goodness and righteousness of God with the existence of evil and gross social injustices like slavery.

EARLY SLAVERY ERA THROUGH ABOLITION ERA (1600-1865)

Northern writers. Early writers most often solved the theodicy dilemma by emphasizing God's sovereignty and ultimately good purposes. With a talent for short comprehensive statements of Christian doctrine, Jupiter Hammon set himself apart as one of the earliest systematizers in African American theological history. Hammon's doctrine of God was what one might expect from an occasional preacher in the Puritan north. He proclaimed that

> [in the Bible] we may learn what God is, that he made all things by the power of his word, and that he made things for his own glory, and not for our glory. That he is over all and above all his creatures and more above them than we can think or conceive—that they can do nothing without him—that he upholds them all and will overrule all things for his own glory.[3]

Such a high view of God's creative power, glory and sovereignty was typically emphasized in Reformed theology—particularly God's sovereignty.

And so it was with the works of Hammon, who emphasized the sovereign rule of God more often than any other attribute. On occasion, he referred to God by title as the "Divine Sovereign," and he extolled God for his rule over all of creation. But most importantly, Hammon recognized God's sovereignty in the affairs and hearts of people.

Hammon displayed his dependence upon the sovereignty of God when he

---

[3]Jupiter Hammon, *An Address to the Negroes in the State of New York,* in Sondra O'Neale, *Jupiter Hammon and the Biblical Beginnings of African-American Literature* (Metuchen, N.J.: American Library Association, 1993), pp. 237-38.

applied the doctrine to tough ethical dilemmas of his time. In the late 1700s, questions about the legitimacy of slavery began to press upon the conscience of people everywhere and prompted a multitude of ethical and theological quandaries. Among the questions was the issue of whether it was morally right for slaves to obey slave owners, a message frequently preached by ministers sympathetic to the institution and rejected by many of its opponents, both slave and free. At times, African American preachers found themselves caught in the ethical dilemma even as they preached:

> Till freedom, I had to preach what they told me to. Master made me preach to the other niggers that the Good Book say that if they obey their master, they would go to heaven. I knew there was something better for them, but I darsen't tell them so, 'lest I done it on the sly. That I did lots.[4]

Some reasoned that because the call to obedience among slaves was inherently connected with the injustice of slavery and its perpetuation, such a call was inevitably self-serving and unethical. To be ethical, then, slaves were to resist, defy and subvert their masters, even if it must be "done on the sly."

On the surface, Hammon's conclusion on the ethical question of the slave's obedience to slave masters was more akin to the preaching of those sympathetic to the continuance of slavery, though for markedly different reasons. Hammon reached his opinion as a result of his theology, while justifiers of slavery very often couched their ideas in nonbiblical appeals to African inferiority. Hammon recognized in difficult imperatives like Ephesians 6:5-8, calling servants to obey their masters, not so much a "duty" born out of the inferiority of the African or the justness of the American chattel system, but the necessity of obeying the sovereign Lord of the Scriptures in all things. He insisted that masters were to be obeyed solely because God commanded such obedience. The slave was to remember that slavery was "permitted . . . by that God who governs all things, who setteth up one and pulleth down another" and that ultimately it was God "who has the hearts of all men in his hands and turneth them as the rivers of water are turned."[5]

The sovereignty of God, then, extended to the daily treatment that Africans received at the hands of both righteous and unrighteous slave owners and

---

[4]James Mellon, ed., *Bullwhip Days: The Slaves Remember* (New York: Grove Press, 1988), p. 191.
[5]Hammon, *Address to the Negroes*, pp. 231, 233.

was the only basis upon which the command to obey could be trusted and hope for peace and comfort could be expected. Emotionally, it was also the only doctrine that relieved Hammon of his despair at the "poor, despised, and miserable state" of his brethren as they labored under the oppressive yoke of twin evils, sin and slavery, each exacerbating the despotic force of the other. If God were not sovereign then there could be no reasonable hope in an emancipation from such evil.

Lemuel Haynes. On the heels of Hammon's brief defense of the sovereignty of God in all things, Lemuel Haynes offered the most developed theological exploration of the doctrine of God among the earliest African American writers and preachers in the North. Lemuel Haynes was born July 18, 1753, in West Hartford, Connecticut. Abandoned by his parents at five months of age, the Rose family raised Haynes as an indentured servant in Middle Granville, Massachusetts. Following his indenture, Haynes volunteered as a minuteman and in October 1776 joined the Continental Army in the American Revolution.

Rev. Lemuel Haynes

It was after the American Revolution, however, and during his time with the Rose family that Haynes demonstrated his interests and talents for theology and ministry. "Haynes was a determined, self-taught student who poured over Scripture until he could repeat from memory most of the texts dealing with the doctrines of grace."[6] Though Haynes also benefited from the devout religious practice and instruction of Deacon Rose, the works of Jonathan Edwards, George Whitefield and Philip Doddrige (1702-1751) most influenced young Haynes. Indeed, Haynes owed much to the revival and evangelism efforts of Whitefield and Edwards, who greatly impacted America and particularly New England

---

[6]Helen MacLam, "Introduction: Black Puritan on the Northern Frontier," in *Black Preacher to White American: The Collected Writings of Lemuel Haynes, 1774-1833,* ed. Richard Newman (Brooklyn: Carlson, 1990), p. xx.

during the 1740s. Haynes began his formal ministerial training by studying Greek and Latin with two Connecticut clergymen, Daniel Farrand and William Bradford. He was licensed to preach on November 29, 1780, and five years later became the first African American ordained by any religious body in America. In 1804, Middlebury College awarded Haynes an honorary master's degree—another first for African Americans.

Owing largely to his Puritanlike experiences with the Rose family and his admiration of Whitefield and Edwards, Haynes adopted a decidedly Calvinistic theology. Calvinism was typical of African American writers during Haynes's lifetime. One biographer, reflecting on a host of African American writers in the late 1700s, observed:

> Indeed, Calvinism seems to have corroborated the deepest structuring elements of the experiences of such men and women as they matured from children living in slavery or servitude into adults desiring freedom, literacy, and membership in a fair society. From Calvinism, this generation of black authors drew a vision of God at work providentially in the lives of black people, directing their sufferings yet promising the faithful among them a restoration to his favor and his presence. Not until around 1815 would African American authors, such as John Jea, explicitly declare themselves against Calvinism and for free-will religion.[7]

In his 1805 sermon titled "Divine Decrees, an Encouragement to the Use of Means," Haynes elaborated Hammon's contentions when he wrote of God's self-existence, sustaining activity, providence, goodness and sovereignty in all things. He distinguished himself from some of his New Divinity colleagues and "the Hopkinsian reserve about the efficacy of the means [of grace] to effect regeneration."[8]

Haynes began his development of the doctrine of God by first exploring the self-existence of God. All things that exist, that have a beginning, that have a cause, according to Haynes depended on the prior existence of God who alone had no cause.[9] He contended that it was "impossible for Deity to communi-

---

[7]John Saillant, *Black Puritan, Black Republican: The Life and Thought of Lemuel Haynes, 1753-1833* (New York: Oxford University Press, 2003), p. 4.

[8]E. Brooks Holifield, *Theology in America: Christian Thought from the Age of the Puritans to the Civil War* (New Haven, Conn.: Yale University Press, 2003), pp. 309-10.

[9]In addition to "Divine Decrees," see also Haynes's "Outline of a Sermon on Acts 26:22" (1833), *Black Preacher to White American: The Collected Writings of Lemuel Haynes, 1774-1833*, ed. Richard Newman (Brooklyn: Carlson, 1990), pp. 233-34.

"A Father to the Fatherless"   69

cate or impart independence to any; this is peculiar to himself; and it would
imply the grossest absurdity and contradiction to suppose it of any other being."[10] And, since God alone was independent and self-existent, it stood to
reason that all other creatures and events relied upon God.

The events of history and the actions of men, Haynes argued, came to pass
by the will and providence of God who guided all things. Moreover, Haynes
emphasized the idea that God was not just the cause of events but also the sus-
tainer of all things. He declared "that all things depend on God for their existence is a sentiment abundantly taught in the word of God." And by "all
things," Haynes meant to include every incident and action in creation.

> Not only events of great, but those of less magnitude, are ascribed to God; even
> the falling of a sparrow, or a hair of our head. It is difficult for us to distinguish
> between great and small events; there is not a superfluous link in the whole
> chain; they all depend on each other. It was necessary that Moses should be born
> at that time; that the careful parents should lodge him in the flags, by the side
> of the river, at such a place; that Thermuses, Pharaoh's daughter, should come
> to such a place to wash; that her eye should be fixed upon the spot, and discover
> something amidst the thicket; that her curiosity should excite her to have it
> fetched; that little Moses should weep, and excite female compassion; that he
> should fall in to the hands of a tender mother, etc. These things are beyond the
> wisdom of mortals; and are parts of the ways of the Almighty.[11]

God governed the minutest details of life. The whole of the created order operated under the superintending and instigating providence of God, where
nothing happened by unguided chance.

Haynes reasoned that because *all* things depended on God for their existence, that because an all-encompassing providence operated, then even the
evil of men was "effected or brought about by the agency or providence of
God."[12] With this conclusion, Haynes risked going further than many orthodox theologians in Christian history were willing to venture. However, he saw
in passages like Romans 11:36; 1 Corinthians 8:6; 2 Corinthians 5:18 and
Genesis 50:20 ample scriptural warrant to promote the sovereignty of God
over even the wicked actions of men. He was certain that men did not create

[10]Haynes, "Divine Decrees," p. 91.
[11]Ibid.
[12]Ibid.

or affect events except "as instruments in the hand of God."[13] He denied the milder explanation of God's relationship to evil that contended that God *permitted* evil but was in no way the cause of evil. Proponents of this view were concerned about the implication that God must be wicked in some sense if he were the cause of moral evil. Haynes responded by distinguishing between the nature of the thing caused and the cause itself.

> Some are unwilling to acknowledge the absolute and unlimited providence and agency of God in the production of all things, especially with respect to the existence of moral evil, that it implies wickedness in Jehovah; as though there must be the same in the cause as in the effect: *should this be admitted, we must deny God in the greater parts of creation and providence.* Would men learn to distinguish between events in their own nature, and the good to which they are made subservient, it would relieve them of many difficulties. However wicked Pharoah was in devoting the Hebrew children to death, yet good was effected thereby, and the hand of God shone conspicuous.[14]

At risk, in Haynes's mind, was the potential separation or alienation of God from creation. Haynes anticipated that a view that too aggressively exonerated God from the charge of evil would lead to an impotent caricature of the great Jehovah of Scripture.

Haynes continued, directly addressing opponents of his view:

> All will allow that God *permitted* or *suffered* sin to take place; But if, on the whole, it is not promotive or made subservient to the highest possible good, then he cannot be vindicated in *permitting* it to be; but if it is best that sin should have existence, why cannot the divine Character be cleared in *causing* it to take place? Some, to relieve themselves of difficulties, suppose sin to be merely negative, consisting in the want of holiness; But can this be criminal only as implying positive exercises of hatred to God? Should I tell my neighbor who stands by me, that the pen with which I now write is crooked—should he reprove me for my impertinence and deficiency of language, and say I had not declared the thing as it is; for it *wants straitness*, should I gain much philosophical instruction by the remark?[15]

Haynes envisioned a moral good as the conclusion of moral evil; God used the evil of men not simply by way of allowance but positively to affect a higher,

---

[13]Ibid.
[14]Ibid., p. 92, emphasis added.
[15]Ibid., italics original.

ultimate purpose. A view of God that simply permitted or allowed evil to exist, in Haynes's estimation, failed to either vindicate God or to adequately explain the providential workings of God. Alternative views lacked explanatory power for reconciling the fact that both moral evil and an omnipotent God existed. Put briefly, Lemuel Haynes attempted to resolve the dilemma of God's righteousness in the presence of moral evil *inside* the character of God by placing the existence of sin and evil within the purview of God's control and divine agenda for good. While he recognized that such a strategy made the question of God's righteousness more acute, he also saw that reducing the control of God in human events by arguing that God *desired* one end but was forced to *permit* another failed to take all of biblical revelation seriously or to offer a helpful pastoral understanding.

Haynes also responded to a second objection to the sovereignty and providence of God in all things, namely, that such a view contradicted the moral freedom and culpability of men for the evil they commit. Haynes flatly rejected the charge, saying, "The agency and government of God is perfectly consistent with the liberty and freedom of men, and with their being the subjects of blame and praise; so that it does not exclude moral good and evil from the system." Far from believing that providence undermined human agency or moral guilt, Haynes argued that "the absolute dominion of Jehovah is *the object and foundation of all true morality*" and that the reason the wicked were to be judged and destroyed was precisely "because they oppose his holy government or plan."[16]

The justice of God and genuine moral guilt were preserved in Haynes's thought through the distinction of primary and secondary causes. While God's will and plan were certain and inviolable, the acts of men occurred, so far as they knew, freely and without coercion. God's plans, Haynes taught, were "hidden" in the details and choices of everyday life, depending "on so many minute circumstances, that we can discover no kind of connexion between the means and the end."[17] Moreover, the fulfillment of God's plans depended upon the "diligent use of means." In other words, though God's decrees necessitated every event according to his will, "without the exertions of

---

[16]Ibid., p. 97, emphasis added.
[17]Ibid., p. 91.

men, it [was] impossible that [God's designs] should take place."[18]

Haynes illustrated this point with a number of examples from biblical literature. He called upon God's promise to Abraham as an instance of God both decreeing an end and using secondary causes to fulfill it:

> God revealed to Abraham, that his seed should go down into Egypt, and at such time be delivered; but this supposed a series of second causes, all dependent on the first cause; without them the event could not take place. One was the edict of Pharoah to destroy the male infants of the Hebrews; that Moses should be born and hid three months; that he should be educated at the expense of the King of Egypt; that the Egyptians should be visited with ten plagues, etc.[19]

While God authored and designed a future according to his will, each of the agents involved acted of their own accord in a way consistent with God's purposes. Thus, in Haynes's view, God was sovereign in all things as the Scriptures indicated, *and* man was genuinely free and responsible for his actions. If men rejected this doctrine, according to Haynes, it was only "because the carnal mind is enmity towards God."[20]

For Haynes and his generation, however, the problem of God's justice and righteousness was not a merely philosophical one. They looked squarely into the actual gross evil of race-based chattel slavery and witnessed the tissue-splitting brutality of the lash. The righteousness of God was a pressing existential conundrum to be solved with eyes—and oftentimes backs—wide open. Astonishingly, that generation of writers and thinkers concluded—in contradiction to the view that made God a disappointed observer of human events and evils like slavery—that God indeed was both sovereign and just. They saw even in his hard providences beneficence consistent with his character, and therefore an ultimate good for African people as they endured untold and seemingly unending horrors.

Haynes, a supporter of the Republic despite its hypocritical toleration of slavery, believed that God sovereignly appointed government for the regula-

---

[18]Ibid., p. 95.
[19]Ibid.
[20]Lemuel Haynes, "Outline of a Sermon on Psalm 96:1," in *Black Preacher to White America: The Collected Writings of Lemuel Haynes, 1774-1833*, ed. Richard Newman (Brooklyn: Carlson, 1990), pp. 39-41.

tion of human affairs and for the support of virtue,[21] especially freedom and equality among men.[22] Other African Americans of this era echoed Haynes's belief in the providence and sovereignty of God. Olaudah Equiano (c. 1745-1797), famous abolitionist and former slave, concluded that he was "a particular favourite of Heaven" despite the bitter trials he combated. Reflecting on his trials as a slave, Equiano wrote, "through the mysterious ways of Providence, I ought to regard [slavery] as infinitely more than compensated by the introduction I have thence obtained to the knowledge of the Christian religion."[23] The first African American woman poet Phillis Wheatley (1753-1784) joined Equiano in thinking that God's sovereign decision to send Africans into slavery wrought his unsurpassed blessing of Christianity to the race.[24] New York Baptist pastor Nathaniel Paul (1793-1839), in the epigraph at the opening of this chapter, concluded that either God was sovereign and just or all of religion was a sham.

The earliest African American Christians in the North held an interpretive framework exalting God's attributes of goodness and righteousness above the apparently contradictory evidence of suffering and moral evil. In all things, God ruled, worked his designs, and produced blessings for his people. These writers staked their theological convictions on the long arc of God's justice revealed in the Bible's redemption narrative and refused to any single event or experience the power to call into question his righteousness.

Southern writers. Questions about the nature of God and of his justice were not limited to northern writers. Questions and ideas also appeared among blacks in the South. Like their counterparts above the Mason-Dixon line, southern blacks also accepted a conception of God that emphasized his sovereignty and goodness. However, in ways more pronounced than their northern

---

[21]Lemuel Haynes, "The Influence of Civil Government on Religion" (1798), in *Black Preacher to White American: The Collected Writings of Lemuel Haynes, 1774-1833,* ed. Richard Newman (Brooklyn: Carlson, 1990), 65-76.

[22]Lemuel Haynes, "The Nature and Importance of True Republicanism" (1801), in *Black Preacher to White America: The Collected Writings of Lemuel Haynes, 1774-1833,* ed. Richard Newman (Brooklyn: Carlson, 1990), pp. 80-81.

[23]Olaudah Equiano, *The Interesting Narrative of the Life of Olaudah Equiano, or Gustavas Vassa, the African,* in *My Soul Has Grown Deep: Classics of Early African-American Literature,* ed. John Edgar Wideman (Philadelphia: Running Press, 2001), ed. John C. Shields (New York: Oxford University Press, 1988), pp. 192, 194.

[24]Phillis Wheatley, *The Collected Works of Phillis Wheatley,* ed. John C. Shields (New York: Oxford University Press, 1988), p. 15.

brethren, southern slaves and freemen developed the traditional attributes of God into a conception of the Father as Deliverer. This Deliverer motif primarily concerned God's timely, active engagement in human affairs.

Slave testimony: The waymaking "Time God" who delivers his people. From the slave exhorter to the field hand and from the secret plantation gatherings in the "hush arbors" to the plaintive songs of labor, the enslaved African worshiped God as the deliverer of the oppressed and downtrodden. And in this view, they found ample support and hope from the Old Testament history of God's intervention in the life of Israel. From the accounts of bondage under Pharaoh to the exodus under Moses, the early African American Christian appropriated the sojourn of Israel as their own. This view of God as Deliverer found expression in the entire tradition of the early black church. It was a doctrinal distinctive "believed and taught everywhere and by all" (to borrow from a Catholic formulation). Evidence of the doctrine's pervasiveness was found in slave conversion testimony, in songs and prayers, and in early preaching.

In the conversion testimonies of many slaves, the Deliverer motif pictured God as the "Waymaker" and the "Time God." The harshness of slave life constantly threatened to crush individuals in sorrow and despair. The deluge of pain and suffering promised to engulf the slave if God did not intervene, if he did not "make a way." The notion of God as a "Time God" pointed to his control and action in space-time history. For the African American in the antebellum South, God appeared in human affairs in an immanent, indeed personal, way. He was not, primarily, a transcendent God, but One who consistently identified with the plight of his people. Mary Reynolds recorded her recollection of a spiritual gathering that included a glimpse of the slave's dependence on this way-making God:

> Once my maw and paw taken me and Katherine after night to slip to 'nother place to a prayin'-and-singin'. A nigger man with white beard told us a day am comin' when niggers only be slaves of Gawd. We prays for the end of trib'lation and the end of beatin's and for shoes that fit our feet. We prayed that us niggers could have all we wanted to eat, 'cause that all we can do. Some say they was glad to [wished for] the time they's dead, 'cause they'd rather rot in the ground than have the beatin's.[25]

---

[25]Testimony of Mary Reynolds in Mellon, *Bullwhip Days*, p. 19.

Slaves concerned themselves in prayer for practical provision to be made for their needs—shoes and food—and for release from the tribulation of the lash. Prayer was their one weapon in this struggle, and they used it even as they longed for death. The idea of a way-making God was a folk expression capturing the faithfulness of God to respond materially, substantially, tangibly even—or perhaps especially—when there seemed to be no way of escape. The Waymaker was adept at providentially fashioning circumstances to relieve his people of their plight in just the right manner, often in ways hidden to the believer.

And in the experience and biblical hope of the African American, God not only promised to intervene but did so "right on time." Consequently, the way-making Deliverer also revealed himself as the "Time God." The testimony of a widowed slave woman concerned about the presence of God in her suffering when everyone else appeared to be faring well illustrated this belief. She recounted, "A voice spoke to me as plain as day but it was inward and said, *'I am a time-god working after the counsel of my own will. In due time I will bring all things to you.* Remember and cause your heart to sing.'"[26] The revelation of God as a Time-God was bound together with his sovereign providence and his promise to provide "all things." She was to rejoice at God's promised faithfulness, knowing that he who promised controlled time and events according to his will.

Though the slaves understood God to be a way-maker and a God of time, it would be a mistake to conclude that they believed their desires or needs in some way dictated his presence and action. According to one, God had "His own time and way of taking hold of His people and His works are more than we read and think about. He is a Time God and He won't make haste."[27] The Time-God remained sovereign and free, deciding when and how to interact with the events of history. Although this conception of God was often "revealed" to the slave in voices or dreams, it is consistent with the biblical revelation (see, for example, Ephesians 1:5, 9, 11). The enslaved somehow found solace in the fact that God was not hurried or moved to action apart from the dictates of his own, often mysterious or hidden, purposes. And they found in his promise of deliverance and timely provision, and in the history of Israel, exculpatory evidence supporting their recognition of the just character of God.

---

[26]Clifton Johnson, ed., *God Struck Me Dead: Religious Conversion Experiences and Autobiographies of Ex-Slaves* (Cleveland: United Church Press, 1969), p. 20, emphasis added.
[27]Ibid., p. 25.

Theology in song. Slave songs and spirituals also provide a glimpse into the theology of antebellum blacks. That literature, while too vast to thoroughly review here, yields good material for understanding the slave's view of God.[28]

In short, the theology of slave spirituals was "consistent with the heart of Protestant theology of [its] era."[29] Benjamin E. Mays (1895-1984) summarized the theology of the spirituals thus:

> God is omnipotent, omnipresent, and omniscient. In both heaven and earth, God is sovereign. He is a just God. . . . In the very nature of things sinners will be punished by God. He will see to it that the wicked are destroyed. God is revengeful. He hardened the heart of Pharoah for the express purpose of trapping him and his host in the Red Sea. This indicates that God is a warrior and He fights the battles of his chosen people. "Go Down Moses" and "Joshua Fit de Battle ob Jericho" are filled with the confidence that God takes care of his own.

Mays continued his summary:

> God is near and there is a feeling of dependence upon Him. In times of distress, He is ever present. The idea that God comforts and consoles in hours of trials is brought out in the Spirituals, "Keep Me From Sinking Down" and "Give Me Jesus When I Come to Die." There is no doubt that God is ever present.[30]

In these summations, Mays related the slave's belief in both some typical orthodox insights into the nature of God (his omnipotence, etc.) and some unique partisan understandings of the immanence of God. Authors and singers of the spirituals defined God in ways that brought to bear his greatness, power, and majesty in the defense of his people. The Waymaker and Deliverer spoken of in slave testimonies and sermons found poetic expression in slave songs. For

---

[28]Several authors have written book-length studies of spirituals and slave songs. The interested reader might find helpful materials in William Francis Allen, Charles Pickard Ware and Lucy McKim Garrison, *Slave Songs of the United States* (New York: A. Simpson, 1867; Electronic Edition available from the University of North Carolina at Chapel Hill); James H. Cone, *The Spirituals and the Blues: An Interpretation* (New York: Orbis, 1972); Howard Thurman, *Deep River and the Negro Spiritual Speaks of Life and Death* (Richmond, Ind.: Friends United Press, 1975); James Weldon Johnson and J. Rosamund Johnson, *The Book of American Negro Spirituals: Volume One* (New York: Viking Press, 1925); James Weldon Johnson and J. Rosamund Johnson, *The Book of American Negro Spirituals: Volume Two* (New York: Viking Press, 1926).
[29]David Emmanuel Goatley, "Godforsakeness in African American Spirituals," in *Cut Loose Your Stammering Tongue: Black Theology in the Slave Narrative*, ed. Dwight N. Hopkins and George C. L. Cummings, 2nd ed. (Louisville, Ky.: Westminster John Knox Press, 2003), p. 135.
[30]Benjamin E. Mays, *The Negro's God as Reflected in His Literature* (New York: Antheneum, 1973), p. 21. First published in 1938.

example, the slave spiritual "Jehovah Hallelujah" juxtaposed the slave's expectation of God's provision with the Lord's own abandonment of his glory:

Jehoviah, Hallelujah, De Lord is perwide,
Jehoviah, Hallelujah, De Lord is perwide.
De foxes have a hole, an' de birdies have-a nest,
De Son of Man he dunno where to lay de weary head.[31]

The slave also sang of God's just identification with their cause. For them, any difficulties with the righteousness of God in this life were satisfied by the ultimate vindication of God in the judgment and life to come. So, for example, the second verse of "Come Along, Moses" proclaimed:

We have a just God to plead-a our cause,
to plead-a our cause, to plead-a our cause,
We have a just God to plead-a our cause,
We are the people of God.[32]

Whether through personal testimony or lyrical artistry, enslaved African American Christians in the South believed in a God of justice and deliverance. They easily identified themselves as the new people of Israel, the new bondmen awaiting the providential hand of God to set them free from their afflictions—either in this life or the one to come. They confidently sang, "We are the people of God." From the earliest writings of Jupiter Hammon to the testimonies of slaves alive at Emancipation, African Americans displayed a consistently orthodox or traditional comprehension of God. Moreover, God was not an abstraction but a present, partisan and powerful reality in their daily lives—making a way when things were most bleak and pleading their cause in both the human and heavenly courts. This theology did not undergo any significant revision until the political and social turmoil of the decades following Reconstruction.

RECONSTRUCTION, "JIM CROW" SEGREGATION, GREAT MIGRATION AND THE "NEW NEGRO" MOVEMENT (1865-1929)

From Emancipation through the 1930s, African Americans experienced

---

[31] Allen et al., *Slave Songs of the United States*, p. 2. The stenographers recorded the hymn with as precise a reflection of the coastal South Carolina dialect as possible. The word rendered "perwide" is translated as "provide," and "dunno" is "doesn't know."

[32] Ibid., p. 104, emphasis added.

several significant social and cultural shifts. Between 1890 and 1930, some 2.5 million African Americans left the depressed economy and racial discrimination of the South to join the Great Migration to the North to seek employment in large urban centers. "This massive movement of people disrupted rural and urban congregations, transplanted southern religious customs North and West, strained the resources of urban churches, and formed in black city neighborhoods new opportunities for religious creativity."[33] The Harlem Renaissance and the "New Negro" movement embodied this burgeoning creativity. Led by men like Alaine Locke (1886-1954) and James Weldon Johnson (1871-1938), these campaigns produced a flood of creative works that explored the varieties and meanings of the black experience, renewed interest in Africa, and promoted a new vision of "blackness" among Negroes in America. These great social changes gave rise to seismic shifts in the way African Americans defined themselves, and the esteem they attached to their culture and history. During this same period, leaders like Booker T. Washington (1856-1915) and W. E. B. DuBois (1868-1963) championed political and economic self-help agendas for African Americans. Not surprisingly, then, African Americans' conception of God changed profoundly.

Marcus Garvey's God as universal intelligence. Jamaican-born Marcus Mosiah Garvey Jr. (1887-1940) immigrated to the United States in 1916 and soon thereafter established the pan-Africanist organization called the Universal Negro Improvement Association (UNIA). The UNIA sought to organize Negroes all over the world for the purposes of instituting an independent government, launching independent black-owned businesses, and the general uplift of African peoples. However, perhaps the greatest impact of the UNIA was the mark it made on the religious and social consciousness and imagination of black Americans. In an October 16, 1920, edition of the *Negro World*, the organization's official newspaper, Garvey likened the movement to a religious conversion. "The masses of the race absorb the doctrines of the UNIA with the same eagerness with which the masses in the days of the supremacy of imperial Rome accepted Christianity. The people seem to regard the move-

---

[33] Albert J. Raboteau, *Canaan Land: A Religious History of African Americans* (New York: Oxford University Press, 2001). See chapter 5, "From Plantation to Ghetto: Religion in the City," for a brief treatment of some of these changes.

Marcus Mosiah Garvey

ment in the light of a new religion."[34] The people's "regard" for the movement as a new religion was not an uninstigated flight of fancy on their behalf. The UNIA intentionally sought to create this impression and to provide a distinctly "African" alternative to white Christianity by offering religious worship services, rituals and symbols appropriate for Negro peoples—including a black Jesus and a black Madonna.

In addition to centering its religious expression upon the ethos of Negro Americans during the height of the Harlem Renaissance, Garvey's theology blended traditional Christian doctrines and themes with the prevailing New Thought philosophies of his time. New Thought philosophy emphasized mental healing and mind mastery as metaphysical theories necessary for success in life. One UNIA official and friend to Garvey proclaimed the leader to

---

[34]Cited in Robert A. Hill and Barbara Bair, eds., *Marcus Garvey: Life and Lessons* (Berkeley: University of California Press, 1987), p. xxxvi.

be "the apostle of New Thought among Negroes." Garvey himself declared that "new thought must be injected into the race" in order to escape racial turmoil and disorder. In 1920, at least one commentator observed a widespread influence of Christian Science and New Thought ideas among American blacks.[35] With the enormous popular appeal of the UNIA movement, Marcus Garvey did much to make this assessment a reality.

Consequently, Garvey spoke often about the nature of God in trinitarian terms. Lessons five and six from his School of African Philosophy were expositions of his view of God, Christ and the Holy Spirit. In lesson five on God, Garvey appropriated traditional Christian language about God and infused that language with New Thought emphases. He taught that God was "not a person nor a physical being. He is a spirit and He is universal intelligence."[36] The commingling of a noncorporeal spirit concept of God from orthodox Christianity with the New Thought emphasis on "universal intelligence" demarcated Garvey's theology as at once familiar in rhetoric but filled with meaning wholly new to the African American understanding of God. As universal intelligence, God was the "embodiment of all intelligence" and beyond the measurement or questioning of man whose intelligence was "unitary" and finite.[37]

Garvey surmised that "The doctrine of the Trinity of God the Father, the Son, and the Holy Ghost is not commonly understandable to the ordinary mind that will not think in the guiding spirit of God." However, he concluded that for "the mind that thinks with the spirit of God it is very pleasingly understood that the Godhead is one in three parts all related and all doing good, you cannot separate them."[38] With this pronouncement, Garvey offered a statement on the Trinity that was orthodox enough on the surface—even hinting at the apostle Paul's teaching on the need for spiritual discernment of divine truth.[39] However, Garvey intended a fairly different meaning than orthodox formulations suggested. For Garvey, the incomprehensibility of the Trinity signaled a New Thought idea of the vastness of universal intelligence

---

[35]Ibid., pp. xxviii–xxix.
[36]Ibid., p. 221.
[37]Ibid., pp. 221, 228.
[38]Ibid., p. 228.
[39]See 1 Cor 2:7-15. The apostle describes the gospel of Jesus Christ and the plan of God to redeem men through the cross of Christ as a mystery revealed only through the Spirit of God who searches both the mind of God and the hearts of men.

or the *"thought* that created the Universe" and "masters the Universe."[40]

Garvey's theology functioned as a call to Negro people to emulate this basic aspect of God by committing to education and the development of their minds. Since a share of the universal intelligence was found in man, and the road to progress was largely an issue of mind over matter, Garvey called his listeners to use their thoughts "to get the best results from the Universe." He reminded them that, "Proper thinking may lead [them] suddenly into the conquest of that which heretofore was mysterious."[41] And since God was ultimately universal intelligence, Garvey's followers were to find companionship with God by seeking the most excellent thoughts. Invoking the parable of the faithful steward, Garvey concluded that man must "lift himself highest to God by his mental industry, and the man who has not mental industry forfeits that mentality to the useful servant who climbs in his excellence to the most *excellent*."[42]

Where earlier conceptions of God encouraged the believer with assurances of God's sovereign rule and just purposes, Garvey's theology functioned as an inducement to intellectual growth and stewardship in the cause of racial self-help and self-development. In many ways, Garvey's thinking foreshadowed New Age and word-of-faith influences in contemporary Christianity.

DEPRESSION AND WORLD WAR II (1930-1949)

In 1922, Marcus Garvey was arrested on spurious mail fraud charges, and he was convicted in June 1923. Following a brief stint in prison, President Calvin Coolidge commuted Garvey's sentence and ordered his deportation from the United States in 1927. What had been a unified political, religious, social and economic program in the philosophy of Marcus Garvey splintered into loosely connected and sometimes independent elements after his deportation. During the rise and fall of Garveyism, African American soldiers returned from European battlefronts with hopes of greater inclusion and freedom in American society. Their hopes were met with rejection, repression and riots. The iron strictures of Jim Crow segregation and U.S. disenfranchisement policies clamped down on upstart expressions of black independence.

---

[40]Marcus Garvey, "The Universe," in *Marcus Garvey: Life and Lessons*, ed. Robert A. Hill and Barbara Bair (Berkeley: University of California Press, 1987), p. 275, italics original.
[41]Ibid.
[42]Ibid., italics original.

Emboldened by brief tastes of social freedom in Europe and the blossoming New Negro aesthetic, black Americans organized and protested in many U.S. cities for social and political liberty. These efforts tilled ground and planted early seeds for what would become the Civil Rights movement. These protests also influenced African American doctrines of God. In the aftermath of the Garvey movement's collapse arose different perspectives on the nature of God and his relationship to the plight of black people. Two such perspectives were the "social rehabilitation" or "social construction" orientation of Benjamin Elijah Mays (1894-1984) and the mystical thought of Howard Thurman.

Benjamin Elijah Mays and The Negro's God as Reflected in His Literature. Born in 1894 to former slaves, Benjamin Elijah Mays grew up in South Carolina. Despite his meager beginnings, Mays graduated from Maine's Bates College in 1920 and was ordained a Baptist minister while pursuing masters and doctoral degrees at the University of Chicago. He later taught at Morehouse College and South Carolina State, and served as dean of Howard University's school of religion and president of Morehouse College. Known mostly for his leadership in civil rights and spiritual mentorship to younger civil rights advocates, including Martin Luther King Jr., Julian Bond and Andrew Young, Mays also authored a number of studies of African American religion and theology.[43]

The 1938 publication of Benjamin Elijah Mays's *The Negro's God as Reflected in His Literature* marked a turning point in African American conceptions of God. Writing more like a literary critic or sociologist than a theologian, Mays provided perhaps the first systematic categorization of African American ideas about God from 1760 to 1938. Though not an explicit statement of Mays's own theology, the work established the parameters for African American writings about God for the following generations, significantly shaping how various writers and thinkers were understood.

In *The Negro's God*, Mays divided the history of African Americans into three time periods: 1760 to the Civil War, the Civil War to 1914 (World War I), and 1914 to 1938. Mays argued that the concept of God evolved in response to the changing social contexts African Americans encountered, developing according

---

[43]Benjamin E. Mays, *Born to Rebel: An Autobiography* (Athens: University of Georgia Press, 2003); Lawrence Edward Carter, ed., *Walking Integrity: Benjamin Elijah Mays, Mentor to Martin Luther King, Jr.* (Macon, Ga.: Mercer University Press, 1998).

to a three-part typology.[44] *Traditional or compensatory* views were mainly orthodox Christian views of God formed from biblical teaching and combined with a "shallow pragmatism" that sought satisfaction of certain psychological or emotional desires of the adherent. For Mays, Christians of this stripe held a view of God that made them "other-worldly," by which Mays meant that such Christians emphasized the ultimate justice of God in spiritual or heavenly terms rather than looking for justice in the present world. Christian ideas of God and heaven were means for keeping the people "submissive, humble, and obedient." They were an "opiate to deaden one's sensibility to slavery and other problems."[45] He categorized the writings of individuals like Jupiter Hammon, Phillis Wheatley and most of the Negro spirituals into this compensatory class.

Thinkers in the *constructive* category emphasized progress and social adjustment in this life. Mays argued that their view of God led them to insist on justice and social change as a priority *over* the end-of-life or heavenly priorities of their traditional counterparts. Exemplars of the constructive category included Henry Highland Garnett (1815-1882) and David Walker (1796-c. 1830), who called slaves to radical action against oppression. Mays approvingly cited figures like Frederick Douglass (1818-1895), Daniel Alexander Payne, and James W. C. Pennington (1807-1870) as men whose view of God prompted them to seek social adjustments that were either universal in scope, particular to the plight of Negroes, or psychological protests against claims of racial inferiority.[46] Mays offered the following summation of the constructive category's view of God, in which God was best recognized as a force and power for change in society:

> God may be defined as the power or force in man and in the world that impels man to seek to transform life in the interest of a healthier and more resplendent life for mankind individually and generally. The ideas are not other-worldly. They place one under obligation to adjust himself to a life of peace where all may enjoy the fruits necessary for resplendent living. They go far beyond the limits of race, but the needs of the race are met in the universality of the ideas of God presented. They are constructively developed in terms of social reconstruction that is universal.[47]

---

[44]Benjamin E. Mays, *The Negro's God as Reflected in His Literature* (New York: Antheneum, 1973), pp. 14-16. First published by Chapman and Grimes in 1938.
[45]Ibid., pp. 26, 59.
[46]Ibid., pp. 15, 107-26.
[47]Ibid., p. 82.

The third category presented in *The Negro's God* was post-War *agnosticism* or *atheism*. Here, Mays discerned a tendency among some writers "to abandon the conception of God 'as a useful instrument' in social rehabilitation." These writers vacillated along a continuum from the denial of God's existence to doubting the value of God in the Negro's struggle. Mays noted this strain of thinking in some of the writers of the post-War period, including some of the poetry of Countee Cullen (1903-1946) and various works from W. E. B. DuBois, James Weldon Johnson and Langston Hughes (1902-1967).[48]

While Mays did not intend to endorse a particular view of God as better or best for black people, he often wrote in terms more sympathetic to a constructive view. For example, Mays rejected Jupiter Hammon and Phillis Wheatley as offering a view of God that sedated the people and ignored their condition. While he showed some appreciation for the comforting power of the theology reflected in Wheatley's poetry, Mays condemned Wheatley as "hardly concerned about transforming society."[49] He censured the "traditional" or "compensatory" writers as utterly other-worldly and only thinly veiled his disdain for their depictions of God, formed as he saw it by their relatively privileged experience of slavery when compared to the masses of chattel with tougher lots.

The Negro's God established a major system of interpreting African American writings that reigned for the remainder of the twentieth century. Mays's study of African American literature set the boundaries for classifying black writers' conceptions of God. As the first to survey and codify African American thinkers along an accomodationist—protest continuum, Mays in some ways helped to lay the foundation for later schools of Black Theology. Though widely influential and historically important for its ambitious grappling with a wide array of black literature, the work suffered from two weaknesses.

First, Mays's study built its dichotomization of traditional views of God and social constructive ideas of God on a false premise. While he acknowledged that the view of God typical to these two categories was the same essentially Christian and orthodox understanding,[50] he continued separating in-

---

[48]Ibid., pp. 15, 223-39.
[49]Ibid., p. 106.
[50]See, for example, Mays's summaries of chapter 2 (pp. 96-97) and chapter 3 (pp. 126-27) where he describes a common idea of God worked out in two different reactions to the social situation. These summaries make it clear that compensatory and social rehabilitative "ideas" of God are the application of the theology and not the theology itself.

dividuals according to this typology *as if* they defined God differently. The distinction between traditional and constructive groups inhered not so much in their perspectives on God *per se* but with the *inferences* or *applications* they drew from their common doctrine. That is, holding the same theology, the two groups emphasized different actions to be taken or the same actions taken in different degrees. By confusing the social ethics of the groups with the groups' theology, Mays erected a false interpretation and division of African American religious thought. He failed to realize that no contradiction existed between holding a traditional or orthodox view of God, on the one hand, *and* mustering social reactions ranging from radical to accomodationist, on the other. The earliest generations of African Americans did not see a contradiction or inconsistency, though some prioritized spiritual salvation over the temporal. Yet, they all resisted, planned, fought and acted against social injustices in their own ways—and did so as much as anyone in later generations would. In fact, later generations could only be "later" and perhaps bolder in their proclamations because they inherited the successes of their orthodox forebears.

Second, *The Negro's God* suffered from an instrumental view of religion in general and of God particularly. In developing his typology partly under the theme of God's usefulness, Mays reduced Christian assumptions about God to a tool for achieving certain social and personal goals. Though he acknowledged the biblical origins of the various views of God, Mays undercut the Christian convictions and sincerity undergirding the earliest writings and songs by assuming the positions were held largely out of a concern for obtaining certain ends. This occurred most explicitly in his assessment of compensatory and post-War agnostic views, with compensatory views reducing God to an end for achieving emotional and psychological balance in the midst of suffering and post-War agnostic views denying the usefulness of God altogether. However, pragmatic or instrumental assumptions also affected Mays's constructive or social rehabilitative view where God was equated to a "power or force . . . to transform life."[51]

That members of these types derived certain benefits from their views of God is not in dispute. However, the weakness of an instrumental interpretation of a people's faith claims is that it fails to take seriously the adherents' be-

---

[51]Mays, *The Negro's God*, p. 82.

lief in the actual veracity of the claim. In other words, an instrumental interpretation does not allow sufficient room for the likelihood that a person
prioritizes spiritual things over earthly things—not because they "feel better"
doing so—but precisely because they understand such prioritization to be the
Bible's prioritization and the truth. An instrumental interpretation of faith
robs the social rehabilitationist of her or his belief that acting for a better society is, in fact, the ethical imperative fostered in the Bible. Such an approach
suggests that what people really believe is less important than how they act as
a result of that belief. *The Negro's God* shifts focus from the nature of God to
the nature of human activity or response to injustice. That shift profoundly affects the evaluation of theological ideas today, as very often the favored theology is one that uncritically places God on the side of the oppressed and treats
any reaction to injustice that does not seek to rehabilitate society as suspect.

   God as "being" in the thought of Howard Thurman. Perhaps no one is more
difficult to categorize in the history of African American theology than
Howard Thurman, whose mystical orientation to theological questions made
him a singular personality in black Christianity. This is particularly true with
regard to his views on the nature of God. It is easier to define what Thurman
did not believe about God than it is to positively identify what he did believe.
For example, Thurman was not trinitarian in his understanding. Though he
did speak of God and the Spirit in terms suggesting divinity, nowhere in his
writing or speaking did he assign divinity to Jesus Christ.

   Moreover, Thurman departs from historical categories for describing the
nature of God, instead defining God as "the source of the vitality, the life, of
all living things." He continued, "It is fundamental to my thought that God is
the Creator of Life, the Creator of the living substance, the Creator of existence, and as such expresses himself through life."[52] Thurman sought out a
"crucial rationale for the aliveness of life," which he contended could only be
God. For Thurman, the "beingness" of God was his most essential characteristic. Here, he echoed Paul Tillich's *Systematic Theology* published in 1951,
which defined God as "being-itself" or "Ground of being."[53] For Thurman,
God was the very ground of existence, of life. Recalling the apostle Paul's

---

[52]Howard Thurman, *Disciplines of the Spirit* (Richmond, Ind.: Friends United Press, 1977), pp. 21, 87.
[53]See Paul Tillich, *Systematic Theology, Volume One* (Chicago: University of Chicago, 1951).

words in Acts 17:28, Howard Thurman contended that communication with God was the most natural thing in the world because it was *in God* that all things consisted.

Though not a pantheist, Thurman appreciated the pantheistic worldview precisely because it intuited the presence of God in all things, a view known as panentheism. That intuition made sense of his childhood experiences with nature:

> As a child I was accustomed to spend many hours alone in my rowboat, fishing along the river, when there was no sound save the lapping of the waves against the boat. There were times when it seemed as if the earth and the river and the sky and I were one beat of the same pulse. It was a time of watching and waiting for what I did not know—yet I always knew. There would come a moment when beyond the single pulse beat there was a sense of Presence which seemed always to speak to me. My response to the sense of Presence always had the quality of personal communion. There was no voice. There was no image. There was no vision. There was God.[54]

Thurman's panentheistic view of God was integral to his idea of religious experience as an individual's conscious and direct exposure to God in a way that includes all the meaning of life. "In the experience defined as religious, the individual is seen as being exposed to direct knowledge of ultimate meaning, *ne plus ultra* being, in which all that the individual is becomes clear as immediate and often distinct revelation. He is face to face with something which is so much more, and so much more inclusive, than all of his awareness of himself that for him, *in the moment*, there are no questions. Without asking, somehow he knows."[55] Such an experience required that "God must be all-inclusive, all-comprehending, and in a profound sense universal."[56] In referring to the all-inclusive and all-comprehending nature of God, Thurman loosely appropriated more typical notions of God's omnipresence and omniscience. However, he understood these concepts not as proofs for God's transcendence but of his immanence. And unlike more orthodox applications of these ideas, Thurman believed it was an individual's spiritual en-

---

[54]Thurman, *Disciplines of the Spirit*, p. 93.
[55]Howard Thurman, *The Creative Encounter: An Interpretation of Religion and the Social Witness* (Richmond, Ind.: Friends United Press, 1954), p. 24.
[56]Ibid., p. 28.

counter with God that yielded real and complete comprehension of these facts about God. Religious experience taught the most important fact about God, namely, that he *is*.

Thurman's theology echoed some of the New Thought themes of Marcus Garvey. While immensely popular in academic circles, he did not strive for or command the kind of popular awareness and adulation that Garvey wielded. His particular theological perspective was not widespread among the masses of black America, but his influence on the pulpit was undeniable. As a revered educator and orator, many African American pastors and leaders acknowledged Thurman as a significant influence in their thinking. And through these pastors and preachers, Thurman's nonsectarian and doctrinally ambivalent theology has no doubt reached many in the pew as well.

CIVIL RIGHTS ERA (1950-1979)

In many respects, the religious syncretism of Marcus Garvey and the theology of Howard Thurman were an interlude between the long-standing view of God established in Hammon, Haynes and other early African American writers up to Reconstruction and the radical reinterpretations of God birthed during the 1960s. In the late 1800s, Bishop Henry McNeal Turner (1834-1915) declared that blacks needed a God that reflected them—a black God. In an 1898 editorial published in *The Voice of Missions*, Turner responded to the white press for mocking his assertion:

> We have as much right biblically and otherwise to believe that God is a Negro, as you buckra, or white, people have to believe that God is a fine looking, symmetrical and ornamented white man. For the bulk of you, and all the fool Negroes of the country, believe that God is white-skinned, blue-eyed, straighthaired, projecting-nosed, compressed-lipped and finely-robed white gentleman, sitting upon a throne somewhere in the heavens. Every race of people since time began who have attempted to describe their God by words, or by paintings, or by carvings, or by any other form or figure, have conveyed the idea that the God who made them and shaped their destinies was symbolized in themselves, and why should not the Negro believe that he resembles God as much so as other people? We do not believe that there is any hope for a race of people who do not believe that they look like God.
>
> Demented though we be, whenever we reach the conclusion that God or even

that Jesus Christ, while in the flesh, was a white man, we shall hang our gospel trumpet upon the willow and cease to preach.[57]

Marcus Garvey obliged Bishop Turner with a black Christ and Virgin Mary. And writers like Countee Cullen gave imaginative, poetic voice to both Turner and Garvey.

God in our own image: The *"black" God of Black Theology*. The nascent desire for a black God or a God for black people did not reach full flower until the advent of the Black Power movement. Black Theology took seriously the musings of Turner and the visual stylizations of Marcus Garvey and attempted a full articulation of a "black" God. James Cone's radical Black Theology project approached this redefinition of God on two fronts: first by reorienting traditional attributes ascribed to God toward the liberation struggles of oppressed blacks in America, and second by breaking from the solution to the theodicy puzzle fashioned in the 1700s and 1800s by declaring God firmly on the side of the oppressed.

Attributes of God in Black Theology. Black Theology dressed all the attributes of God in the cloak of black liberation. The black theologian presupposed the existence of God and focused on discerning the meaning of that existence as revealed both in biblical literature and the historical condition of black people. The traditional attributes of God developed

Bishop Henry McNeal Turner

in orthodox theological circles became in Black Theology handmaidens for understanding the disposition of God toward the plight of African Americans. For example, the historical definition of God's immanence, traditionally referring to the closeness or presence of God to his creation, became in James Cone's Black Theology an encounter with God in a "situation of historical liberation." Likewise, the doctrine of God's transcendence lost any spatial meaning—any sense of otherness and exaltedness—in Cone's view. Drawing from

---

[57]Henry McNeal Turner, "God Is a Negro," *The Voice of Missions* (February 1898); reprinted in Henry McNeal Turner, *Respect Black: The Writings and Speeches of Henry McNeal Turner,* comp. and ed. Edwin S. Redkey (New York: Arno Press and the New York Times, 1971), p. 176.

Tillich, Cone argued that God's transcendence referred to the human purpose, dignity and value revealed in the liberation struggle of black people.[58]

With regard to the providence of God—a doctrine integral to the earliest resolutions of apparent contradictions between the righteousness of God and human suffering—Cone rejected the formulations of Emil Brunner, who shared much with the positions of Haynes, Hammon, Wheatley, Equiano and others. Cone insisted that "God can't be the God of blacks *and* will their suffering."[59] He opted instead for a definition that turned away from the long-term view of providence that guaranteed God's good purposes in his own time and according to his own plan, and placed emphasis on the present reality of blacks and God's liberating activity on their behalf. Cone redefined both providence and omnipotence. According to Cone, omnipotence did not "refer to God's absolute power to accomplish what he wants," but to his "power to let blacks stand out from whiteness and to be."[60] While he rightly warned against "an easy acceptance of human injustice" in the name of providence, Cone ultimately saw a contradiction between suffering and the sovereign providence of God where earlier African American Christians saw none.

Cone also provided a critique of the tendency, *á la* Marcion and others, to emphasize God's love to the exclusion of his righteousness. The central question for Black Theology was "whether the love of God . . . can be properly understood without focusing equally on the biblical view of God's righteousness. Is it possible to understand what God's love means for the oppressed without making *wrath* an essential ingredient of that love?" Cone occluded a one-sided view of God and proclaimed that:

> A God without wrath does not plan to do too much liberating, for the two concepts belong together. A God minus wrath seems to be a God who is basically not against anything. All we have to do is behave nicely, and everything will work out all right.[61]

By holding the righteousness of God in unbreakable tension with the love of God, Cone sought a theological justification for condemnation of and judg-

---

[58]James H. Cone, *A Black Theology of Liberation: Twentieth Anniversary Edition* (Maryknoll, N.Y.: Orbis, 2003), pp. 76-78
[59]Ibid., p. 81, italics original.
[60]Ibid.
[61]Ibid., pp. 69-70, italics original.

ment against oppression. According to Cone, preserving the unity of God's righteousness and love allowed blacks to know whose side God was on in the revolution. He concluded, "There is no use for a God who loves white oppressors *the same as* oppressed blacks."[62] For whites, the love of God could only come in the form of God's wrath. For blacks, considering their drive for liberation against racist forces, Cone insisted "that God's love and righteousness [were] two ways of talking about the same reality. Righteousness means that God is addressing the black condition; love means that God is doing so in the interests of both blacks and whites."[63]

Black Theology posited that the love of God for humankind was demonstrated in God becoming black. God assumed solidarity with the oppressed, taking upon himself the condition of blacks. "God is black because God loves us," decided Cone, and "righteousness is that side of God's love which expresses itself through black liberation."[64] It's difficult to imagine a more radical redefinition of God in Christian history, especially African American Christian thought.

Theodicy in Black Theology: God becoming black. As is the case with every doctrinal issue in Black Theology, the question of the nature of God begins with and is viewed from the vantage point of black suffering and liberation. The central question for Black Theology's formulation of God is, "How do we dare speak of God in a suffering world, a world in which blacks are humiliated because they are black?"[65]

Cone rested his answer to this question and his view of God upon two hermeneutical principles. First, the Scriptures revealed God through the history of Israel's liberation from oppression beginning with the Old Testament exodus narratives and culminating in Jesus Christ. Second, the same God revealed in the history of Israel and the person of Jesus Christ remained active in the liberation struggle of black Americans during the Black Power movement. Thus, Black Theology rejected a "docetic" understanding of God that sought what Cone regarded as a merely philosophical definition of God's aseity instead of grappling with the "material" or real presence and activity of God in history.

---

[62]Ibid., p. 70, italics original.
[63]Ibid., pp. 72-73.
[64]Ibid., pp. 73-74.
[65]Ibid., p. 60.

From these two suppositions, Cone argued that God is black and that any conception of God that hinders the self-determination efforts of blacks must be rejected. The "blackness" of God entailed the idea that God makes the condition of the oppressed his own condition, and that God's essential nature is found in the concept of liberation.[66] The "heart of the Black Theology doctrine of God" was this conception of the blackness of God, which insisted that either God identified with the struggles of black people "to the point that their experience becomes God's experience or God is a God of racism."[67] Having rejected the traditional attribute of divine providence, an inescapable need for a theodicy pressed in on Cone's interpretation. Other writers deemed this dilemma irreconcilable with traditional theological tools and proffered a "humanocentric theism" that stressed the exercise of human choice and freedom as the basis for solving problems of evil.[68] Cone rejected this hypothesis and asserted that the dilemma of God's righteousness in the presence of such suffering and evil could only be resolved by positioning God on the side of the oppressed against the oppressor. Otherwise, Cone could conceive of no just God.

Cone rejected out of hand any view of God that limited the self-determination of black people. God's identification with blacks was the essence of biblical revelation demonstrated in God's election of Israelite slaves as his people and "becoming the Oppressed One in Jesus Christ." Just as God worked in the history of Israel to free them from bondage and overthrow their ancient oppressors, so too was God working in the experience of African Americans to liberate them from unjust racial oppression. So, Cone concluded, anyone wishing to know God must know who black people are and know something of their engagement in liberation activity. Liberation became the quintessential nature of God.[69] Cone explained:

> This does not mean lending a helping hand to the poor and unfortunate blacks of society. It does not mean joining the war on poverty! Such acts are sin offerings that represent a white way of assuring themselves that they are basically "good" persons.

---

[66]Ibid., pp. 63-64.
[67]Ibid., p. 63.
[68]William R. Jones, *Is God a White Racist? Prolegomenon to Black Theology*, rev. ed. (Boston: Beacon, 1997; first published in 1973 by Doubleday). For a brief treatment of Jones's thesis, see James H. Evans, *We Have Been Believers: An African-American Systematic Theology* (Minneapolis: Fortress, 1992), pp. 62-67.
[69]Cone, *Black Theology of Liberation*, pp. 63-64.

Knowing God means being on the side of the oppressed, becoming *one* with them, and participating in the goal of liberation. *We must become black with God!*[70]

The exodus, incarnation and crucifixion expressed this figurative "blackness" of God, that is, God identifying with the liberation activity of oppressed people. Cone interpreted these events to mean that, "God is free to be for us."

> The biblical God is the God of Jesus Christ who calls the helpless and weak into a newly created existence. God not only fights for them but takes their humiliated condition upon the divine Person and thereby breaks open a new future for the poor, different from their past and present miseries. Here is the central meaning of the cross, dramatically revealed in the Markan account in Jesus' cry of dereliction: "My God, my God, why hast thou forsaken me?"[71]

In Black Theology, the cross of Jesus Christ revealed a God who suffered for and with his people and joined them in the cause of liberation. God was not a distant conductor of providence moving chess pieces to suit his will, but a God who entered into the suffering of his people and established the grounds for their freedom and resistance. Cone critiqued historical philosophical definitions of the problem of evil for leaving out any consideration of political action against evil. He found such definitions too theoretical, too concerned with a rational reconciliation of God's omnipotence and the presence of moral evil, and not nearly practical enough. He issued a sweeping condemnation of Western theologians from the early church fathers to the Reformers Luther and Calvin to ethicist Reinhold Niebuhr (1892-1971) for their "theological blindness" in not making racial oppression a central problem in their deliberations.[72] While confessing appreciation for the answers to the problem of evil developed by earlier African Americans, Cone ultimately departed from their perspectives because of what he saw as too much emphasis on providence. He defended early writers against the charge of making black people submissive and servile, but he was unprepared to completely endorse their views apparently because their perspectives lacked sufficient emphasis on Christ's crucifixion as an event with liberation implications in *this* life.[73]

---

[70]Ibid., p. 65, italics original.
[71]James H. Cone, *God of the Oppressed* (Maryknoll, N.Y.: Orbis, 1997; first published by Seabury Press in 1975), p. 128.
[72]Ibid., pp. 181-85.
[73]Ibid., pp. 170-78.

James Cone set out to establish a theology sufficient for explaining the Black Power movement of the 1960s and the African American fight for liberation. He contributed theological ammunition to a war for reclaiming black life. While he drew upon earlier African American writers as a source for interpreting the nature and work of God, his conclusions represented a significant innovation in the theological discourse of black peoples. He defined a radical liberal theological perspective and spawned the first uniquely black academic approach to theological inquiry.

Yet, to the extent that the Reformed theological position of men like Lemuel Haynes and the generally orthodox view of African American slaves were appropriate standards for the doctrine of God, Cone's innovation was also a departure and a decline. Lost in Black Theology was the ability to think and write of God's person apart from the narrow confines of blackness as struggle and suffering. While Cone extended to black people a God of liberation with one hand, he ironically enslaved God to the mono-vocal local narrative of black life with the other hand. Because Cone so firmly entrenched God in the struggle of black people, his theology ultimately featured a small, provincial deity incapable of the kind of complex and universal rule of creation understood by African Americans through Reconstruction. This diminution of God muted the significant advance of Black Theology, which was to raise the concern of black suffering and oppression for Christian doctrines of God.

END OF CENTURY, POSTMODERN ERA (1980-PRESENT)

African American Christians closed the twentieth century with three major views of the doctrine of God. First, they held to traditional and orthodox perspectives found in the Scriptures and bequeathed through centuries of Christian history, emphasizing God's sovereignty, power, love, righteousness and holiness. This traditional orthodox view of God stood as an unchallenged phalanx over black faith and practice until Reconstruction and the social changes that followed. The second view might be considered a theologically liberal view of God—beginning with the New Thought metaphysics of Marcus Garvey and continuing with the liberal and mystical ideas of Howard Thurman. The liberal view gained wider acceptance in the 1950s and informed the thought of Dr. Martin Luther King Jr., who carried some of Howard Thurman's ideas into the populist Civil Rights movement of the 1950s and 1960s.

The liberal school of thought also gained momentum from the rise of denominational liberalism spreading throughout most major mainline branches of Protestantism. Black Theology, spearheaded by the writings of James Cone, represented a third approach to the doctrine of God, echoing the politically radical voices of earlier generations and of the Black Power movement. Black Theology's perspective on the doctrine of God focused more adamantly on political strivings than any theological system before it.

Each of these streams of thought continues into the present era, with new voices appearing on the scene for each.

Reviving old heresies: Bishop T. D. Jakes and the Oneness controversy. However, perhaps the most significant conflict regarding the doctrine of God among African Americans at the close of the twentieth century coincides with the rise and prominence of Bishop Thomas Dexter (T. D.) Jakes (1958-) of the Dallas, Texas–based Potter's House Ministries. Writers at *The New York Times* speculate that Bishop Jakes may be the "next Billy Graham," while journalists at *Time Magazine* dub him "the best preacher in America" and one of the twenty-five most influential evangelicals in America.[74] His influence extends to millions worldwide through his television outreach, speaking tours and popular books. Regrettably, his doctrine of God is taken from doctrinal errors roundly rejected by many modern Pentecostal and evangelical churches as well as the early Christian church.

Bishop Jakes subscribes to a Oneness Pentecostal doctrine of God. Oneness Pentecostalism is a branch of Pentecostalism with its modern roots extending to the Azusa Street revival of 1906 and revival meetings featuring Canadian preacher R. E. McAlister (1880-1953) and evangelist Frank Ewart (1876-1947) between 1913 and 1915. McAlister and Ewart departed from traditional and orthodox trinitarian views of the Godhead and taught the radical unity of God by denying that God existed in three Persons. They held that the one God appeared in three distinct "modes" or "manifestations"—as Father in creation, as the Son in redemption, and as Holy Spirit in regeneration and indwelling—but that there was only one real Person in the Godhead,

---

[74]Gustav Niebuhr and Laurie Goodstein, "The Preachers: A Special Report—New Wave of Evangelists Vying for National Pulpit," *The New York Times*, January 1, 1999; David Van Biema, "Spirit Raiser," *Time Magazine*, September 27, 2001; "Time Magazine 25 Most Influential Evangelicals in America," *Time Magazine*, February 7, 2005.

namely Jesus. Also known as "Modalism" in the early church, Ewart's teachings spread rapidly through Pentecostal denominations. At its 1916 General Assembly, the Assemblies of God, a major branch of Pentecostalism, rejected the Oneness doctrine of God and required adherence to trinitarian theology. Following that decision, nearly 160 Oneness ministers formed their own denominations and alliances. The Pentecostal Assemblies of the World formed in 1918 as a multiracial denomination, but split in 1924 along racial lines to become a predominantly African American organization.[75]

Bishop T. D. Jakes stands as a contemporary, though reluctant, representative of Oneness theology. Jakes tends to eschew doctrinal disputes and offers a passing defense of his theology by saying, "Christians have always had diversity in their theology and will continue to do so."[76] Nonetheless, historically orthodox churches condemn or exclude heretical views as misrepresentations of biblical faith—including the Oneness doctrine of God for its denial of the Trinity.

The Potter's House "Doctrinal Statement" reads:

THREE DIMENSIONS OF GOD (I John 5:7; Matthew 28:19; I Timothy 3:16)
We believe in one God who is eternal in His existence, Triune in His manifestation, being both Father, Son and Holy Ghost AND that He is Sovereign and Absolute in His authority.[77]

The very title of the section, emphasizing *dimensions* of God, signals Jakes's heretical doctrinal stance. The brief exposition that follows uses typical Modalist or Oneness language referring to God as *"Triune in his manifestations"* but not in his Person.

Outside of this doctrinal statement, Jakes rarely explicates the theology informing his ministry. In one place, he writes, "One of the greatest controversies in all the Bible concerns the Godhead."[78] He explains his sense of the controversy with rhetorical questions intended to undermine the credibility of trinitarian doctrine: "If there is one God, as Scripture teaches, how can there be a Son who says that He and His Father are one? If there is only one God,

---

[75]"Oneness Pentecostalism," *Interfaith Belief Bulletin* (Alpharetta, Ga.: North American Mission Board, 1999).

[76]Downloaded from the Potter's House website May 17, 2005; available at <www.thepottershouse.org>.

[77]Ibid.

[78]T. D. Jakes, *Anointing Fall on Me: Accessing the Power of the Holy Spirit* (Lanham, Md.: Pneuma Life Publishing, 1997), p. 7

how can there be 'three that bear record in heaven, the Father, the Word, and the Holy Ghost: and these three are one'?"[79] Aside from the fact that the biblical writers did not record any intra-Christian "controversy" involving the trinitarian nature of God, Jakes's own admission of the "mystery" involved in understanding the Trinity should steer him away from attacking orthodox theological positions. However, intrepid in his conclusions, Jakes's error revives and popularizes the ancient, denounced heretical opinions of Sabellius in the third century A.D.[80] And in doing so, he does more than merely depart from tradition; Bishop T. D. Jakes's Oneness doctrine of God "indirectly undermines the Christian view of God's character, God's revelation, and God's salvation by grace."[81] Millions of people are influenced by Jakes's subtle representation of aberrant theology. And given the importance the Bible attaches to accurately knowing God, his revival of heresy is no small matter.

SUMMARIZING THE DECLINE

While theological changes from the 1800s to the present gave rise to the diversity of views in black religious thinking, such changes also produced significant changes to prevailing theological frameworks among African Americans. Though subtle to most untrained theologians, these shifts in understanding are profound in their implications. For example, the earliest black Christians maintained a tendency toward a Reformed or orthodox view of God as sovereign Ruler of all events. African Americans built this understanding upon the teachings of Scripture and aligned it with the historic definitions of Christianity. A high view of God's sovereignty allowed early black Christians, despite the horrors of slavery, to trust that God had the necessary power to deliver them from oppression and that he would ultimately do so. Any perceived contradictions between this doctrine of God and the evil afflicting black people were resolved *in* the character of God. Such a belief im-

---

[79]Ibid.

[80]For good treatments of Sabellianism or Modalist theology in the early church, see Jaroslav Pelikan, *The Christian Tradition: A History of the Development of Doctrine—Volume 1: The Catholic Tradition, 100-600* (Chicago: University of Chicago Press, 1971), pp. 176-80; for a brief discussion of the effect of Sabellianism on more contemporary theologians, see John D. Hannah, *Our Legacy: The History of Christian Doctrine* (Colorado Springs: NavPress, 2001), pp. 77-79, 98, 100.

[81]Gregory A. Boyd, *Oneness Pentecostals and the Trinity* (Grand Rapids: Baker Academic, 1992), p. 12; as cited in Jerry L. Buckner, "The Man, His Ministry, and His Movement: Concerns About the Teachings of T. D. Jakes," *Christian Research Journal* 22, no. 2 (1999).

plied at least two conclusions. First, these saints concluded that the events of their lives remained in the sovereign control of God. And second, they concluded that the proper response before the ineffable wisdom and providence of God was humility and faith. Both resolutions stirred more faith in God.

As generations and theologians after the Harlem Renaissance pursued New Negro and New Man ideologies, with their emphasis on self-help and independence, reliance on God evaporated into man-centered political programs. This theology resolved the perceived contradiction of God's righteousness *outside* the nature of God. In other words, it put forth a view of God that excused him from the exalted position of sovereign Ruler and placed control of human events outside his immediate control. These new views either marginalized God in the case of some writers like DuBois and Countee Cullen, or forced God into a black history-sized box in the case of James Cone and Black Theology. Faith in God became synonymous with "the struggle." Trust in God became reliance on one's self and assuming that God was "on your side" in the struggle. The idea that God purposed some ultimate good beyond suffering and evil died a sudden and hard death. The theological shift from pre- to post-Reconstruction doctrines of God reduced the incomprehensible God of pre-Reconstruction Christians to the imaginable "black" God of the Black Power movement. And once God is unambiguously proclaimed to "be on the side of" a certain people as in the case of Black Theology, there is no way to prevent the more solipsistic and materialistic partisan claims of prosperity teachers.

This decline from an orthodox definition of God leaves African American Christians vulnerable to "every wind of doctrine." Without critical reflection upon and, if need be, rejection of developing theologies, there is no effective way of protecting the faithful from serious error. The New Thought metaphysics of Garvey finds comfortable clothing in New Age ideas promulgated from some pulpits today. The long-rejected heresies of Oneness theology are espoused as acceptable diversity as some African American pastors and leaders clamor for a false unity.[82]

For many people, the importance and effect of these different doctrines of God will seem like academic nitpicking divorced from the "reality" of living

---

[82]The Trinity Broadcasting Network aired on March 8, 1999, a discussion between Trinitarian Bishop Clarence McClendon and Oneness advocate Bishop Noel Jones on the ways the two groups can learn from each other's theologies to "restate the Godhead" and foster unity.

the Christian faith. However, one's view of God profoundly shapes real-life decisions and actions.

The difference between the Reformed, liberal and radical views of God might be discerned by asking, "How central is the doctrine of God in each system?" For the earliest writers, nearly all of whom were Reformed in their theology, the doctrine of God was the distinctive tenet of their perspectives.[83] In other words, all other doctrinal issues and world events were interpreted in light of their basic understanding of God. Whether intentionally or not, later generations moderated their view of God with other biblical or temporal assumptions. Once this change occurred, the line between a true or biblically accurate view of God and certain political proclivities dressed in the name of God was obscured. Radical Black Theology, for example, assumed that one must fashion an idol in order to justify certain political stances—which is simply not true. The first generation of black writers proved that there was no contradiction between activist opposition to injustice and an orthodox theology and that it was unnecessary to surrender either theological orthodoxy or righteous indignation for the sake of the other. In fact, these writers demonstrated that an orthodox theology provided the best seedbed for long-term opposition to injustice.

We must avoid the mistaken conclusion that earlier generations opted for "pie-in-the-sky" or "opiate" forms of religion because they applied their theology in politically less strident or radical ways than we would prefer. We must avoid that anachronistic tendency that reads our freedoms back into earlier eras as a normative standard for action. If we make that mistake, we run the risk of misjudging the integrity and sophistication of the earliest writers' conceptions of God and of too harshly or wrongly judging their motives. We are better off humbly accepting and returning to the wisdom they articulated.

---

[83]I am indebted to Dr. R. C. Sproul for this insight. Dr. Sproul correctly points out that Reformed theology affirms along with nearly all other Protestant evangelical denominations most of the historical doctrines of Christianity. What makes Reformed theology distinctive is the centrality of the doctrine of God in all matters theological and temporal.

3

"Ain't I a Man?"

African American Anthropology

Cowardly and cruel are those Blacks Innate,
Prone to Revenge, Imp of inveterate hate.
He that exasperates them, soon espies
Mischief and Murder in their very eyes.
Libidinous, Deceitful, False and Rude,
The spume Issue of Ingratitude.
The Premises consider'd all may tell,
How near good Joseph they are parallel.

JOHN SAFFIN (1701)

[God] hath made of one blood all nations of men
for to dwell on all the face of the earth.

ACTS 17:26 (KJV)

GENERAL INTRODUCTION AND CONTEXT

Unlike any other religious issue, the doctrine of man, or anthropology, ener-
gized the theological and ethical energies of African Americans. Slave trading
rapidly became a central feature of southern life and northern colonies alike,
and profoundly shaped the economics and politics of the New World.[1] The in-

---

[1]See, for example, Allan Kulikoff, *Tobacco and Slaves: The Development of Southern Cultures in the Ches-*
apeake, 1680-1800 (Chapel Hill: University of North Carolina Press, 1986).

stitution of slavery with all of its inhumane brutality demanded a psychologically satisfying justification. The panacea offered by proslavery adherents involved the denial of the African's humanity. As the epigraph at the beginning of this chapter reveals, proponents of slavery multiplied arguments designed to emphasize fabricated differences between Africans and European whites—the African had no soul, was the result of human–ape intercourse, was subhuman or at least a lower species of humanity, was uneducable and uncivilized, and so on.[2] At their heart, these arguments betrayed historical Christian tenets regarding the nature of man.

In the historical Christian doctrine of man, God constituted man with both a physical body and an immortal soul. God created humanity "in his own image" and endowed him with certain faculties uncommon to the rest of the created order. However, man corrupted himself through sin and "fell" from his original state. Early Christian debates centered on how the Fall affected the freedom of man's will and the relationship between man's will and the grace of God. The Augustinian formulation persisted into the Reformation, where it was again debated and refined in the theology of Luther, Calvin and others who contended that the will of man was not free but bound by his sinful nature.[3]

Nearly all of the controversies from the early church fathers through the Reformation concentrated on the spiritual nature of man and rarely focused on the kind of ethical applications of anthropology relevant to the experience of Africans in America. That theological contribution remained for African Americans to make in defense of their humanity. The two hundred year war between African Americans and white Americans over the humanity of African-descended peoples represented the most prolonged and significant theological encounter between the two groups.

---

[2]For treatments of white justifications and attitudes towards Africans during the slave trade, see Stephen R. Haynes, *Noah's Curse: The Biblical Justification of American Slavery* (New York: Oxford University Press, 2002); Larry Tise, *Proslavery: A History of the Defense of Slavery in America, 1701-1840* (Athens: University of Georgia, 1987); and Winthrop D. Jordan, *White Over Black: American Attitudes Toward the Negro, 1550-1812* (Chapel Hill: University of North Carolina Press, 1968).

[3]Jaroslav Pelikan, *The Christian Tradition: A History of Development of Doctrine, Volume 1: The Emergence of the Catholic Tradition, 100-600* (Chicago: University of Chicago Press, 1971), pp. 278-331; and, *Volume 4: Reformation of Church and Dogma* (Chicago: University of Chicago Press, 1983), pp. 132-72. For a short treatment of Augustine's view on human freedom, see, Augustine *On Free Choice of the Will*, trans. Thomas Williams (Indianapolis: Hackett, 1993); Luther's views are expressed in Martin Luther, *Bondage of the Will*, reprint ed. (Grand Rapids: Revell, 1990).

EARLY SLAVERY ERA THROUGH ABOLITION ERA (1600-1865)

Though whites and blacks would eventually clash over the humanity of Africans, the earliest shots in the anthropological battles were fired between rival white theologians and churchmen. Judge Samuel Sewall (1652-1730) issued an antislavery response in 1700 to proslavery positions, notable for its review of Old and New Testament arguments against slavery and for liberty. In 1706 New England Puritan Cotton Mather (1663-1728) published *The Negro Christianized*, a tract defending the humanity of black men but failing to attack slavery as a system. The Reverend Samuel Willard (1640-1707) retorted against proslavery arguments that the soul of a slave was of equal worth to that of his owner and as precious in the sight of Christ. Quaker thinkers like John Woolman and Anthony Benezet (1713-1784) launched the most pervasive and steady assaults on proslavery sentiment.[4] However, their defense of the African's humanity and condemnation of slavery notwithstanding, "For virtually all the antislavery advocates, the Negro's color was not a mark of brotherhood but a defect which brotherhood must ignore."[5] Hence, many of the early defenders of African humanity stopped well short of extending their theological position to an ethical conclusion entailing the social and civil equality of Africans with whites. And though the Great Awakening buried any contentions regarding the African's soul and spiritual conversion, leading theologians and preachers of the awakening like Jonathan Edwards and George Whitefield owned slaves and left the institution of slavekeeping fairly untouched.[6] But, on the heels of the awakening arose the first generation of African American writers who put forth perhaps the most complete anthropology in Christian history, emphasizing both the full spiritual, physical and intellectual humanity of all peoples and parlaying that emphasis into a call for justice and equality in all spheres of human life.

Northern writers. The earliest African American thinkers and writers faced

---

[4]Jordan, *White Over Black*, pp. 193-204, 271-76; Noll, *History of Christianity in the United States and Canada* (Grand Rapids: Eerdmans, 1992), pp. 77-79; Kenneth Silverman, *The Life and Times of Cotton Mather* (New York: Welcome Rain Publishers, 1984), pp. 263-64.

[5]Jordan, *White Over Black*, p. 196; for a good treatment of the history of Christendom's assessment of blackness, see Robert E. Hood, *Begrimed and Black: Christian Traditions on Blacks and Blackness* (Minneapolis: Fortress Press, 1994).

[6]Noll, *History of Christianity in the United States and Canada*, pp. 108-10; Sherard Burns, "Trusting the Theology of a Slave Owner" in *A God-Entranced Vision of All Things: The Legacy of Jonathan Edwards*, ed. John Piper and Justin Taylor (Wheaton, Ill.: Crossway, 2004), pp. 145-71.

the strongest onslaught from white supporters of the slave trade and some white Christian sympathizers attempting to lend biblical justification to the practice. The early rationalizations for slavery appeared in two broad categories. First, proponents argued that since Africans were subhuman and had no soul, then the practice of slavery was permissible in the same way that domestication of cattle was allowable. This amounted to a spiritual assault on the humanity of the African. Second, slavery's apologists asserted that since Africans lacked acceptable levels of intelligence and moral virtue their enslavement was not only permissible but also good for both the African and white society. This attack on the natural endowments of the African formed the second category of proslavery rationalization.

Jupiter Hammon and spiritual equality between black and white. One of the earliest writers to respond to the spiritual misanthropy directed toward Africans was Jupiter Hammon (1711-1806). Hammon's most unique contribution among early African American writers included his forceful articulation of the spiritual equality all men shared given the corrupted nature and behavior of man and the need for repentance toward a savior. Each of Hammon's surviving sermons or essays developed these themes in detail. In *A Winter Piece*, for example, Hammon enunciated a standard view of original sin and the depravity of man. He wrote, "My brethren, it is not we servants only that are unworthy; but all mankind by the fall of Adam became guilty in the sight of God (Gen. 2:17). Surely then, we are sinners by nature and are daily adding thereto by evil practices."[7] Elsewhere, he elaborated:

> In the Bible likewise, we are told what man is. That he was at first made holy, in the image of God, that he fell from that state of holiness and became an enemy to God, and that since the fall, all the imaginations of the thoughts of his heart are evil, and only evil and that continually. That the carnal mind is not subject to the law of God, neither indeed can be. And that all mankind was under the wrath and curse of God and must have been forever miserable if they had been left to suffer what their sins deserve.[8]

Two things were observable in Hammon's brief formulation of original sin.

---

[7]Hammon, *A Winter Piece,* in Sondra O'Neale, *Jupiter Hammon and the Biblical Beginnings of African-American Literature* (Metuchen, N.J.: American Library Association, 1993), p. 106.

[8]Hammon, *An Address to the Negroes,* in Sondra O'Neale, *Jupiter Hammon and the Biblical Beginnings of African-American Literature* (Metuchen, N.J.: American Library Association, 1993), p. 238.

First, where some other African American writers were intent on demonstrating the essential equality of man in creation, and thereby justify the universal freedom of all men, Hammon began his anthropology and soteriology with the equality of men *in sin*. Addressing the African "brethren," Hammon moved on to conclude that not only "servants" but "all mankind" was unworthy and guilty before God. The nature that blacks, whites and all people shared was a common nature *as sinners*. Second, Hammon argued that we were not only natural sinners but active sinners as well. Perhaps he had in mind Ephesians 2:2-3 when he wrote that all were "daily adding [to their sins] by evil practices." In Hammon's view and that of the orthodox Calvinism to which he adhered, man was both "born" with a nature corrupted at its roots (radical depravity) and actively sinful against God in practice. In Hammon's words, "man was prone to evil, as the sparks to fly upward."[9]

Alluding to Matthew 13:20-21, the parable of the sower, Hammon equated the depravity of man with a "hard heart" towards God. In *An Evening's Improvement*, he extended this view, arguing:

> There is such a depravity in our natures that we are not willing to suffer any reproach that may be cast on us for the sake of our religion; this, my brethren, is because we have not the love of God shed abroad in our hearts; but our hearts are set too much on the pleasures of this life, forgetting that they are passing away.[10]

Hammon saw depravity as a problem in the disposition of man. Unreceptive to religion, man lacked any love for God in his heart and preferred instead the fleeting pleasures of the world. He was bent toward earthly pleasures that have no eternal value, perhaps referring to John's diagnosis of this same problem in 1 John 2:15-17:

> Love not the world, neither the things that are in the world. If any man love the world, the love of the Father is not in him. For all that is in the world, the lust of the flesh, and the lust of the eyes, and the pride of life, is not of the Father, but is of the world. And the world passeth away, and the lust thereof: but he that doeth the will of God abideth for ever. (KJV)

[9]Hammon, *Winter Piece*, p. 101.
[10]Hammon, *An Evening's Improvement*, in Sondra O'Neale, *Jupiter Hammon and the Biblical Beginnings of African-American Literature* (Metuchen, N.J.: American Library Association, 1993), p. 163.

The hard heart of man made him an enemy of God and a slave to sin and Satan. Hammon knew well the biblical data supporting this claim, and he argued persuasively in order to make his hearers aware of their condition. "Now you may think you are not enemies to God and do not hate him, but if your heart has not been changed and you have not become true Christians, you certainly are enemies to God and have been opposed to Him ever since you were born."[11]

Here, Hammon codified a simple, systematic statement on the nature and condition of man. He alluded to a wide range of biblical passages: Genesis 2 and 3 regarding the original creation and the Fall of man; Genesis 6:1-6 and others regarding the consistent evil of man; 1 Corinthians 2:14 regarding the "carnal mind" and its relationship to God; and John 3:36 in reference to the curse of God's wrath on the sinful creature. In doing so, Hammon displayed his sweeping knowledge of Scripture on this point and offered perhaps the first written statement on spiritual anthropology by an African American writer.

Hammon detailed the effects of this sinful condition on both man and society. He wrote that man's sins "have made us unworthy of the mercy of the Lamb of God,"[12] and "made all flesh guilty in the sight of God."[13]

AN

A D D R E S S

TO THE

NEGROES

IN THE

STATE OF NEW-YORK.

by JUPITER HAMMON,
Servant of JOHN LLOYD, jun. Esq. of the Manor of Queen's Village,
Long-Island.

" Of a truth I perceive that God is no respecter of
" persons :
 " But in every Nation, he that feareth him and work-
" eth righteousness, is accepted with him."—
Acts x. 34, 35.

NEW-YORK :
Published by SAMUEL WOOD, No. 362 Pearl-street.
1806.

Title page of Jupiter Hammon's *Address to the Negroes of the State of New York*

Moreover, continuing in sin ruined the commonwealth, by which Hammon meant the negative consequences visited on the public. He writes, "If men in general were more humble and more holy, we should not hear the little children in the street taking God's holy name

---

[11] Hammon, *Address to the Negroes*, p. 237.
[12] Hammon, *Evening's Improvement*, p. 161.
[13] Hammon, *Winter Piece*, p. 111.

in vain."[14] Hammon even speculated about the effect of free Africans' sins on the common good or potential freedom of the enslaved:

> One great reason that is given by some for not freeing us, I understand, is that we should not know how to take care of ourselves and should take to bad courses, that we should be lazy and idle, and get drunk and steal. Now all those of you who follow any bad courses and who do not try are doing more to prevent our being free than anybody else. Let me beg of you then, for the sake of your own good and happiness in time and for eternity, and for the sake of our poor brethren who are still in bondage, to "lead a quiet and peaceable life in all godliness and honesty" (I Tim. 2:2).[15]

For Jupiter Hammon, man's spiritual depravity ruined society and his eternal prospects before God, a position typical of northern writers and a Reformed and more broadly evangelical understanding of the nature of man.

Extended liberty in the thought of Lemuel Haynes. Lemuel Haynes (1753-1833) shared much with his Calvinist brother Jupiter Hammon in his basic understanding of the doctrine of man. Like Hammon, Haynes underscored the radical depravity of all men fallen in Adam and personal sin. Yet Haynes went a step further in his doctrinal defense by arguing for the full inclusion of Africans in the developing republic. To arguments deduced from the universality of sin and natural law, Haynes added that the innate impulse toward liberty was an indication of the full humanity of the African.

A veteran of the Revolutionary War, Haynes saw an inescapable compatibility between the republican political polity he ardently supported and the teachings of Scripture regarding the freedom of man. In his 1776 essay, *Liberty Further Extended: Or Free Thoughts on the Illegality of Slave-keeping*, written during the transition from colonial fragmentation to national solidarity embodied in the Declaration of Independence, and his 1801 essay, *The Nature and Importance of True Republicanism*, Haynes put forth anthropological claims that struck at the heart of the newborn country's identity. *The Nature and Importance of True Republicanism* defended the natural endowments of Africans and highlighted the corrupting effects of slavery on those capacities. Haynes wrote, "Our beneficent creator has furnished us with moral and natural endowments, and they ac-

---

[14]Ibid., p. 104.
[15]Hammon, *Address to the Negroes*, p. 241.

cording to common sense, are our own." These God-given faculties were "invaluable blessings, which equally belong unto all men as their birthright." The suppression of these faculties by despotic slaveholders "reduced [Africans] to their present pitiful, abject state" and "taught them to view themselves as a rank of beings far below others" suppressing "in a degree, every principle of manhood" making them "despised, ignorant, and licentious."[16] Haynes not only saw the error of anthropological claims that justified slavery based upon the denial of African humanity but also the actual retarding effects of slavery on the African. Lemuel Haynes's insights were similar to Olaudah Equiano's and John Jea's, and they paralleled those made by Quaker abolitionist John Woolman, who delineated similar psychological and spiritual corruptions in whites by linking the African's outward conditions with the European's inward corruption.[17]

Haynes began *Liberty Further Extended* by reminding readers of the deleterious effects of the Fall, which tended to corrupt the habits of men and society. The effects of the Fall, according to Haynes, continued in the lives of individuals and society even after persons were converted to Christian faith. However, resident in all people despite the Fall was "an innate principle, which is unmoveably placed in the human Species." That innate principle was "Liberty and freedom," which Haynes styled as "a Jewel which was handed Down to man from the cabinet of heaven . . . Coaeval [*sic*] with his Existance [*sic*]" and proceeding "from the Supreme Legislature of the universe." Man's equality with man was evident in the universal impulse toward freedom written by God into the very nature of man and the laws of nature. Efforts to deny this impulse were futile attempts to deny one's self in the case of the bondsman or to usurp the prerogative of God in the case of the enslaver.[18]

Haynes appealed to the thirst for liberty recently expressed by Englishmen in their overthrow of colonial rule as an argument against racial superiority and for the universality of liberty as an innate principle.

---

[16]Haynes, "The Nature and Importance of True Republicanism," in *Black Preacher to White America: The Collected Writings of Lemuel Haynes, 1774-1833,* ed. Richard Newman (Brooklyn: Carlson, 1990), pp. 80-82.

[17]Olaudah Equiano, *The Interesting Narrative,* in *My Soul Has Grown Deep,* ed. John Edgar Wideman (Philadelphia: Running Press, 2001), p. 206; John Jea, *The Life, History, and Unparalleled Sufferings of John Jea, The African Preacher, Compiled and Written by Himself,* in *Pioneers of the Black Atlantic: Five Slave Narratives from the Enlightenment, 1772-1815,* ed. Henry Louise Gates Jr. and William L. Andrews (Washington, D.C.: Civitas, 1998), pp. 369-74; *Jordan, Black Over White,* pp. 272-76.

[18]Haynes, "Liberty Further Extended," in *Black Preacher to White America,* pp. 17-18.

One man may bost [*sic*] a superorety [*sic*] above another in point of Natural priviledg [*sic*]; yet if he can produse [*sic*] no convincive arguments in vindication of this preheminence [*sic*] his hypothesis is to Be Suspected. To affirm, that an Englishman has a right to his Liberty, is a truth which has Been so clearly Evinced, Especially of Late, that to spend time in illustrating this, would be But Superfluous tautology. But I query, whether Liberty is so contracted a principle as to be Confin'd to any nation under Heaven; nay, I think it not hyperbolical to affirm, that Even an affrican [*sic*], has Equally as good a right to his Liberty in common with Englishmen.[19]

The contraction of liberty solely to men of English descent lacked justification; it presumed differences in natural physical abilities based upon distinctions in natural privilege obtained through environmental circumstances. For Haynes, "God has been pleas'd to distinguish some men from others, as to natural abilitys [*sic*], But not as to natural *right*, as they came out of his hands."[20]

Against such spurious differentiations, Haynes cited Acts 17:26—God "made of one blood all nations of men" (KJV)—and concluded that liberty for the African was not out of the realm of judicious expectation. Freedom for the African followed naturally from a correct anthropology. If the African bore within himself a drive for freedom common to all men, thus affirming his humanity, and if Africans like Europeans were made by God of the same blood as other men as Acts 17:26 declared, then the African should be free. Haynes drove home the point:

> We may suppose, that what is precious to one man, is precious to another, and what is irksome, or intolerable to one man, is so to another, consider'd in a Law of Nature. Therefore we may reasonably Conclude, that Liberty is Equally as precious to a Black man, as it is to a white one, and Bondage Equally as intollerable [*sic*] to the one as it is to the other: Seeing it Effects the Laws of nature Equally as much in the one as it Does in the other. But, as I observed Before, those privileges that are granted to us By the Divine Being, no one has the Least right to take them from us without our consent; and there is Not the Least precept, or practise [*sic*], in the Sacred Scriptures, that constitutes a Black man a Slave, any more than a white one.[21]

---

[19]Haynes, "Liberty Further Extended," p. 18.
[20]Ibid., p. 20, italics original.
[21]Ibid., p. 19.

And not only should the African be freed but whites should recognize that "others can have no demand on [Africans] for what they never gave or for which [Africans] are in no sense indebted to them." Failing to do so by holding men in bondage ruined the virtues of a true Republic and opposed the law of heaven. "The laws of the commonwealth are to defend mankind in the peaceable possession of these invaluable blessings" and "those who oppose such a [republican] form of government, would invert the order of nature, and the constitution of heaven, and destroy the beauty and harmony of the natural and moral worlds." A true republican government, according to Haynes, depended for its security on a correct understanding of the nature of man and tended "to destroy those distinctions among men that ought never to exist."[22] The ethical conclusion followed logically from the theological supposition as Haynes simultaneously affirmed an anthropology that made the African equal with all other men and denounced the slave trade—something many white theologians, preachers, church leaders and missionaries with the Society for the Propagation of the Gospel could not bring themselves to do.

One by one, Haynes responded to proslavery arguments. Against the supposed curse of Ham, he wrote: "But allowing they were actually of Canaans posterity, yet we have no reason to think that this Curse Lasted any Longer than the comeing [sic] of Christ: when that Sun of riteousness [sic] arose this wall of partition was Broken Down." If the curse had existed in precisely the way slaveholders fantasized—a contention Haynes refuted—the death, burial and resurrection that inaugurated "a more glorious Oeconomy [sic]" surely overthrew bodily as well as spiritual imperfections in Ham's offspring and required full communion among all believers. For those arguing that slavery was endorsed in the New Testament by the apostle Paul's injunctions for servants to obey their masters, Haynes retorted that, though the ancient world practiced slavery, such interpretations of the apostle's words overlooked his emphasis on spiritual freedom and the "lawful" pursuit of physical freedom as in 1 Corinthians 7:21. Moreover, the mere prevalence of a practice did not reverse the "unchangeable Laws of God, or of nature" that demanded liberty among all men. For their ignorance of key Bible texts like Romans 3:8 and 6:1 forbidding commission of intentional sins under the pretense of some greater

---

[22]Haynes, "The Nature and Importance of True Republicanism," pp. 80-81.

good, Haynes reproved slave traffickers daring to say that slavery was necessary for Christianizing those from the "Dark Continent." Moreover, the barbarous treatment of slaves and the failure to actually take the gospel message to nearly all Africans contradicted any such claim.[23]

For over fifty years, Lemuel Haynes wrote about and preached the gospel of Jesus Christ and opposed the unfair practice of slavery that contradicted every true republican virtue. He stood as the head of the first wave of theologian-pastor-abolitionists. With keen insight he surveyed the American cause at its infancy and saw the arrested development she faced if she did not wean all her children on the milk of liberty. No writer of the period was as consistently republican in ideals and unswervingly orthodox in Christian theology and ethics as Lemuel Haynes. John Saillant summarized Haynes's contribution thus:

> Haynes subsumed a traditional ethos of charity into a modern insistence on the right to liberty, which should have been granted charitably but was also to be enforced by the state at the peril of the dissolution of society itself. Freedom was not a privilege, but a right. Charity was not merely a desideratum, but an essential part of republican society. As with the antislavery commitment written into the Vermont state constitution, there was public context in Haynes's adopted state that made his way of looking at race, slavery, and freedom seem reasonable at a time when both slavery and racism were becoming stronger in America.[24]

Southern writers. The propaganda supporting slavery was not completely ineffective. In 1860, roughly 4 million of the 4.5 million African-descended peoples in the United States were slaves. Most were unexposed to the raging debates carried on between white slavocrat factions and white and black abolitionists.[25] Consequently, a few former slaves reported believing in some pro-slavery justifications. For example, Gus Rogers seemed to swallow the myth of the Hamitic curse without gagging:

> Noah had three sons, and when Noah got drunk on wine, one of his sons laughed at him, and the other two took a sheet and walked backwards and threw it over

[23]Haynes, "Liberty Further Extended," pp. 24-27.
[24]John Saillant, *Black Puritan, Black Republican: The Life and Thought of Lemuel Haynes, 1753-1833* (New York: Oxford University Press, 2003), p. 71.
[25]Mia Bay, *The White Image in the Black Mind: African-American Ideas about White People, 1830-1925* (New York: Oxford University Press, 2000), p. 113. This is the only treatment, to my knowledge, of the image of white people in the cultural imagination of black people.

Noah. Noah told the one who laughed, "'You' children will be hewers of wood and drawers of water for the other two's children, and they will be known by their hair and their skin being dark." So, Miss, there we are, and that is the way God meant us to be. We have always had to follow the white folks and do what we saw them do, and that's all there is to it. You just can't get away from what the Lord said.[26]

More fantastic than Rogers's perspective was Katie Sutton's gullibility at believing her white Mistress's tale that "the stork brought the white babies to their mothers, but that the slave children were all hatched out from buzzard's eggs."[27] Apparently, Rogers benefited little from the exegetical refutations of Ham's curse expounded by both white and black abolitionists and preachers. Though Rogers and Sutton were certainly not alone in their errors, folk superstitions and exegetical fallacies did not predominate in the thinking of enslaved Christians.[28] Rather, southern blacks were just as likely to respond to white creation myths with myths of their own. Historian Lawrence Levine catalogued black folk tales that explained the origin of white people. The stories included explanations ranging from the originally black Adam and ginger-colored Eve who turned white from fear after Adam's transgression or Cain's murder of Abel to the more typical tales of an all-black creation of man with descendant whites following.[29]

Though southern writers of the antebellum period marshaled arguments less elegant and sometimes more fanciful than their northern peers, they were every bit as aware that the claim to humanity was at stake. As Mia Bay pointed out:

> They confronted race and racism in different ways than the educated blacks who read and rebutted racist doctrine. Steeped in a universalist understanding of Christianity and wholly unaware of scientific questions about the origins of the races, ex-slaves did not worry about tracing the biblical descent of their own race. Nor did they share the black intellectual's anxieties about being mistaken for monkeys or apes—species largely unfamiliar to uneducated black Southerners. Instead,

---

[26]James Mellon, ed., *Bullwhip Days: The Slaves Remember* (New York: Grove Press, 1988), p. 185.
[27]Ibid., p. 39.
[28]Mia Bay points out that often where such folk tales were believed they served other important functions, like shielding the identity of white fathers who impregnate women slaves or obscuring paternity and maternity in a context where children could not rely on natural parents to care for them (*White Image in the Black Mind*, p. 120).
[29]See Lawrence W. Levine, *Black Culture, Black Consciousness: Afro-American Folk Thought from Slavery to Freedom* (New York: Oxford University Press, 1977); cited in ibid., pp. 122-23.

these African Americans worried about being taken for animals of a different kind, complaining that whites made little distinction between black people and domestic animals. . . . Ex-slaves remembered being fed like pigs, bred like hogs, sold like horses, driven like cattle, worked like dogs, and beaten like mules.[30]

Despite their lack of biblical finesse and the animallike treatment they received, slaves and former bondsmen pounded their opponents with untutored arguments worthy of their cause. They understood that slavery's advocates regarded them as brute beasts, and they responded by distinguishing themselves from animals. Their declarations were clear, precise and baldly honest.

Most slaves recognized the hypocrisy and lunacy of slave master ideology. They perceived the contradiction between the practices of slavery predicated upon the invented inhumanity of Africans, on the one hand, and the tacit admission of humanity in the required church attendance of slaves on the other. Malinda Discus recalled, "Our master took his slaves to meetin' with him. There was always something that I couldn't understand. They treated the colored folks like animals and would not hesitate to sell and separate them, yet they seemed to think they had souls and tried to make Christians of them."[31] Others saw straight through the contradiction and proclaimed, "Us niggers has a soul an' a heart an' a mine. We ain't like a dog or a horse."[32] The slave never doubted his humanity and cried for recognition of this basic fact.

Charles Williams, in his autobiography "I'se Much a Man," upheld black humanity when he wrote,

God pick up handful of dust and perform you like a Man. You ourt to know that Christ didn make you to jest lay down like a hog or a Dog and be no more to you. It is a grand mistake on you side. Jest Keep the gate to you Mind open & see more better into the future. You ourt to know that God didn intend for His Son to go through all what he did without the Good Spirit come to visit every man & Woman.[33]

The evidence of black humanity was revealed in both a common creation with other men and not animals, and in the redemptive purposes of Christ. If

---

[30]Ibid., p. 119.
[31]Mellon, *Bullwhip Days*, p. 190.
[32]Ibid., p. 182.
[33]Cited in Bay, *White Image in the Black Mind*, p. 118.

Christ died for men, then wallowing like an animal or accepting the slave drivers' premise of inhumanity was a "grand mistake." Black men and women were a part of the "worl full of mans" that God created.

Recognition of Williams's declaration of full humanity occurred even among the newest enslaved exiles in America. KA-LE, a Mendi-speaking native of Sierra Leone and a rebel aboard the famous slave ship *Amistad*, wrote effectively to John Quincy Adams about his predicament at the hands of white Englishmen and slave traders. "Some people say Mendi people got no souls," KA-LE began. "Why we feel bad we no got souls? We want to be free very much." He explained that Mendi people, and by extension all Africans, were capable of thought, a faculty indicating humanity as surely as any. Moreover, Africans possessed moral faculties that made them aware of divine retribution and justice. KA-LE wrote, "Mendi have got souls. We think we know God punish us if we tell lie. We never tell lie we speak the truth. What for Mendi people afraid? Because they got souls."[34] All that the African was seemed to proclaim his humanity in defiance of white mythologies, stereotypes and mistreatment to the contrary.

Perhaps most amazingly, the folk theology of slaves proved resilient against tendencies to denigrate white people as a class or to make pejorative associations with white skin color. In the folk thought of black people, there were no equivalents to white-made black stereotypes like Sambo, mammy and Jezebel. Most African Americans, slave and free, southern and northern, showed little preoccupation with skin color in defending their own humanity or advancing their own anthropology. As Bay concluded, "if African-Americans assigned any set of racial personality traits to white people, it has remained largely unrecorded. Black folk culture challenged racial stereotypes rather than revising them. In recounting their life experiences, ex-slaves assigned no personal characteristics to white folks that they did not also see in themselves."[35] Slaves sensibly concluded, "there is some white folks will treat you right, and some will take everything away from you. They ain't all alike." Freedman Cal Woods succinctly described the matter—"some folks good no matter what dey color,

[34]Letter from KA-LE to John Quincy Adams, New Haven, 4 January 1841, in *Slave Testimony: Two Centuries of Letters, Speeches, Interviews, and Autobiographies*, ed. John Blassingame (Baton Rouge: Louisiana State University Press, 1977), p. 34.
[35]Bay, *White Image in the Black Mind*, p. 166.

other folks bad."[36] The equality desired by the black bondperson manifested itself partly through fair depiction of whites even in the face of brutal black misrepresentation at the hands of many of those same white people.

RECONSTRUCTION, "JIM CROW" SEGREGATION, GREAT MIGRATION AND THE "NEW NEGRO" MOVEMENT (1865-1929)

With the emancipation of Africans from slavery came a significant shift in the theological debates between whites and blacks over the nature of man. Until the defeat of slavery, the battle lines were drawn along two fronts—arguments over whether Africans were people with souls and contentions over whether Africans possessed certain natural endowments making them socially equal to whites. Northern victory in the Civil War helped to vanquish those ideas that denied African possession of souls and spiritual equality. In their place, the War helped erect a new orthodoxy that first mushroomed during the Great Awakening and subsequent revivals. That new orthodoxy maintained that blacks were indeed human beings with a soul and a human body. However, the social attitudes and corresponding dogma of social separatism, invented during the country's experience with slavery, survived the war. Even if African Americans were to be regarded as fully human in a theological or religious sense, they were not to be accorded the same rights and privileges belonging to white men or to be treated as though their natural faculties were equal to those of whites. Jim Crow was born of this obstinate refusal of white prejudice to die along with more formal theological bigotry.

African American thinkers and writers shifted their emphasis to counter such racial bias and to insist on a social reality commensurate with the spiritual equality of all men. For example, William Christian (1856-1928), a former slave and founder in 1889 of the church of the Living God (Christian Workers for Fellowship), took a strong stance against racism and faulty anthropological claims. Drawing upon numerous biblical texts,[37] the church held a doctrine of man that from the beginning

> tried to combat certain racist teachings, and particularly the claims of some Baptist preachers in the latter part of the nineteenth century that Negroes were not

---

[36]Ibid., pp. 176-77.
[37]Num 12:1; Ps 119:83; Job 30:30; Jer 8:21; 13:23; Gal 3:28.

men, but the outcome of a human father and a female beast. Opposing this teaching, the Church of the Living God assert[ed] that the saints of the Bible belonged to the black race. Since Jesus has no earthly father, He is considered to belong to all people and to be "colorless."[38]

Christian put forth a polygenesis theory of the origins of man, with the biblical creation account describing the origins of the African race and Asian and European accounts occurring at some other time. "Within the racial politics of the era, Christian's reading of the Scriptures challenged the biblical interpretation of the Hamitic curse that purported to defend black inferiority by reinterpreting the curse as an intra-African, not interracial, affair. Thus Christian debunked black inferiority without making claims to black racial superiority."[39] Though Christian's anthropology represented a novel response to post-Emancipation racism, it never gained widespread adherence.

African Americans vested their hopes for equality in the historical viewpoint that all men were equal and their mantra became God "made of one blood all nations of the earth." This egalitarian impulse helped answer the strategic question of whether to acquiesce to Jim Crow and the Black Codes or to fight for full equality.[40] Leading churchmen stood ready to arm civil and political protestors with a theology that further emphasized the "brotherhood of man" and the "ideal of black manhood" as justification for full citizenship and impartiality in social affairs.

Elias Camp Morris and the brotherhood of man. One thematic emphasis in the anthropology of African Americans that seemed to gain wide acceptance was the notion of the "brotherhood of man." Elias Camp Morris (1855-1922), a Baptist pastor from Arkansas and long-time leader of the National Baptist Convention, popularized this concept among black Baptists of his day. In a sermon entitled "The Brotherhood of Man," Morris expounded his under-

---

[38]George E. Simpson, "Black Pentecostalism in the United States," in *Native American Religion and Black Protestantism*, ed. Martin E. Marty, *Modern American Protestantism and Its World*, vol. 9 (New York: K. G. Saur, 1993), p. 148.

[39]David D. Daniels, "Charles Harrison Mason: The Interracial Impulse of Early Pentecostalism," in *Portraits of a Generation: Early Pentecostal Leaders*, ed. James R. Goff, Jr. and Grant Wacker (Fayetteville: University of Arkansas Press, 2002), p. 259.

[40]For a good discussion of white counter-responses to Emancipations and Reconstruction, see Armstead L. Robinson, "Full of Faith, Full of Hope: The African-American Experience from Emancipation to Segregation," in *Upon These Shores: Themes in the African-American Experience, 1600 to the Present*, ed. William R. Scott and William G. Shade (New York: Routledge, 2000), pp. 141-66.

standing of the idea. Choosing Genesis 45:4 as his text, Morris took the opportunity to explain that although slavery existed from the most ancient times
and although "those who traffic in human flesh lose their respect for pious,
consecrated humanity," the providential workings of God often "proved to be
a blessing in disguise" as in the case of Joseph being sold into bondage by his
brothers. Such occasions, according to Morris, revealed "an unexplored field
of humanity which recognizes one common Father—God, and one common
brother—man."[41] Writing after the proliferation of church splits along racial
lines, Morris recognized that, unless Christian anthropology asserted the
common origins and brotherhood of all men, the church and the country
would be imperiled. He wrote, "Class and race antipathy has carried so far in
this great Christian country of ours, that it has almost destroyed the feeling of
that common brotherhood, which should permeate the soul of every Christian
believer, and has shorn the Christian Church of that power and influence
which it would otherwise have, if it had not repudiated this doctrine."[42]

Elias Morris saw in the now commonplace citation of Acts 17:26 an ancient
mandate for multiracial Christian unity. He wrote:

> The whole world is to-day indebted to Paul for the prominence he gave to this
> all-important doctrine at Mars Hill. We know that the doctrine is not a popular
> one and that none can accept and practice it, except such as are truly regener-
> ated. But the man who has been brought into the new and living way by the
> birth which is from above, by contrasting his own depraved and sinful nature
> with the pure, immaculate character of the Son of God after meditating what
> that matchless Prince underwent for him, can get inspiration and courage to ac-
> knowledge every man his brother who has enlisted under the banner of the
> Cross, and accepted the same Christ as his Saviour.[43]

For Morris, acknowledgement of the common humanity of all people—
especially the kinship of all Christians regardless of race—was a matter of true
repentance and conversion. Only the "truly regenerated" accepted and practiced Morris's doctrine of the brotherhood of man. Those who failed to wel-

---

[41]Elias C. Morris, *Sermons, Addresses and Reminiscences and Important Correspondence*, (Nashville: National Baptist Publishing Board, 1901) p. 37; an electronic edition of this publication is available from
   the Documenting the American South project at the University of North Carolina at Chapel Hill.
[42]Ibid., p. 38.
[43]Ibid.

come racially different others as brothers
failed to properly consider the character of
Jesus and the effects of the cross in redeeming
men from such prejudices and proved themselves not to be Christians.

Morris echoed Jupiter Hammon concerning the equality of man in their depravity.
Morris regarded mankind as having "volun-
tarily imprisoned his own soul" to sin. With
poignancy applicable to both the spiritual

Elias Camp Morris

state of all people and the peculiar circumstance of African Americans, Morris likened spiritual bondage to sin to the imprisonment of a patriot in his
own country. He wrote:

> The awful depths into which sin had plunged man can better be imagined than
> described in words. The fact that man had lost favor with his Creator, was shut
> out of Paradise and held under the dreadful penalty that "the soul that sinneth
> must die," rendered him a most miserable creature. Think of one who has been
> tried under the laws of his country by a jury of his countrymen, and, having been
> convicted, still cherishes hope in executive clemency, his longing eyes filled with
> tears of hope as he looks to see coming to him a pardon, which will free him
> from the awful guillotine or gallows. Who can contemplate or portray the joy of
> one doomed to death when he has been assured, just before the time appointed
> for execution, that a full pardon has been granted? And yet it is the great privi-
> lege of every man to receive such a pardon. Indeed, every man is in need of a
> pardon, for all have sinned and all are doomed to eternal death, except such as
> receive the pardon which is found only in the Gospel of Jesus Christ and borne
> to a guilty world by the heralds of the cross.[44]

But, in addition to the equality of man in their depravity and their need for
spiritual clemency, Morris also emphasized the spiritual equality of all men
calling themselves Christians as a consequence of spiritual conversion. In his
view, segregated worship was emblematic of a faulty gospel and insincere
Christian profession. Morris concluded that "the commission which (God)
gives is without race, color or condition, but is that the gospel be preached to

---

[44]Elias C. Morris, "Sermon Delivered to the Holy Trinity Baptist Church, Philadelphia, Penn., April
1900," *Sermons, Addresses and Reminiscences and Important Correspondence*, pp. 46-47.

every creature, not over the telephone or through the medium of the phono-
graph, but by the human voice, coming in direct contact with the people, all
the people. . . . 'Christ Jesus came into the world to save sinners,' not white
sinners, nor black sinners, nor red sinners, but sinners."[45] The Scriptures demanded Christian unity across racial barriers and the success of the church in
the twentieth century depended upon razing such barriers.

   Francis Grimké: The ideal of black manhood. For over five decades, Dr.
Francis J. Grimké (1850-1937) led as pastor the 15th Street Presbyterian
Church in Washington, D.C. A former slave and nephew to the famous abo-
litionists Angelina and Sarah Moore Grimké, Francis studied at Lincoln and
Howard University and received his theological education at Princeton under
the tutelage of Charles A. Hodge (1797-1878).[46] In his years as pastor of 15th
Street Presbyterian, Dr. Grimké championed the cause of biblical orthodoxy
and racial equality inside and outside the church.

   Francis Grimké countered the racial prejudice of the early 1900s with a direct denouncement and echoed his contemporary, Elias C. Morris, with a call
to Christian unity. In his 1910 address, "Christianity and Race Prejudice,"
Grimké asserted that racial bigotry was in almost absolute control of the practice of churches, congregations, and professing Christians and lamented the
existence of "white churches" and "black churches." Grimké asked,

> Why should there be churches made up of white Christians, and churches made
> up of colored Christians in the same community, and, where all speak the same
> language; why should white Christians and colored Christians not feel perfectly
> at home with each other in the same religious gatherings, if they are all Chris-
> tians, if they all believe in the Fatherhood of God, and the brotherhood of man,
> in doing by others as they would be done by, in loving each other as they love
> themselves, in their oneness in Christ Jesus, and if the same Holy Spirit dwells
> alike in all their hearts?[47]

Like most other writers of his period, Grimké understood that one's anthropology entailed acute ethical considerations. He linked the brotherhood

---

[45]Ibid., p. 39.
[46]Henry J. Ferry, *Francis James Grimké: Portrait of a Black Puritan* (Yale University, Ph.D. dissertation,
   1970). Ferry's dissertation is the only book-length treatment of the life of Grimké.
[47]Francis J. Grimké, "Christianity and Race Prejudice (June 5, 1910)" in *The Works of Francis Grimké,
   Volume 1*, ed. Carter G. Woodson (Washington, D.C.: Associated Publishers, 1942), p. 458.

of man to observance of "the golden rule" and love for one's neighbor. He maintained that "every principle of Christianity, every sentiment of true religion was totally, absolutely opposed to race prejudice in every shape and form." Therefore, white Christians should either renounce Christianity and with integrity embrace race prejudice or they should repent, practice true Christianity, and embrace their black brothers and sisters.[48] He saw no impediment inherent in the nature of men that should prevent them from living together peacefully and respectfully, provided whites would recognize the humanity of blacks and realize the moral imperatives of the Scriptures.[49]

But, Grimké also parlayed his conception of the brotherhood of man into an attempt to stir the African American conscience and to develop their social and economic potential. Not only did the doctrine of man's fraternity through common origin require whites to grant full acceptance to blacks, but it also required blacks to apply themselves in every available pursuit. The pulpit was to stimulate "a true manhood and womanhood" by making African American Christians "good husbands and wives, good citizens and neighbors" and yielding "the largest returns in purity, in honesty, in sobriety, in sweetness, in gentleness." Attaining true manhood and womanhood was to be the subject of fervent prayer:

> What are we to pray for, then? That God would help us by His grace to be true men and women; that He would put deep down into our souls a divine unrest, a holy ambition to be something, and to make something of ourselves; that He would kindle in our heart of hearts a desire for the things that are true, and just, and lovely, and of good report; that he would help us all to come in the unity of the faith and of the knowledge of the Son of God, unto a perfect man, unto the measure of the stature of the fullness of Christ. What we need is development along every line that makes for righteousness, for a better, purer, nobler manhood and womanhood.[50]

Grimké campaigned for the development of Christian character in the pulpit, the pew and the streets. "Every Negro, in every part of the country, by

<hr/>

[48]Ibid., pp. 454-55, 461-62.
[49]Francis J. Grimké, "The Remedy for the Present Strained Relations Between the Races in the South (June 25, 1899)," in *The Works of Francis Grimké, Volume 1*, ed. Carter G. Woodson (Washington, D.C.: Associated Publishers, 1942), pp. 317-33
[50]Francis J. Grimké, "God and Prayer As Factors in the Struggle (December 11, 1900)" in *The Works of Francis Grimké, Volume 1*, ed. Carter G. Woodson (Washington, D.C.: Associated Publishers, 1942), p. 282.

some means should be made to feel, and to feel at once, the transcendent importance of character." He contended that Christian virtue was more important to Negroes than anything else and that "to make our people strong in morals is to render them invincible in the battle of life."[51] Grimké perceived that "the battle of life" involved rising white resistance to black advancement. In 1900, Dr. Grimké commented:

> The determination to keep us in a state of civil and political inferiority and to surround us with such conditions as will tend to crush out of us a manly and self-respecting spirit is stronger now than it was at the close of the war. The fixed purpose and determination of the Southern whites is to negative these great amendments [Fourteenth and Fifteenth Amendments to the Constitution], to eliminate entirely the Negro as a political factor. And this purpose is intensifying, is growing stronger and stronger each year. The sentiment everywhere is: This is a white man's government. And that means, not only that the whites shall rule, but that the Negro shall have nothing whatever to do with governmental affairs.[52]

Grimké began to see this rising political oppression and mob violence against blacks as an assault on their "manhood." Any failure by blacks to respond, or worse, to willingly acquiesce, signaled treasonous cowardice. "The hungry bloodhounds of Southern democracy" were to be resisted to the last. Black Americans needed determination and intensive cultivation of their "manhood" through intellectual, moral, social and political exertions.

In Grimké's sermons and writings, political agitation became a litmus test for his anthropology. One's active demand for civil and political justice verified his claim to personhood. For Grimké, the solution to the "Negro question" was simple: "the Negro is a man *and* an American citizen, and . . . he will never be satisfied until he is *treated as a man, and as a full fledged citizen.* Until his manhood is recognized, and all his rights, civil and political, are accorded to him,

[51]Francis J. Grimké, "Afro-American Pulpit in Relation to Race Elevation (1892)" in *The Works of Francis Grimké, Volume 1*, ed. Carter G. Woodson (Washington, D.C.: Associated Publishers, 1942), pp. 223-24, 234; see also "The Paramount Importance of Character, or Character, the True Standard by Which to Estimate Individuals and Races" (October 27, 1911), in *The Works of Francis Grimké, Volume 1*, ed. Carter G. Woodson (Washington, D.C.: Associated Publishers, 1942), pp. 473-88.
[52]Francis Grimké, "Discouragements: Hostility of the Press, Silence and Cowardice of the Pulpit (November 20, 1900)," in *The Works of Francis Grimké, Volume 1*, ed. Carter G. Woodson (Washington, D.C.: Associated Publishers, 1942), pp. 237-38.

he will never hold his peace, will never cease to cry aloud, to agitate, to make trouble."[53] Elsewhere he wrote, "As long as he lives, as long as there is one manly, self-respecting Negro in this country, the agitation will go on, will never cease until right is triumphant." Conversely, any Negro who accepted or justified the burgeoning policy of racial oppression and marginalization was "a traitor to his race, and shows that he is deficient in manhood, in true self-respect."[54] In this way, Grimké's anthropology curved back onto the African American himself and demanded certain ethical responses to the anti-Reconstruction circumstances facing him. Earlier appeals had mostly been outward-focused attempts to persuade whites. Grimké identified an intra-racial element as well.

At the very least, true Negro men were to repudiate "the pernicious doctrine of race-effacement" because of its unquestioning acceptance of assumptions supporting racial inferiority. But, the more grand goal emphasized the centrality of the home where parents were to teach their children an anthropology combining equality before God with equality under the law—"that though they may have a dark skin, they are just as much the children of God, are just as dear to him, and are entitled to the same rights and privileges, under the Constitution, as the whitest child." Grimké exhorted his listeners to let children "take in these ideas with the first breath they breathe, with the milk that they suck from the breast of motherhood, and let them strengthen with their age" until "everywhere there will be found a sturdy manhood."[55]

The anthropology that emerged between the Civil War and the early 1900s wove together the traditional concept of fallen man with an affirmation of the essential equality of all men and an appeal for civil and political enfranchisement. This anthropology represented a subtle but significant shift in emphasis. While all of these elements could be discerned in the writings of men like Lemuel Haynes and Jupiter Hammon, the earliest generation of writers had properly stressed spiritual equality in sin and the need for salvation largely be-

---

[53]Francis Grimké, "Sources From Which No Help May Be Expected—The General Government, Political Parties (November 27, 1900)," in *The Works of Francis Grimké, Volume 1*, ed. Carter G. Woodson (Washington, D.C.: Associated Publishers, 1942), p. 256; emphasis added.

[54]Grimké, "Discouragements: Hostility of the Press, Silence and Cowardice of the Pulpit (November 20, 1900)," in *The Works of Francis Grimké, Volume 1*, ed. Carter G. Woodson (Washington, D.C.: Associated Publishers, 1942), pp. 238-39.

[55]Grimké, "Sources From Which No Help May Be Expected—The General Government, Political Parties," in *The Works of Francis Grimké, Volume 1*, ed. Carter G. Woodson (Washington, D.C.: Associated Publishers, 1942), p. 257.

cause slavery's advocates questioned the spiritual constitution of Africans. The Civil War officially ended that aspect of the dispute over the African's personhood (though the proslavery argument had been declining since the Great Awakenings) and ushered in a new degree of mobility, freedom and political aspiration for African Americans. Consequently, the post-Civil War generation of Grimké and Morris placed greater stress on the need for social and political equality, for a true "brotherhood of man," while retaining the traditional conception of fallen man. African Americans extended their theological insights into the realm of social and political power, undercutting inconsistent claims to Christian profession and segregation based on race. This post-Emancipation shift in emphasis gave theological justification to calls for full parity, but in subsequent generations would begin to supplant and neuter the gospel in more liberal quarters of black Christianity.

DEPRESSION AND WORLD WAR II (1930-1949)

During the 1930s and 1940s African American religious intellectuals focused intently on the nature of race relations. The issue of black and white coexistence achieved international prominence as blacks ventured abroad either as military patriots or as cultural ambassadors of one sort or another. For instance, Howard Thurman on behalf of the World Student Christian Federation toured India, Burma and Ceylon during which he met with Mahatma Gandhi and discussed U. S. race relations with multiple student groups.[56] Benjamin Elijah Mays attended the 1937 Church Conference on Church, Community and State in Oxford, England, where he informed conference participants that racial pride, hatreds, persecutions and exploitation were evil sins. Again in 1939, at the Conference of Christian Youth in Amsterdam, Holland, Mays blasted anti-Semitism and anti-black racism in the United States and South Africa and rejected appeals for slow approaches to church desegregation. The heightened international profile of black religious intellectuals provided "transnational significance" that helped advance the philosophical, theological and practical foundations of the 1950s Civil Rights campaign.[57]

---

[56]Howard Thurman, *With Head and Heart: The Autobiography of Howard Thurman* (Orlando: Harcourt Brace, 1979), pp. 103-36.

[57]Dennis C. Dickerson, "African American Religious Intellectuals and the Theological Foundations of the Civil Rights Movement, 1930-55," *Church History* (June 2005): 217-35.

An anthropological unanimity of opinion filtered through the public comments and writings of this generation of thinkers. That unanimity, like the generation before, stressed the Fatherhood of God and the common brotherhood of man. Individuals possessed intrinsic worth, made as they were in the image of God.[58]

Howard Thurman's theology illustrated the generally high view of man included in the theology of the era. Thurman's anthropology stressed the importance of the individual personality, which required the nurturance of an appropriate self-love. The protection and preservation of both individual and group personality, Thurman contended, occurred in an integrated community context where the oneness of all humanity is affirmed. Thurman believed that human beings were essentially good and that that goodness was trying to realize itself in history.[59] To the extent that Thurman's view typified the understanding of others in this period, the anthropology of the 1930s and 1940s began to disentangle itself from the traditional conceptions of original sin, depravity and the need for spiritual redemption. This cadre of churchmen directed their energies at fashioning a sustained attack on the racial phalanx of segregation and legalized racism.

The eradication of racism and segregation was axiomatic. "To segregate a man because his skin is brown, or black, red or yellow," declared Mays, "of all immoral acts, this is the most immoral," because "it inflicted a wound upon the soul of the segregated and so restricted his mind that millions of Negroes now alive will never be cured of the disease of inferiority."[60] Mays and his cohorts were hopeful that true Christian character or enlightened moral conscience could overcome and transform the damning effects of racism and seg-

[58]Ibid., pp. 229-31.
[59]Luther E. Smith, *Howard Thurman: The Mystic as Prophet* (Richmond, Ind.: Friends United Press, 1991), pp. 53-56, 60, and 130-32. Thurman's anthropology was shaped by the philosophical Personalism popular at the Boston University School of Theology where Bordon Parke Bowne (1847-1910) and Edgar Sheffield Brightman (1884-1953) popularized and institutionalized the philosophy. Bowne expounded the same pluralistic idealist version of Personalism combined with theistic beliefs that Howard Thurman maintained. For more on Personalism, see, John H. Lavely, "Personalism," in *The Encyclopedia of Philosophy, Volume 6*, ed. Paul Edwards (New York: Macmillan, 1967), pp. 107-10.
[60]Freddie C. Colston, ed., *Benjamim E. Mays Speaks: Representative Speeches of a Great American Orator* (Lanham, Md.: University Press of America, 2002), pp. 61-62; cited in Dickerson, "African American Religious Intellectuals," p. 229. See also Mark Chapman, "'Of One Blood': Mays and the Theology of Race Relations" in *Walking Integrity: Benjamin Elijah Mays, Mentor to Martin Luther King, Jr.*, ed. Lawrence Edward Carter Jr. (Macon, Ga.: Mercer University Press, 1998), pp. 233-61.

regation. Looking to the success of Gandhi in India, they sought a strategy that combined direct nonviolent tactics with the Christian ethic of love to pursue social change. The greatest benefactor of their contributions was Dr. Martin Luther King Jr., an undergraduate student of George Kelsey (1911-1996) and Benjamin E. Mays while at Morehouse College and a doctoral candidate at Boston University during the tenure of Howard Thurman.

CIVIL RIGHTS ERA (1950-1979)

The first major shift from an egalitarian emphasis in African American anthropology to a critical denial of white humanity occurred during the more radical phase of the Civil Rights era. Militant spokesperson for the Nation of Islam, Malcolm X, arraigned white people as "devils" breeded by a renegade demi-god named Yakub. The Yakub myth of the Nation of Islam never gained widespread belief, but the "devilish" nature of white brutality towards blacks did captivate the imagination of many African Americans. The label seemed to succinctly illustrate the three hundred years of debasement African Americans suffered at the hands of whites. The Black Power arm of the Civil Rights movement grew impatient with the exhortations to love and brotherhood espoused by moderate and mainstream leaders like Dr. King. For radicals, King's ethical demands and restraint were incongruous with the scenes of attack dogs, fire hoses and church bombings witnessed on the evening news.[61] Such brutality demanded a revised doctrine of man that better accounted for the capacity of whites to commit or ignore such atrocities. George Kelsey offered a strong condemnation of racism in his 1965 work *Racism and the Christian Understanding of Man.*[62] However, the theological anthropology most consonant with the emergent radicalism of the 1960s was that of James Cone's Black Theology.

James Cone: Reversing the color symbolism of the anthropology debate. The

---

[61]For example, Joseph R. Washington, Jr. called for black churches and theologians to articulate a theology that supported violent revolution instead of the ultimately deceptive and self-defeating Civil Rights agenda of integration which was fundamentally fought for within the framework of white power. See Joseph R. Washington Jr., *Black and White Power Subreption* (Boston, Mass.: Beacon Press, 1969).

[62]George D. Kelsey, *Racism and the Christian Understanding of Man* (New York: Charles Scribner's Sons, 1965). For a brief but good review of Kelsey's work, see James H. Evans, *We Have Been Believers: An African American Systematic Theology* (Minneapolis: Fortress Press, 1992), pp. 104-7; Harold Dean Trulear, "George Kelsey, Christianity and Race: A View from the Academy," *The Princeton Theological Review* 10, no. 2 (Spring 2004), pp. 35-40.

founding of the school of Black Theology by James Cone in the late 1960s opened a new stream of African American anthropology. Cone recognized that historically white theological anthropology and ethics had followed two courses, either decreeing that blacks were nonhuman animals whose enslavement was good for them and society or assimilating blacks into mainstream white society by destroying black identity. In response, he proposed that blacks instead "destroy the oppressor's definition of blackness by unraveling new meanings in old tales." He believed that history was a vital source for asserting black personhood and developing a perspective independent of whites.[63]

Cone's first step in developing such an anthropology was to deny the claims to universalism that had characterized earlier discussions. He followed Tillich in the assertion that "man discovers himself when he discovers God."[64] He embraced a view of theology that harkened back to the subjective experience and mystical personalism of Howard Thurman[65] and the cultural relativism of New Negro intellectuals like Alaine Locke (1886-1954).[66] Cone defiantly proclaimed that truth could only be ascertained from within a particular community:

> We can say that the definition of truth for the black thinker arises from a passionate encounter with black reality. Though that truth may be described religiously as God, it is not the God of white religion but the God of black existence. There is no way to speak of this objectively; truth is not objective. It is subjective, a personal experience of the ultimate in the midst of degradation.[67]

---

[63]James H. Cone, *A Black Theology of Liberation: Twentieth Anniversary Edition* (Maryknoll, N.Y.: Orbis, 2003), p. 13.

[64]Ibid., p. 14.

[65]See chapter 1 for Thurman's view of revelation as subjective experience.

[66]William J. Moses, "From Booker T. to Malcolm X: Black Political Thought, 1895-1965," in *Upon These Shores: Themes in the African-American Experience, 1600 to the Present,* ed. William R. Scott and William G. Shade (New York: Routledge, 2000), pp. 198-220. Moses points out that the black intellectual tradition underwent a significant shift in tone and strategy during the Harlem Renaissance era. Up to the 1920s, most defenses of black humanity relied on "vindicationism" and "Ethiopianism." Vindicationism defended African humanity by highlighting African contributions to world civilization, especially through the achievements of ancient Egypt. Ethiopianism was a religious emphasis on the conversion of African peoples to Christianity based on the biblical text, "Ethiopia shall stretch forth her hands unto God." However, some intellectuals of the 1920s abandoned these approaches and adopted the "cultural relativism" of white scholars like Franz Boas and Melville Heskovits and the social Darwinian themes of William Graham Sumner. African Americans used these theories and assumptions to "argue that African manners and customs were intelligent adaptations to the conditions of life in Africa, rather than evidence of genetic or moral inferiority." So a nascent cultural pluralism and relativism seeped into the thinking of black intellectuals.

[67]Cone, *Black Theology of Liberation*, p. 19.

Later, Cone wrote in *God of the Oppressed* that "what theologians mistake for God is nothing but the latent nature of humanity" and that "theology is *subjective* speech about God, a speech that tells us far more about the hopes and dreams of certain God-talkers than about the Maker and Creator of heaven and earth."[68] This subjective understanding of the nature of theological discourse shaped both James Cone's view of revelation and his anthropological conclusions.

Second, as far as his doctrine of man was concerned, Cone negated any claims for the compatibility of racial prejudice and true Christianity. He proclaimed that "the essence of the gospel of Christ stands or falls on the question of black humanity, and there is no way that a church or institution can be related to the gospel of Christ if it sponsors or tolerates racism in any form."[69] Here, Cone was consistent with the conclusion drawn by nearly every African American preacher, theologian and thinker since the publication of Lemuel Haynes's 1776 essay *Liberty Further Extended: Or Free Thoughts on the Illegality of Slavekeeping*. Like early African American intellectuals and some white abolitionists, Cone recognized the destructive aspects of white racial ideology, calling white racism "an insanity comparable to Nazism." He recognized how white assessments of blackness historically entailed social oppression and coercion.

In order to be human, then, one needed to reject white social and political power and to affirm what whites found degrading—blackness.

> In a world in which the oppressor defines right in terms of whiteness, *humanity means an unqualified identification with blackness.* Black therefore is beautiful; oppressors have made it ugly. We glorify it because they despise it; we love it because they hate it. It is the black way of saying 'To hell with your stinking white society and its middle-class ideas about the world. I will have no part in it.'[70]

This identification with blackness revealed three problematic distinctions in Cone's anthropology. First, Cone inched closer to an outright rejection of whiteness and white humanity than any writer before him. Second, Cone adopted a reactionary definition of blackness where earlier writers attempted positive articulations of black humanity. Blackness was loved *because* whiteness

---

[68]James H. Cone, *God of the Oppressed* (Maryknoll, N.Y.: Orbis, 1997), pp. 37-38, italics original.
[69]Cone, *Black Theology of Liberation*, p. 14.
[70]Ibid., p. 15, emphasis added.

was hated, not because there was an affirmation of anything essential to blackness. Third, Cone's anthropology opened the way for a more radical political
philosophy favoring either black separatism or an "integration" on black terms.
James Cone was not the first to recognize such implications. Proponents of
African emigration and colonization in the 1800s had reached similar conclusions, though the majority of black intelligentsia and black masses preferred
some form of full integration.[71] Cone's ethical applications moved in a different direction than that of his predecessors. Cone was one of the first black
theologians to flat-out reject white institutions *while simultaneously insisting
upon full American citizenship and the formation of black institutions* rather than
forsaking any claims to the country as earlier emigrationists had. Cone believed that white political structures limited European theology's ability to adequately define humanity, because it systematically overlooked the suffering of
the oppressed.[72]

   An anthropology of suffering and freedom. Cone positively linked his anthropology with the concrete condition of oppressed blacks and bound together his
conception of man with human suffering. Black Theology's definition of the human being was "limited to what it means to be liberated from human oppression." He condemned the brand of theological anthropology that defined man
with a list of properties as too abstract and convenient for those willing to ignore
the plight of subjugated peoples. Instead, Cone preferred a view of humanity
that revealed itself in the "being-in-the-world of human oppression." In such a
context, Cone opined, one could observe humanness for what it was—"being in
freedom." In other words, "To be human was to be free, and to be free was to be
human."[73] Circumscribing freedom was to circumscribe humanity.

   Moreover, limiting freedom tarnished the image of God in which man was
made. Cone reproved western theologians for their inadequate doctrines of
man. For example, Cone appreciated Luther's addition of a personal dimension capturing the relationship of man to God through grace, but he lamented
the failure of Luther and later neo-orthodox theologians to extend their anthropology to the social and political conditions and liberation impulses of the
oppressed. Cone concluded:

---

[71]Moses, "From Booker T. to Malcolm X: Black Political Thought, 1895-1965," pp. 209-10.
[72]Cone, *Black Theology of Liberation*, pp. 86-87.
[73]Ibid., pp. 84-87.

The image of God refers to the way in which God intends human beings to live in the world. The image of God is thus more than rationality, more than what so-called neo-orthodox theologians call divine-human encounter. In a world in which persons are oppressed, the image is human nature in rebellion against the structures of oppression. It is humanity involved in the liberation struggle against the forces of inhumanity.[74]

The freedom inherent in the image of God required, according to Cone, identification with the oppressed community, entrance into the economic and social suffering of the oppressed, and, thus, becoming "black." "To be free is to participate with those who are oppressed," he wrote.[75] By implication, failure to side with the oppressed revealed inhumanity.

Again, faint echoes of Lemuel Haynes surfaced in Cone's theorizing. But, where Haynes recognized a universal impulse toward freedom as an indication of a universal humanity to which Africans and Europeans belonged, Cone paradoxically asserted that "only the oppressed are truly free" and therefore fully human. Haynes interpreted the drive for freedom as an "innate principle"; Cone derived definitions of human freedom from the concrete existential circumstance of oppressed and suffering people. One looked to the internal constitution of man to define his anthropology; the other looked to external limitations. What had properly belonged to all people in Haynes devolved into the property of only the oppressed in Cone.

Fallenness and color symbolism in Black Theology. Just as he reconceptualized freedom in his anthropology, James Cone also redefined human fallenness. He equated fallenness with sin, as had most writers in Christian history, but he defined sin fundamentally as "estrangement from the source of meaning and purpose in the universe." Sin and fallenness was an attempt to reject one's identity in the source of being and to attempt to be what one was not.[76] Cone developed this view of fallenness along two dimensions: community and race.

Sin, according to Cone, could only be understood in the relative context of an oppressed community. The community was the "source of being" that provided personal and group identity. For Cone, "Sin [was] not an abstract idea

---

[74]Ibid., p. 94; Cone also comments on the limitations of Barth's analysis for the image of God in *God of the Oppressed*, pp. 133-34.
[75]Cone, *Black Theology of Liberation*, p. 94.
[76]Ibid., pp. 103-4.

that defines ethical behavior for all and sundry." Rather, to be in sin was "to deny the values that make the community what it is" and to live "according to one's private interests and not according to the goals of the community."[77] "Because sin represents the condition of estrangement from the source of one's being, for blacks this means a desire to be white. It is the refusal to be what we are. Sin, then, for blacks is loss of identity."[78] Cone's anthropocentric intent seems clear here. Sin, which had been defined throughout Christian history as an affront to a holy God, became an identity conflict in Black Theology. Cone imagined no greater marring of black humanity than to accept the world on the terms of white people. Living apart from the tribe constituted a sacred violation, harming both the group and the individual.

But the concept of sin in Cone's construction of Black Theology also included a racial dimension. Spurred on by the cultural relativism that lay at the heart of his view of theology, Cone believed blacks and whites defined and experienced sin differently, relative to their position in the struggle for liberation. For instance, Cone held that blacks were the only people who could talk about sin because their condition of oppression located them where God and sin were revealed. Apart from failing to resist white oppression, there seemed to be little concern for any sin on the part of African Americans. Lost in his analysis of blacks' sin was the historical Christian concern for moral corruption and need for reconciliation with God. Cone easily envisaged such corruption in whites, as their sin pervaded their entire being, blinding them to the concrete struggle for liberation and coaxing them to "simplistic" ideas about "broken relation to God."[79] But for blacks, such pervasive corrosion of mind and soul only occurred if they "sold out" to white ideals, solutions and culture. What needed redeeming, then, was not the soul but the self-conception of black people scarred and warped by injustice and violence.

Whites, on the other hand, were incapable of perceiving the extent and depth of sin *because* they were white. Because whites generally did not enter into the liberation of the oppressed, they were outside the revelation event that made sin concrete and knowable and human response possible. "In a word, sin is whiteness," concluded Cone, "the desire of whites to play God in the realm

[77]Ibid., p. 104.
[78]Ibid., p. 108.
[79]Ibid., p. 107.

of human affairs."[80] At least symbolically, Cone came close to repudiating white humanity as he equated whiteness with sin and decried the "filthy manifestations of whiteness" in society. At this point, his anthropology was more reminiscent of the mythology of the Nation of Islam with its Yakub myth[81] than historical Christian doctrines of man.

Escape from subhuman status required white expiation before God and black people. Whites must "die to whiteness" and receive the approval of "every single black person" as they identified with and supported black liberation.[82] Cone concluded his 1969 book *Black Theology and Black Power* with an elaboration of the idea of white reconciliation:

> For white people, God's reconciliation in Jesus Christ means that God has made black people a beautiful people; and if they are going to be in relationship with God, they must enter by means of their black brothers, who are a manifestation of God's presence on earth. The assumption that one can know God without knowing blackness is the basic heresy of the white churches. They want God without blackness, Christ without obedience, love without death. What they fail to realize is that in America, God's revelation on earth has always been black, red, or some other shocking shade, but never white. *Whiteness*, as revealed in the history of America, *is the expression of what is wrong with man. It is a symbol of man's depravity.* God cannot be white, even though white churches have portrayed him as white. When we look at what whiteness has done to the minds of men in this country, we can see clearly what the New Testament meant when it spoke of the principalities and powers. To speak of Satan and his powers becomes not just a way of speaking but a fact of reality. When we can see a people who are being controlled by an ideology of whiteness, then we know what reconciliation must mean. The coming of Christ means a denial of what we thought we were. It means destroying the white devil in us. *Reconciliation to God means that white people are prepared to deny themselves (whiteness), take up the cross (blackness) and follow Christ (black ghetto).*[83]

---

[80]Ibid., p. 108.
[81]The cultic anthropology of the Nation of Islam held that white people were created by a rogue demigod named Yakub, who in successive experiments took the original man, the African, and removed his purity. The result was that other shades of men were created until reaching the most debased group, white people. In the Nation of Islam's mythology, white people were regarded as "blond haired, blue eyed devils."
[82]Cone, *God of the Oppressed*, p. 222.
[83]James H. Cone, *Black Theology and Black Power* (Maryknoll, N.Y.: Orbis, 1997), p. 150, emphasis added.

Cone's anthropology effectively reversed the color symbolism and dehuman-
izing rhetoric once applied to blacks and departed from the near unanimous
African American tradition of rejecting negative associations with blackness
without sinking to deny white humanity. Whiteness in Black Theology became the emblem of depravity, moral corruption and satanic power, while
blackness intimated purity and salvation.

In one sense Cone displayed a high regard for black identity, since God
was said to be "black" through his identification with black people in their
suffering. He even claimed that God was the source and ground for blackness.[84] But Cone's anthropology led to other problems. First, his doctrine of
man produced insurmountable contradictions with the biblical record,
where God "made all men of one blood" and "in his own image." If blackness
and God were so reflective of one another, where, then, was the theological
room for creation "in the image of God" of not only whites, but also Asians,
Native Americans, Latinos and Middle Eastern peoples? Second, his view
of black humanity ultimately did more to lower the image of God than to
raise the stature of African Americans. In order to closely associate God
with the condition of downtrodden peoples, Cone needed to eschew "universal" conceptions of God and to choose instead a "local" deity for blacks.[85]
Third, Black Theology's anthropology risked being both singular and superficial in its depiction of African Americans. Suffering and oppression were
the only expressions of black existence.

Cone could not conceive of a black station in life that was not characterized
by such extremities. This assumption curtailed the application of his theology.
And his anthropology risked being superficial with its emphasis on contemporary fads as cultural being. Being black embodied "natural hair cuts, wearing
African daishikis, and dancing to the sound of Johnny Lee Hooker or B. B.
King, knowing that no matter how hard whitey tries there can be no real
duplication of black soul."[86] A group of 250 black Methodists in "The Black
Paper" (1968) exhibited similar shallowness, confessing their "failure to be reconciled with themselves as black men" by denying their blackness, parenthet-
ically defined as "hair texture, color and other God-given physical character-

[84]Cone, *A Black Theology of Liberation*, pp. 63-65, 75.
[85]Ibid., p. 85.
[86]Ibid., p. 25.

istics."[87] The prevailing cultural ethos of the 1960s certainly emphasized such stylistic identifications with Africa, and a good case can be made that these displays were necessary corrections for years of black self-hatred and white ridicule. And, though it is unthinkable that James Cone believed blackness *only* or *merely* entailed transient cultural fads, his anthropology nonetheless set the bar of blackness well below the ideals of true manhood, brotherhood and spiritual equality promulgated by earlier black folks, intellectuals, preachers and theologians.

END OF CENTURY, POSTMODERN ERA (1980-PRESENT)

The blazing fires of 1960s revolution smoldered to ashen decay in little over a decade. In their aftermath stood a growing number of African Americans with both a lower view of the Christian faith and, not incidentally, a lower view of man. Liberal theology's enthusiasm for the unlimited possibilities of man and the promise of God's kingdom on earth were squelched by the Vietnam War, the failed war on poverty, government scandal, assassinations of revered leaders and an overwhelming drug epidemic.

No significant Christian anthropology to answer the dashed hopes of liberalism or liberation theology has been written. James Evans, in his work *We Have Been Believers*, reviewed earlier efforts and proposed three questions for future attempts at a Christian anthropology to embrace: Who are we, how shall we live and where do we belong? These questions, observed Evans, would provide a possible framework for constructing a new anthropology encompassing fallen humanity, geographical, psychological and social dislocation, and the ethical correlates of God's redemption. Evans called for Black Theology to develop a "definition of what it means to be human . . . conceived in relation to both God and one's neighbor."[88] At the close of the millennium, that call remained unanswered.

SUMMARIZING THE DECLINE

In one sense, "decline" is not the best word to describe African American views of man. For most of their history, African Americans maintained and

---

[87]Cited in Cone, *Black Theology and Black Power*, pp. 109-10.
[88]James H. Evans Jr., *We Have Been Believers: An African-American Systematic Theology* (Minneapolis: Fortress Press, 1992), pp. 113-17.

expanded Christian anthropology in ways that strengthen Christian theology and appealed to higher ethics in human interaction. The African American abolitionists of the nineteenth century fought valiantly for a view of man that recognized the spiritual equality of all people and the freedom from bondage that such equality demanded. African American writers of the Reconstruction and Great Migration eras took up the mantle of advocating for full civil and political rights premised upon the social equality of all people. Their efforts gave rise to the Civil Rights struggles and victories from the 1940s through the 1960s. In all of these periods, it should be noted that African Americans held a theological understanding of man superior to their white Christian counterparts who attempted to justify chattel slavery, Jim Crow segregation, Black Codes, and political oppression. African Americans understood the sinful contradiction that enslaved their white brothers and responded with what they regarded as the only true Christian option of both affirming their own humanity and that of their enemies. African American preachers and theologians called all humanity to a greater recognition of the destructive effects of racial prejudice, both for the victim and the perpetrator.

Though the anthropology of black Christians remained strong through most of African American history, subtle shifts in emphasis did create some weaknesses. Following the ministries of Elias Camp Morris and Frances Grimké, a generation of thinkers and churchmen adopted the ideals of "true manhood" and the "brotherhood of man" but began to leave off the gospel imperatives that leaders up to Morris and Grimké had held so firmly. As William J. Moses observes, "From the mid-1930s to the mid-1960s, black intellectual leadership was overwhelmingly committed to integrationism" as opposed to either acquiescing to white-ordained segregation or black separatism. However, with the advent of "cultural pluralism" and "cultural relativism" expressed in the writings of the influential Howard University scholar Alain Locke, crucial aspects of previous pleas for egalitarian and democratic tolerance were lost. "What Locke and his cohorts seemed to forget was that nineteenth-century intellectuals had argued no less convincingly for a religious universalism *as the basis of* democracy and egalitarianism."[89]

---

[89]Moses, "From Booker T. to Malcolm X: Black Political Thought, 1895-1965," pp. 209-10, emphasis added.

Abstracted from gospel-centered convictions—what William Moses terms "religious universalism"—the brotherhood of man and true manhood ideals became moralistic exaltations of natural man with declining concern for man's fallenness and need for spiritual redemption. In an ironic twist, arguments for the spiritual nature of black people, which led to many post-Emancipation freedoms, became obsolete as African Americans actually began to exercise those freedoms. A narrower anthropology emerged, one that overlooked the spiritual aspect of man in favor of conceptions grounded more exclusively in contemporary social and physical circumstance. Instead of cogent gospel appeals for conversion and Christian unity as the basis for a just society, abstracted moral ideals to which any man could attain became the basis for social justice. Liberal theology's high estimations of man's ability and progress supplanted the old orthodoxy of radical depravity. Though neo-orthodox opponents of liberalism, and even some liberal leaders like Dr. Martin Luther King Jr. opposed liberal theology's depreciation of sin and man's moral wickedness, nevertheless the gospel-corrupting effects of an optimistic view of man permeated many African American churches.

The consequences of this overly optimistic anthropology were many. First, it lowered in African Americans' collective conscience the importance of man's spiritual needs. Where there was no urgency prompted by a concern for sin, there was no urgency for preaching the gospel and spiritual reconciliation with God. Today, clear gospel appeals elicit obdurate responses from many people in churches because they believe sin and guilt to be psychological maladjustments left over from a superstitious bygone era. In such cases, the gospel of Jesus Christ is relegated to secondary status.

Second, the emergence of high estimations of man's moral ability leads many to overemphasize political and social freedom. If man no longer needs rescuing from the effects of sin and the wrath of God to come, and if he is capable of ushering in a temporal utopia of sorts, then the logical focus of his energies becomes societal inequities and social structures. Salvation becomes a matter of reconstructing an inefficient but salvageable society. Great hope is placed in the great society. Churches move more aggressively toward becoming the "one stop centers" for all the physical and social needs of their communities—launching housing, credit union, education and social service endeavors. Many seem to forget or overlook the Lord's incisive question, "What does it profit a man to gain the whole world and lose his own soul?" Gaining the whole world seems more and more like the sole quest of man once anthropological amnesia obscures the church's memory of man's depravity.

4

"What a Friend We Have in Jesus"

The Christology of African Americans

We believe in one God, the Father Almighty,

Maker of heaven and earth, and of all things visible and invisible;

And in one Lord Jesus Christ, the Son of God, the Only-begotten,

Begotten of the Father before all worlds, Light of Light, Very God of Very God,

Begotten, not made; of one essence with the Father, by whom all things were made:

Who for us and for our salvation, came down from heaven, and was incarnate of the

Holy Spirit and the Virgin Mary, and was made man.

And was crucified also for us under Pontius Pilate, and suffered and was buried;

And the third day He rose again, according to the Scriptures;

And ascended into heaven, and sitteth at the right hand of the Father;

And He shall come again with glory to judge the quick and the dead,

Whose kingdom shall have no end.

And we believe in the Holy Spirit, the Lord, and Giver of life,

Who proceedeth from the Father, Who with the Father and the Son together is worshiped

and glorified, Who spake by the Prophets;

And we believe in one, holy, catholic, and apostolic Church.

We acknowledge one Baptism for the remission of sins.

We look for the Resurrection of the dead,

And the life of the world to come. Amen.[1]

NICENE-CONSTANTINOPOLITAN CREED (A.D. 381)

---

[1]The Nicene-Constantinopolitan Creed (A.D. 381), adopted at the first council of Constantinople, which revised the original version adopted at Nicaea in A.D. 325. This version omits the contested *filioque* clause of the later Latin version.

GENERAL INTRODUCTION AND CONTEXT

The Council of Nicaea (A.D. 325), the first ecumenical meeting of the subapostolic church, assembled to resolve major disputes regarding the Person of Jesus Christ. Having recently emerged to enjoy its first period of peaceful existence, the church conferred with disputing parties threatening to split Christianity into factions. At issue was whether Jesus was to be understood as the eternal God and how the Father and Jesus were therefore related. At stake was the church's understanding of God, as well as the unity of both the ecumenical church and the Roman Empire.

Arius (d. 336), a presbyter in Alexandria, argued that the persons in the Godhead were not equal. Attempting to avoid the problems of Modalism or Sabellianism, which emphasized the unity of the Godhead at the expense of the distinct Persons, Arius asserted that there was a time when the Son of God or Logos of God was not, that he did not share eternality with the Father, and that he was created in eternity. Athanasius (c. 296-373) charged Arius with dismembering the Godhead and insisted that the Father and the Son were coequal. In an attempt to resolve the dispute, the Council at Nicaea adopted the Nicene Creed. However, the debate over the deity of Christ and his relationship to the Father continued until the second ecumenical council at Constantinople (A.D. 381) where the council held up the Nicene Creed and clarified its position on the Trinity by including comments on the Holy Spirit. The consensus forged at Nicaea and Contantinople—though surrounded by political, ecclesial and theological challenges—survived as the reigning orthodoxy through the Middle Ages, the Great Schism between Eastern and Western churches in 1054, the Protestant Reformation, and into the New World.

This orthodoxy bequeathed to the early colonists and the early American church a trinitarian view of God, which posited the coequal, cosubstantial, co-eternal deity of Jesus Christ with the Father and the Holy Spirit.[2] African American Christianity inherited this orthodox framework and maintained it with no significant revisions until the rise of theological liberalism in the late 1800s and early 1900s. Yet around this time and into

---

[2]For a complete survey of the biblical and historical roots of orthodox Christology, see David F. Wells, *The Person of Christ: A Biblical and Historical Analysis of the Incarnation* (Westchester, Ill.: Crossway, 1984).

the Civil Rights movement, African Americans modified their inherited evangelical Christology. How African Americans have answered two questions—who was Jesus and what did he come to do?—is the subject of this chapter.

EARLY SLAVERY ERA THROUGH ABOLITION ERA (1600-1865)

With rare exception, most Africans brought to the American shores as slaves were not Christians. To be certain, Christianity had found major inroads into Africa prior to the transatlantic slave trade, but during the beginning and peak of the slave trade to the Americas most enslaved West and West Central Africans practiced indigenous religions and a few practiced Islam.[3]

Having been ripped from the familiar cultural contexts of Africa, enslaved Africans attempted to turn to their native religious understandings to make sense of the horrors of slavery. However, plantation abuses and official laws in the colonies systematically drove "underground" the practice of native religion. Slaves discovered observing African religions and rites were summarily punished and subject to being killed. Given such oppression and the prolonged condition of slavery, the question "Who is God?" broke into their conscience and experience in a radical new way.

Some Africans attempted to retain elements of their African religious heritage and to reject European notions of deity. Other Africans—despite persistent oppression by Europeans often "in the name of Christ" coupled with widespread white indifference to spreading the gospel to the slaves—found themselves attracted to Christianity and began to consider whether the claims of Christ's deity were in fact true. Charles H. Long writes poignantly about this dilemma:

> To whom does one pray from the bowels of a slave ship? To the gods of Africa?
> To the gods of the masters of the slave vessels? To the gods of an unknown and
> foreign land of enslavement? To whom does one pray? From the perspective of
> religious experience, this was the beginning of African American religion and

---

[3]Sylvia R. Frey and Betty Wood, *Come Shouting to Zion: African American Protestantism in the American South and British Caribbean to 1830* (Chapel Hill: University of North Carolina Press, 1998). In chapter one, Frey and Wood include an excellent discussion of African encounters with missionary efforts in West and West Central Africa. In chapter two, the authors provide a good analysis of indigenous African religious practices that survived the Middle Passage.

culture. In the forced silence of oppression, in the half-articulate moans of desperation, in the rebellions against enslavement—from this cataclysm another world emerged. . . . African's first expressions of the meaning of the New World took place in the experience of daemonic dread as they were forced into history as terror. . . .

African American religion and its subsequent cultures began in the Middle Passage, in that in-betweenness of the continents of Africa, Europe, and the Americas.[4]

The "in-betweenness" of the African experience gave birth to the African's reflection on the question, "Who is God?" and more specifically, "Who is this God called Jesus Christ?" Answers to these questions varied somewhat between the northern and southern writers of the period, with African Americans in the North focusing on orthodox statements of the work of Christ and those in the South developing unique depictions of the person of Christ.

Northern Christology in the works of Jupiter Hammon and Phillis Wheatley. African American writers in the North adopted the orthodox Christology of Reformed and evangelical Christianity extant through Emancipation and World War I. Though they felt the "in-betweenness" of being African in Antebellum America, they rarely revised their Christology according to the dissonance experienced in chattel bondage. Despite the prevailing social condition and the hypocrisy inherent in a "Christian" slave-owning society, these writers unhesitatingly promoted Jesus as the Son of God and the only Savior of the world. Like the long train of theologians in Christian history before them, African Americans developed their Christology by thinking about both the Person and the work of Jesus Christ. This understanding of Christ was well represented in the religious poetry of Jupiter Hammon and Phillis Wheatley, the father and mother of African American literature.

Jupiter Hammon. Jupiter Hammon's opening couplet to "An Evening Thought: Salvation by Christ, with Penitential Cries" fused together both the work of Jesus in salvation and his unique personhood in the Trinity as the Son of God:

---

[4]See Charles H. Long, "Passage and Prayer" in *The Courage to Hope: From Black Suffering to Human Redemption*, ed. Quinton Hosford Dixie and Cornel West (Boston: Beacon Press, 1999), p. 17.

Salvation comes by Jesus Christ alone,
The only Son of God[5]

"An Evening Thought" stressed Jesus' Sonship from beginning to end. By employing common Christian parlance like Lord, King and Author of Salvation when referring to Jesus, Hammon revealed his acceptance of traditional christological precepts. Hammon's Christology represented the understanding of his northern peers who typically adopted—usually with the briefest of references—the Protestant evangelical theology of their time.[6]

Hammon's orthodoxy extended to his characterization of Jesus' salvific work. The themes of ransom and sacrifice that dominated Christian views of Jesus' atonement found expression in Hammon as well.[7] He wrote:

Salvation comes from God we know,
    The true and only One;
It's well agreed and certain true,
    He gave his only Son.

Dear Jesus by thy precious Blood,
    The World Redemption have:
Salvation comes now from the Lord,
    He being thy captive Slave.[8]

These two stanzas, "well agreed and certain true" in Hammon's mind, poetically echoed the universal church's understanding of the eternal decree of God the Father in giving his Son and the Son's voluntary self-sacrifice in shedding his "precious Blood" to redeem the world. Consistent with Protestant evangelical teachings, Jesus in Hammon's theology was "our Savior, who came down from heaven to save men who were lost and undone without an interest in the merits of Jesus Christ. The blessed Jesus then gave his life, a

---

[5]Jupiter Hammon, "An Evening Thought: Salvation by Christ, with Penitential Cries," in Sondra O'Neale, *Jupiter Hammon and the Biblical Beginnings of African-American Literature* (Metuchen, N.J.: Scarecrow Press, 1993), p. 59, italics added.

[6]For example, in the extant sermons and notes of Lemuel Haynes only the brief statement "the Son of God, who was co-equal, co-eternal, and co-essential with the Father" stands as a forthright statement on the deity of Christ. However, everywhere in Haynes's writings the divinity of Christ is assumed. See "A Sermon on John 3:3," in *Black Preacher to White America: The Collected Writings of Lemuel Haynes, 1774-1833*, ed. Richard Newman (Brooklyn: Carlson, 1990), p. 33.

[7]John D. Hannah, *Our Legacy: The History of Christian Doctrine* (Colorado Springs: NavPress, 2001), pp. 149-99.

[8]Hammon, "An Evening Thought," p. 60.

ransom for all that come unto him by faith and repentance."[9] For Hammon
and his colleagues, the work of Christ centered primarily on his role as Sub-
stitute and Sacrifice for sins.

Phillis Wheatley. Regarded by some as "the progenitor of the black literary
tradition," Phillis Wheatley (1753-1784) birthed the creative writing tradition
of African Americans and African American women with the publication of
her *Poems* in 1773.[10] A slave from the age of six, Wheatley learned to read and
write under the tutelage of her owner. Her most famous collection, simply entitled *Poems*, reflects a rather sophisticated knowledge of Scripture and theology. She was obviously acquainted with the work of preachers and theologians
of her period—most of whom were Reformed in their theology. For example,
"On the Death of the Rev. Mr. George Whitefield," written in 1770, provided
poetic eulogy for the late evangelist of the Great Awakening. While Wheatley
and Hammon were certainly more educated than most fellow slaves of their
period, they were reasonable proxies for Protestant theological thinking prevalent in both the Northeastern white American and the African American
"church."

In a 1767 poem entitled "To the University of Cambridge, in New England," Wheatley demonstrated a rather articulate and orthodox view of the
gospel and the work of Christ in salvation. Her work was all the more impres-
sive considering she was only about thirteen at the time of its composition.
She wrote:

> Students, to you 'tis giv'n to scan the heights
> Above, to traverse the ethereal space,
> And mark the systems of revolving worlds.
> Still more, ye sons of science ye receive

---

[9]Hammon, "A Winter Piece," in Sondra O'Neale, *Jupiter Hammon and the Biblical Beginnings of African-American Literature* (Metuchen, N.J.: Scarecrow Press, 1993), p. 107. Elsewhere, taking as his
text "Behold the Lamb of God" in Jn 1:29, Jupiter Hammon referred to Jesus as the Lamb of God:
"the King immortal, eternal, invisible, and the only Son of God," "as coming in the clouds of heaven
with great power and glory," "having power to make the blind see, the dumb speak, and the lame to
walk, and even to raise the dead," "as crucified for us," as having "boundless riches of free grace," having "power to give everlasting life," and "as being the door of eternal life." See, Hammon, "An
Evening's Improvement," in Sondra O'Neale, *Jupiter Hammon and the Biblical Beginnings of African-
American Literature* (Metuchen, N.J.: Scarecrow Press, 1993), pp. 160-70.
[10]Henry Louis Gates Jr., "In Her Own Write," foreword to *The Collected Works of Phillis Wheatley*, ed.
John Shields (New York: Oxford University Press, 1988), p. x.

The blissful news by messengers from heav'n,
How Jesus' blood for your redemption flows.
See him with hands out-stretcht upon the cross;
Immense compassion in his bosom glows;
He hears revilers, nor resents their scorn:
What matchless mercy in the Son of God!
When the whole human race by sin had fall'n,
He deign'd to die that they might rise again,
And share with him in the sublimest skies,
Life without death, and glory without end.[11]

Wheatley admonished the students of Harvard (commonly referred to by its location as Cambridge) to pay more attention to "the blissful news by messengers from heav'n" than to their studies in science. This "blissful news" was the good news or gospel of Jesus Christ. And the substance of that good news, Wheatley clearly posited, was the substitutionary atonement of Christ. She seemed to marvel at the matchless mercy displayed in "Jesus' blood for your redemption flows" and promise of resurrection as "He deign'd to die that they might rise again."

Another work, "To a Clergyman on the Death of his Lady," comforted a grieving husband by reminding him of Christ's sacrifice on his and his deceased wife's behalf. The promise of that sacrifice was a future eternity with Christ and his wife in heaven. Wheatley, adopting the perspective of the deceased wife in heaven, wrote:

O come away, her longing spirit cries,
And share with me the raptures of the skies.
Our bliss divine to mortals is unknown;
Immortal life and glory are our own.
There too may the dear pledges of our love
Arrive, and taste with us the joys above;
Attune the harp to more than mortal lays,
And join with us the tribute of their praise
To him, who dy'd stern justice to atone,
And make eternal glory all our own.

---

[11]This poem was first published in 1773 in a collection titled "Poems on Various Subjects." See Wheatley, *Collected Works.* Emphasis added.

He in his death slew ours, and, as he rose,
He crush'd the dire dominion of our foes;
Vain were their hopes to put the God to flight,
Chain us to hell, and bar the gates of light.[12]

For Wheatley, through the voice of the deceased wife, the death of Jesus was an atoning answer for the justice of God—"who dy'd stern justice to atone." Wheatley's picture of God's justice being satisfied in the crucifixion of Christ indicated her familiarity with historical Christian understandings of the atonement. That historical orthodoxy required the offering of a perfect sacrifice to propitiate the wrath of God on behalf of the penitent faithful. That substitutionary atonement secured ultimate victory over the death owed by the sinner, spiritual foes desiring our banishment to hell, and "eternal glory all our own." Phillis Wheatley affirmed that conception of the person and work of Jesus in her poetry and likely represented the religious ideas of most other northern black Christian writers of the period, who were exposed to the strong orthodox Calvinist theology dominant in the era.

Southern writers: Jesus, friend of slaves. As is the case with most doctrines, the Christology of African Americans in the antebellum South bore several unique characteristics. Africans from southern regions of the New World left sparse evidence in narratives and songs that their basic view of Jesus Christ

Phillis Wheatley

Frontispiece from Phillis Wheatley's
*Poems on Various Subjects, Religious
and Moral*

---

[12]Wheatley, *Collected Works*, p. 54.

conformed more or less to the understandings of the Baptist and Methodist missionaries of the late eighteenth century. The spotty success of plantation missions combined with recalcitrant slave owners' anti-literacy measures made a thorough imbibing of classical Christology difficult. Consequently, Charley Williams announced somewhat paradoxically, "'Course, I love my Lord Jesus same as anybody, but you see I never hear much about Him until I was grown, and it seem lak you got to hear about religion when you little to soak it up and put much by it."[13] Former slave Neal Upson recounted a humorous episode involving his Aunt Flora's examination before joining the church:

> Dem days dey 'zamined folses 'fore dey let 'em jine up wid de church. When dey started 'zaminin' Aunt Flora, de preacher axed her, "Is you done been borned again, and does you believe dat Jesus Christ done died to save sinners?" Aunt Flora, she started to cry, and she said, "Lordy, is He daid? If my old man had done 'scribed for de paper lak I told him to, us would have knowed when Jesus died."[14]

Southern African Christians loved what they knew of Jesus, even though their knowledge was often incomplete. The conspicuous absence or limited references to the name "Jesus" in many slave testimonies and interviews spoke to their untutored Christology.[15]

Where christological thoughts of slaves survived and were explicit, the orthodox view predominated. For example, several slave songs succinctly rehearsed the events of Jesus' crucifixion and resurrection. The lines from "The Resurrection Morn" recounted the events at the tomb where Jesus first appeared to Mary:

1 O run, Mary, run, Hallelu, hallelu!
   O run, Mary, run, Hallelujah!

2 It was early in de mornin', Hallelu, hallelu!
   It was early in de mornin', Hallelujah!

3 That she went to de sepulchre, (chorus)

---

[13]James Mellon, ed., *Bullwhip Days: The Slaves Remember* (New York: Grove Press, 1988), p. 113.
[14]Ibid., p. 363.
[15]The conversion testimonies in Johnson's *God Struck Me Dead* and the recollections in Mellon's *Bullwhip Days* contain surprisingly few references to Jesus by name. The more ambiguous "Lord" is often used to refer to both God the Father and Jesus Christ. And even these references fail to provide much information on what the slaves thought about the person and work of Jesus.

4 And de Lord he wasn't da.

5 But she see a man a-comin',

6 And she thought it was de gardener.

7 But he say, "O touch me not,

8 "For I am not yet ascended.

9 "But tell to my disciples

10 "Dat de Lord he is arisen."

11 So run, Mary, run, etc.[16]

Other songs revealed that slaves knew more than the bare facts of the Passion and resurrection. Songs like "The Hypocrite and the Concubine" indicated an adequate grasp of the meaning of the resurrection for the sinner:

Hypocrite and the concubine,
Livin' among the swine,
They run to God with the lips and tongue,
And leave all the heart behind.
Aunty, did you hear when Jesus rose?
Did you hear when Jesus rose?
Aunty, did you hear when Jesus rose?
He rose and he 'scend on high.[17]

The need to respond to and believe the good news of the resurrection was implicit in the refrain "did you hear when Jesus rose?" The resurrection of Jesus demanded sincere repentance and faith, not a feigned submission by "running to God with the lips and tongue, and [leaving] all the heart behind." Antebellum lyrics carried an urgent appeal of salvation through faith in Jesus Christ, depicted in standard orthodox fashion as the one who rose from the dead and "'scend on high."

But in addition to the work and nature of Jesus assumed from European co-religionists, and despite efforts to dissuade religious innovation among the enslaved, Africans found in Jesus more than the God-man taught and controlled

---

[16]William Francis Allen, Charles Pickard Ware and Lucy McKim, eds., *Slave Songs in the United States* (New York: A. Simpson, 1867), p. 54.
[17]"The Hypocrite and the Concubine," in ibid., p. 70.

by European missionaries and revivalists. The Jesus preached and taught by most planter-sanctioned evangelists and preachers tended to be a bystander to the atrocities of slavery. But enslaved Africans intuited in Jesus a Friend and a Comforter in their trials and affliction.

Southern slaves emphasized the closeness of Jesus in history and his friendship to them in their plight. The worshiper's lament in spirituals like "Nobody Knows the Trouble I've Seen" revealed an understanding Jesus whose awareness of their difficulties not only surpassed that of every other person but turned solitary sorrow into ebullient praise and rejoicing:

> Nobody knows de trouble I've had,
> Nobody knows *but Jesus,*
> Nobody knows de trouble I've had,
> (Sing) Glory hallelu![18]

Despite their bondage, or perhaps because of it, enslaved Africans knew that somehow "Just a little talk with Jesus" made their survival possible. When ethnic and language differences between Africans placed potential brethren beyond mutual empathy, Jesus knew their troubles. He stuck closer than any brother.

In one hymn, Jesus' friendship is juxtaposed to the sabotaging industry of Satan:

> Ole Satan is a busy ole man,
> He roll stones in my way;
> *Mass' Jesus is my bosom friend,*
> *He roll 'em out o' my way.*[19]

For the slave, Jesus was both "bosom friend" and "Mass"—two characteristics no earthly slave owner could reconcile in himself. Jesus' lordship was revealed in his removal of hindrances and spiritual attacks, thereby making known his closeness and alliance.

With this accent on the friendship of Jesus, the slaves evolved a view of the immanence of Christ altogether different from that of traditional Western theology. If the slave had resigned himself to the Savior of European sermons, he would not have found a Friend in such preaching. But in the vacuum created by the intentional intellectual suppression foisted upon bondservants arose a Savior whose affinity for the faithful surpassed anything imagined by

---

[18]Ibid., p. 55.
[19]Ibid., p. 57.

Western orthodoxy. Perhaps the early Anglican failures of the Society for the Propagation of the Gospel in Foreign Parts occurred partly because the Jesus preached appeared too disinterested in African chattel.[20] Were that limitation overcome by the SPG, their catechetical rigor might have produced an African American conception of Jesus more in line with the longer tradition of Christian discourse even as it retained certain African distinctives. As it was, Africans were left with sufficient freedom to fashion a view of the person and work of Jesus that both conformed to their limited knowledge of the Scriptures and spoke to their antebellum circumstance. However, the absence of theological precision or rigor left African Americans essentially open to christological innovations of a more significant and harmful sort.

RECONSTRUCTION, "JIM CROW" SEGREGATION, GREAT MIGRATION AND THE "NEW NEGRO" (1865-1929)

With the rise of a more radical abolitionist movement in the 1830s, the open hands that once received the orthodoxies passed on from European Puritans, Protestants, and evangelicals tightened into clinched fists of protest. The European theological canon faced its first direct onslaught in the Americas and began to wobble under the assault of African Americans attending independent churches and now free to challenge, modify or reject inherited assumptions. Such responses did not begin with overt attempts at overthrowing the old orthodoxy; rather, the first changes in African American Christology resulted in expanded understandings of Christ's atoning work.

William J. Seymour's view of the atonement. At the head of the first christological revision in African American theology stood William J. Seymour, pastor of the Azusa Street Mission and leader of the Azusa Street revival from 1906-1909. Seymour's movement, egalitarian at its inception, significantly impacted both black and white churches. His view of the atonement spread worldwide along with the "revival fire" that ignited it.

Specifically, Seymour taught that the atoning work of Jesus not only included spiritual salvation but physical healing as well. According to Seymour, "The sacrifice on Calvary was a twofold sacrifice. When we have the atonement in all its fullness, we have health and salvation to the uttermost." The

---

[20]Frey and Wood, *Come Shouting to Zion*, pp. 63-79.

Pentecostal leader asserted that Christians "have just as much right to look to Jesus for the health of these bodies as for the saving and sanctifying of our souls."[21] Seymour reasoned that just as original sin accompanied the birth of a child, so did physical sickness. Sickness in Seymour's scheme was a "work of the devil" that, like spiritual bondage to sin, Jesus destroyed in his earthly mission and work on the cross.[22] All those who believed in Jesus were eligible to receive healing.[23]

The Azusa Street doctrine of the atonement appeared in the movement at or near its inception. In an article entitled "The Precious Atonement," Seymour listed three benefits accruing to the Christian believer. First, the atonement provided forgiveness for sins. Second, Jesus' atonement ensured sanctification leading to adoption as sons of God and freedom from sin. Third, the atonement destroyed sickness and disease and healed physical bodies. According to Seymour's Christology, the "stripes" of Jesus referred to in Isaiah 53:5 secured physical sanctification:

> How we ought to honor that precious body which the Father sanctified and sent into the world, not simply set apart, but really sanctified, soul, body and spirit, free from sickness, disease and everything of the devil. A body that knew no sin and disease was given for these imperfect bodies of ours. Not only is the atonement for the sanctification of our souls, but for the sanctification of our bodies from inherited disease.[24]

Seymour predicated his view of the atonement upon the purity of Christ's physical body. He wrote, "If His flesh had seen corruption, then we could not have healing for the body nor look for an immortal body from heaven."[25] Conversely, if Christ were without physical blemish, and if he took upon himself the infirmities of fallen man, then physical salvation was purchased on the cross. "He gave his blood for the salvation of our souls and He gave a perfect body for these imperfect bodies of ours."[26]

"By His stripes we are healed" served as Azusa Street's mantra for a "two-

---

[21]William J. Seymour, "Salvation and Healing," *Apostolic Faith* (December 1906): 2.
[22]Seymour, "Healing," *Apostolic Faith* (September 1907): 1.
[23]Seymour, "Questions Answered," *Apostolic Faith* (January 1908): 2.
[24]Seymour, "The Precious Atonement," *Apostolic Faith* (September 1906): 2.
[25]Seymour, "Virtue in the Perfect Body of Jesus," *Apostolic Faith*, (February-March 1907): 1.
[26]Seymour, "Salvation and Healing," *Apostolic Faith* (December 1906): 2.

fold salvation" understanding of the atonement. The theological justification of the doctrine was Exodus 15:26 where the Lord God proclaimed, "I am the Lord thy God that healeth thee." Seymour held that since God revealed himself as a healing God and gave His Son to accomplish His promise then it was the duty of all Pentecostal Christians to seek the promised healing for their bodies.[27] Writers at the official newspaper for the movement, *Apostolic Faith*, concluded that if a saint were not healed then "the fault is either in [the believer] or in Jesus Christ." They continued, "There is nothing can stop my healing but myself. God is not a moment behind in doing His work."[28] Consequently, failure to obtain a healing and the loss of a healing were attributed to deficiencies in the faith of the adherent who wavered in believing or resorted to medicines and doctors that were forbidden for the faithful.[29]

The emphasis on physical healing as one aspect of the atonement foreshadowed later Charismatic preoccupation with healing. As much as anyone, Seymour provided the theological justification for such a view. The Azusa Street movement also anticipated later word-of-faith teachings on the centrality of faith in receiving healings and other miracles. In either case, an expanded view of the atonement that included physical as well as spiritual benefits in this life was firmly established through the Azusa Street revival.

Marcus Garvey and Jesus the universal man. With the rise of the Marcus Garvey movement came another departure from historical views of the person and work of Jesus Christ. Marcus Garvey, with his emphasis on Negro self-help and New Thought philosophy, developed a view of Jesus that lauded him as an example of the potential for human progress inherent in all men. Garvey more often spoke of Jesus as an object lesson in human capacity for self-realization than as a Savior come to take away the sins of the world. Two precepts defined his Christology.

First, Garvey defined the person of Christ in ways consistent with his New Thought depiction of God the Father. He wasted no ink on delineating the dual nature of Christ or the miracle of the virgin birth; he flatly insisted that

---

[27] Seymour, "He Bore Our Sicknesses," *Apostolic Faith* (December 1906): 3.

[28] *Apostolic Faith* (December 1906): 1.

[29] See the following front page stories: "Pentecost with Signs Following," *Apostolic Faith* (December 1906): 1; "Beginning of World Wide Revival," *Apostolic Faith* (January 1907): 1; and the catechetical article "Questions Answered," *Apostolic Faith* (January 1908): 2.

Jesus' perfect life made it "evident and fair" to assume he was "the begotten Son of God." Though he used traditional trinitarian terms for Jesus, Garvey opted for a nontraditional definition of what Sonship entailed. Where the Father was "universal intelligence," the sum of all intelligence and wisdom in existence, Garvey rendered Jesus universal man, the apex of all human potential. He argued "that Christ had in his veins the blood of all mankind and belonged to no particular race. Christ was God in the perfect sense of his mind and soul." Though Garvey taught there was "no cause to doubt that Christ lived" or that a historical Jesus existed, he presented Christ merely as the human embodiment of divine intelligence—a "soul which acted on the advice of God's spirit." Jesus' faultless obedience to God made him "a superior creature" but not the eternally coequal and co-substantial second person of the Godhead of orthodox Christian theology.[30]

Second, Garvey spiritualized the work of Jesus Christ in a way that harmonized the meaning of the resurrection with his New Thought suppositions. Since Jesus was the embodiment of human potential, "The mission of Christ, therefore, was to redeem man from sin and place him back on the pinnacle of goodness as God intended when he made the first two creatures." Though Garvey spoke of redemption from sin, his concept of sin merely referred to failing to develop one's human capacity—not rebellion against God and his law. The great sin was falling from "the pinnacle of goodness" God intended in the creation account. "The life of Christ (was) intended to show man that *he could lift himself by obedience* to the highest soul expression."[31]

In a sense, then, Garvey's understanding of the work of Christ harkened back to Peter Abelard's (1079-1142/3) and Hugo Grotius's (1583-1645) ethical and moral interpretations of the atonement.[32] These men believed that the sacrifice of Christ was not necessary for satisfying the justice of God or to pay for the penalty of sin; it was merely to exemplify the virtuous life and to encourage the would-be faithful to imitate that life. In a 1922 Easter sermon entitled "The Resurrection of the Negro," Garvey summarized his ethical and moral view of the cross:

---

[30]Marcus Garvey, "Christ." In Robert A. Hill and Barbara Bair, eds., *Marcus Garvey: Life and Lessons* (Berkeley: University of California Press, 1987), pp. 225-27.
[31]Ibid., emphasis added.
[32]Hannah, *Our Legacy*, pp. 163-66, 174.

As Christ triumphed nearly 2,000 years ago over death and the grave, as He was risen from the dead, so do I hope that 400,000,000 Negroes of today will triumph over the slavishness of the past, intellectually, physically, morally and even religiously; that on this anniversary of our risen Lord, we ourselves will be risen from the slumber of the ages; risen in thought to higher ideals, to a loftier purpose, to a truer conception of life.[33]

Garvey believed that stultifying and entangling debates over Christian doctrine were remnants of the "slavishness of the past." So, he poured new meaning into the resurrection for the Negroes of his day.

He continued drawing out the ethical implications of the resurrection:

Today as we think of our risen Lord may we not think of the life He gave to us— the life that made us His instruments, His children—the life that He gave to us to make us possessors of the land that He himself created through His Father? How many of us can reach out to that higher life; that higher purpose; that creative world that says to you you are a man, a sovereign, a lord—lord of the creation? On this beautiful spring day, may we not realize that God made Nature for us; God has given it to us as our province, our dominion? May we not realize that God has created no superior being to us in this world, but Himself? May we not know that we are the true lords and creators of our own fate and of our own physical destiny?[34]

Among other things, historical Christian understandings of the work of Christ emphasized the substitutionary nature of his sacrifice. That orthodoxy interpreted the Bible's teachings on the cross and resurrection as a necessary sacrifice for sin to satisfy the just wrath of God the Father. Garvey's Christology supplanted the biblical and historical understanding with an idealized man exemplified in the life of Jesus. Gone in Garvey's theology was any serious view of sin, any orthodox conception of the deity of Christ, any need to satisfy God's character, and any need therefore for Christ's death. In their place stood a New Thought monument to the possibilities of man.

DEPRESSION AND WORLD WAR II (1930-1949)

Marcus Garvey denied the deity of Jesus Christ—at least in terms of how that de-

---

[33]Marcus Garvey, "The Resurrection of the Negro" (April 16, 1922), in *Selected Writings and Speeches of Marcus Garvey*, ed. Bob Blaisdell (Mineola, N.Y.: Dover, 2004), pp. 66-67.
[34]Ibid., p. 67.

ity was historically understood by the church—by infusing traditional theological terms with new meanings, amplifying the human nature of Jesus and spiritualizing the atonement. His denial was not overt, but it opened the door for future explicit rejections of the orthodox Christian consensus. The rise of modern liberalism and higher criticism triggered a rejection of historical tenets and prompted a quest for the "historical Jesus" in contrast to the "Christ of faith."

Howard Thurman, Jesus and the disinherited. Among African Americans, perhaps the first direct rejection of doctrines widely understood to teach the deity of Christ came in the theology of Howard Thurman. Thurman consistently avoided historically accepted doctrines like the incarnation and the atonement, which Christians regarded as evidence of Jesus' divine status. But beyond these outright rejections, there was in Thurman's thought a measured attempt to identify Jesus with the oppressed and downtrodden.

Jesus: An ordinary man with a profound religious experience. Luther E. Smith Jr., in his biography of Howard Thurman, concluded that Jesus, in Thurman's theology, is not God but is "the *for instance* of the mind of God." Smith observed a conspicuous silence from Thurman on fundamental Christian doctrines like the incarnation, sacrificial atonement for sin and the bodily resurrection. Further, "the life of Jesus exercises a moral and spiritual influence over contemporary lives." According to Smith, Thurman's theology followed the typical liberal viewpoint as he searched for the "essence" of religious meaning in the Jesus of history and the Christ of faith, rejecting traditional Christianity for a purer "religion of Jesus."[35] Dr. Thurman denied the uniqueness of Jesus implied in the formula "the only begotten Son." He believed that "anyone who is as sure of God as was Jesus, can hear for himself: 'Thou art my son, my beloved, this day I have begotten thee'."[36] Moreover, becoming the son of God in the sense of acquiring the mind of Christ and having a similar relationship to God, according to Thurman, "may be achieved without any necessity whatsoever of making a God out of Jesus."[37]

Howard Thurman's theology began with the removal of any extraordinary claims to divinity for Jesus. Consistent with liberal convictions and the

---

[35]Luther E. Smith, *Howard Thurman: The Mystic as Prophet* (Richmond, Ind.: Friends United Press, 1991), pp. 67-72.

[36]Howard Thurman, *Deep Is the Hunger* (Richmond, Ind.: Friends United Press, 1951), p. 173.

[37]Howard Thurman, *The Creative Encounter* (Richmond, Ind.: Friends United Press, 1954), p. 83.

thought of Marcus Garvey, Jesus was merely an exemplar. Jesus was *not* the Son of God in any divine or unique sense as historic Christianity held.

Rather, Jesus of Nazareth was simply a man who had a "fundamental and searching—almost devastating—experience of God." However, this encounter between Jesus and God was not unique to the Father and the Son. Thurman maintained that, while extremely profound, Jesus' religious experience was available to all people and its effects should be expected and pursued. In fact, Thurman argued in contradiction to biblical teaching that it was Jesus who insisted that, "all men are children of God, and therefore stand in immediate candidacy for that experience."[38]

In a sermon titled "Not by Bread Alone," Thurman speculated about the effect of Jesus' contact with God. He wrote, "This experience was so fontal and so fundamental to the very grounds of his being that he had to deal with the implications of this experience whenever he raised any question about the meaning of his own life." According to Thurman, the contact between Jesus and God was so extraordinary that it *"seemed to him"* (Jesus) that the heavens opened and that the living Spirit of the living God descended upon him like a dove. . . . And then he left; shaken to his core."[39] The encounter, while real in its effects on Jesus, leaving him "shaken to the core," was also mythical. The baptism account recorded in all four gospels and characterized by a descending dove and the voice of God, long held in orthodox theology to be visible and audible signs of Jesus' divinity, were merely an apparition in Thurman's interpretation of Jesus. Instead of affirming his deity, the vision and voice authenticated Jesus' mystical awareness and transformation, a position typical of liberal theology.

This transformation and mystical awareness was not easily handled by the "ordinary" Jesus of Thurman's theology. "Shaken to his core," Thurman pictured Jesus as doubtful and anxious about the meaning and purpose of his life. In this way, Thurman underscored the humanity of Jesus and emphasized Jesus' identification with the existential angst that afflicted so many of his listeners. Portraying Jesus' uncertainty through an imagined litany of questions, Thurman's Jesus asked:

---

[38]Ibid., p. 135. For an example of a New Testament passage featuring Jesus' teaching to the contrary, see Jn 6:65 and surrounding context.

[39]Howard Thurman, *Temptations of Jesus* (Richmond, Ind.: Friends United Press, 1962), pp. 16, 17-18; emphasis added.

What shall I do with my life if I am going to be true to the tremendous experience of God which I have had? How can I live so that my life will not deny the glory which I saw and felt? Or was the glory which I saw and felt completely other-worldly and beyond any thing that human experience can seek to implement? Is it something that is separate and is not to be a part of the warp and woof, the stuff of human experience? Was I invaded by something that does not belong to the nature and the character of the normal working paper of human life?[40]

Thurman's portrayal is void of the certainty and steadfastness characteristic of Jesus in the gospel accounts. And not only does Thurman's view of Jesus' humanity present itself in imagined doubts about his mission, Thurman also imagines that Jesus is tempted to forsake his mission for a more comfortable life:

So, shall I go north? Back home?

If I go back home now, I can live in the place with which I am familiar, and from all the ends of the region these people could come and be blessed and helped. What a comfort I would be to my mother who finds it so difficult to accept the fact that her oldest son has walked out from under the responsibilities left when the head of the family died. All this is the will of God, isn't it?

If I go home, then I can die in my bed. And how long I could live doing good, helping, teaching. The world needs somebody to teach it. If I could have a long time interval to make available to all who seek, that which moves in me, of which I am so fully conscious and aware, isn't that enough? What is wrong with that?[41]

The Jesus of Howard Thurman's theology dwelt fully in his humanity. He was tempted, and quite possibly could have made wrong decisions.[42] Thurman accented the humanity of Jesus in a way that made him at one with the rest of humanity. The "Jesus idea"—the identification of divine love with the name and spirit of Jesus of Nazareth—"placed at the disposal of men a resource, available to each of them, upon which they may draw for strength and power to enable and to sustain them in the great enterprise of living."[43] He eschewed any historical or fundamentalist claims to the divinity and exclusivity of Jesus as inherently negative and divisive, as "paving the way in the promulgation in

---

[40]Ibid., p. 18.
[41]Ibid., p. 51.
[42]Ibid., pp. 52-53.
[43]Thurman, *Creative Encounter*, p. 137.

the world of a Cult of Inequality that puts man against man and group against group."[44] Thurman biographer Luther Smith Jr. noted, "Thurman's focus on Jesus does not mean, as in many churches, that Jesus should be worshipped. Jesus should be known as an example for the needs of individuals. He demonstrated a proper sense of self. He experienced God. He committed his life to the vision of God. He loved all with whom he came in contact. And he helped create community."[45]

Smith continued:

> The practical consideration here is that Jesus as life example is a unifying principle. It should satisfy the basic affirmation of Christians and not offend (perhaps even appeal to) non-Christians. Jesus as religious object (God) excludes those who cannot make this proclamation, who have come to know God through some other great teacher. So for Thurman, the deification of Jesus is not only theologically unsound, but contrary to the community building mission of the church.[46]

And through his various posts as lecturer and pastor, Thurman's view of Jesus made inroads with a significant number of future preachers and churchmen.

The work of Christ: Jesus identifies with the disinherited. If Thurman's view of the Person of Jesus Christ departed from the mainstream of Christian theology, his emphasis on the work of Jesus was equally as innovative. In 1935, serving as chairman of an African American delegation of the World Student Christian Fellowship, Thurman led a tour through India. The decision to lead the delegation was not an easy one to make. He wrote of the trip:

> My central concern was whether I could in good conscience go to India, or any other missionary field, as a representative of the Christian religion as it was projected in the West, and primarily from America. I did not want to go to India as an apologist for a segregated Christianity, yet how could I go under the auspices of the Student Christian Movement without seeming in fact to contradict my intention?[47]

---

[44]Ibid., pp. 147-48; Howard Thurman, *Disciplines of the Spirit* (Richmond, Ind.: Friends United Press, 1977), p. 35.

[45]Smith, *Howard Thurman*, pp. 85-86.

[46]Ibid.

[47]Howard Thurman, *With Head and Heart: The Autobiography of Howard Thurman* (Orlando: Harcourt Brace, 1979), pp. 103-4.

Members of the World Student Christian Fellowship later persuaded Thurman to lead the delegation precisely because of his hesitations and convictions. During the tour, Thurman met with Mahatma Gandhi and encountered scores of college students posing challenging questions about the integrity of American Christianity in the face of racial segregation and oppression. One questioner attacked Thurman as a "traitor to all the darker peoples of the earth" for representing Christianity as a Negro.[48] However, Thurman resisted being identified with that form of Christianity that accepted bigotry and intolerance. And yet, he could not escape the dogged dissonance caused by the enmity between his own profession of Christian discipleship and the hypocritical religious practice of white American Christians. Thurman came to believe it imperative that Christianity, or rather "the religion of Jesus," demonstrate the relevance of Jesus for black and oppressed people by identifying "what Christianity has to say to the conditions of the oppressed and poor." And given the explosive truths contained in the faith, "Why is it that Christianity seems impotent to deal radically, and therefore effectively, with the issues of discrimination and injustice on the basis of race, religion and national origin? Is this impotency due to a betrayal of the genius of the religion, or to a basic weakness in the religion itself?"[49]

Thurman's resolution of this dilemma shaped and informed his Christology. He maintained that "the sin of pride and arrogance . . . tended to vitiate the missionary impulse and to make it an instrument of self-righteousness on the one hand and of racial superiority on the other," making "a basic relationship between the simple practice of brotherhood in the commonplace relations of life and the ethical pretensions of our faith"[50] impossible to achieve. In other words, the radical eradication of racism and injustice seemed nearly impossible because Christian people refused to meet the height of another's need with the depth of their love.

"The sin of pride and arrogance," as Thurman saw it, caused many Christians to wrongly equate moral good with giving to the needs of others out of one's affluence. Thurman understood how this orientation fostered a certain kind of missionary zeal but prevented serious consideration of what Christian-

---

[48]Ibid., p. 114.
[49]Howard Thurman, *Jesus and the Disinherited* (Boston: Beacon, 1976), p. 7.
[50]Ibid., pp. 12-13.

ity had to say to those "with their backs against the wall," the poor, despised, dispossessed, and disinherited of society. Finding out what Christianity offered as a solution for the plight of the disinherited was "perhaps the most important religious quest of modern life" in Thurman's opinion.[51] And, indeed, framing the claims of Christianity in a manner that addressed the cause of the dispossessed represented a significant improvement in theological discourse regarding the work of Jesus Christ.

From the vantage point of the disinherited, Thurman contended, determining the terms of survival and the appropriate attitude to display toward social, economic and political rulers were the key questions of life. Thurman proposed that Jesus' historical condition provided the Christian solution to these questions. Specifically, three facts from the life of Jesus seemed relevant. First, the historical Jesus was a Jew. His Jewishness identified him with a particular people (Israel) suffering disenfranchisement at the hands of Roman occupiers. Second, Jesus was a poor Jew, which meant that he was placed alongside the great masses of humanity in their deprivation. Third, Jesus belonged to a minority group in the midst of a larger and dominant group. These factors left open to Jesus and Israel two options for surviving and responding to their political situation—resistance or acquiescence.[52]

Assuming this historical backdrop, Thurman posited a view of Jesus' work that redefined redemption partly in terms of its audience. Jesus' work included all the downtrodden of every generation. Thurman recognized that, "the underprivileged everywhere have long since abandoned hope that [a theological and metaphysical interpretation of] salvation deals with the crucial issues by which their days are turned into desolation without consolation." The real Jesus and the genius of Christianity allowed the oppressed to "gather fresh courage; for he announced the good news that fear, hypocrisy, and hatred, the three hounds of hell that track the trail of the disinherited, need have no dominion over them." Christians and theologians, according to Thurman, overlooked the fact that Jesus intended Christianity to be a technique for survival. There was no defect in the religion of Jesus; it possessed the power to heal and motivate. The defect occurred in that conception of Christianity that removed

---

[51]Ibid., pp. 12-13.
[52]Ibid., pp. 15-28.

Jesus from his historical context and rendered him a tool of oppression in the hand of the dominant and powerful.[53]

More specifically, Thurman argued that the historical Jesus and his context most resembled the context of American Negroes of his day:

> The striking similarity between the social position of Jesus in Palestine and that of the vast majority of American Negroes is obvious to anyone who tarries long over the facts. We are dealing here with conditions that produce essentially the same psychology. There is meant no further comparison. It is the similarity of a social climate at the point of a denial of full citizenship that creates the problem for a creative survival.[54]

As Luther Smith pointed out, Thurman's comparison of Jesus' social condition to that of American Negroes "completely upset a norm for much of American theology and religion which have assumed that Jesus' life and ministry more closely resembled the status and values of privileged, white Americans."[55] In explicating Jesus' historical context and applying it to the disinherited of the world, Thurman began articulating a populist Christology with import for oppressed and deplored peoples. Thurman's depiction of Jesus ever so slightly forced open the door to an overtly political interpretation of the life and work of Jesus. Thurman meditated little on the classical meaning of the cross and the atonement, but creatively fashioned a view of Christ's work that reinvigorated theological concern for people and conditions long ignored by traditional theology.

CIVIL RIGHTS ERA (1950-1979)

Reaching back to the earliest antecedents of the "black Christ"—the speculations of Bishop Turner, the religio-political imagery and rhetoric of Marcus Garvey, the artistic influence of the New Negro movement, and the nascent political Christology of Howard Thurman—writers in the Civil Rights and Black Power eras crystallized what had previously been marginal suggestions into a full-blown Christology featuring a black Jesus. Two figures led the charge in this reinterpretation. Albert Cleage (1911-2000), founder of the

---

[53]Ibid., p. 29.
[54]Ibid., p. 34.
[55]Smith, *Howard Thurman*, p. 110.

Albert Cleage

Pan-African Orthodox Christian Church, made an attempt at defending a literal depiction of Jesus as a black man,[56] while James Cone offered a figurative understanding of the blackness of Jesus. Amidst the clamor of competing voices, from the continuing efforts of black evangelicals[57] to the marginal calls of Albert Cleage, James Cone's formulation of Black Theology emerged as the most novel and attractive for many black church leaders and academics.

James Cone's Christology: Jesus "was," "is" and "will be" black. While not following Thurman in an explicit manner, Cone nevertheless saw the theologian's task and the person and work of Jesus Christ in terms very much akin to Thurman. Both Thurman and Cone held that the essential task of the theologian was to articulate the relevance of Jesus Christ for oppressed peoples in their social context. Both recognized Jesus Christ as the point of departure for answering ethical and political challenges associated with being a member of an oppressed community.

However, the Christologies of Thurman and Cone differed in two signifi-

---

[56]Albert Cleage Jr., *The Black Messiah* (New York: Sheed and Ward, 1968).
[57]See, for example, Tom Skinner, *How Black Is the Gospel?* (Philadelphia: J. B. Lippincott, 1970).

cant ways. First, where Thurman emphasized the *psychological* benefits of including the dispossessed in the redemption plans of Jesus' ministry, Cone recognized a greater *political* solidarity between Jesus and the oppressed community. Cone's theology emphasized Jesus' legitimization of a certain political stridency and resistance against oppression. Second, where Thurman's analysis limited itself to the social and historical setting of first century Palestine as a source for interpreting the person and work of Jesus, Cone's approach cited both socio-historical contexts and biblical passages for support. Beyond these basic similarities and differences between Thurman and Cone, there emerged in Black Theology a Christology decidedly more black-centered than any theory before it.

The Christology that emerged from the writings of James Cone grew out of a significant recentering of theological tasks and questions. For Cone, social contexts determined the questions and interests pursued in theological inquiry. He believed that the queries and formulations of the longer Western tradition were not meaningfully connected to black reality. So, he wrote of the first ecumenical councils, "I respect what happened at Nicaea and Chalcedon (A.D. 451) and the theological input of the church fathers on Christology; but that source alone is inadequate for finding out the meaning of black folks' Jesus." Regarding Athanasius's discussion of the Son's *homoousia*, or one substance with the Father, Cone replied, "the *homoousia* question is not a black question. Blacks do not ask whether Jesus is one with the Father or divine and human, though the orthodox formulations are implied in their language. They want to know whether Jesus is walking with them, whether they can call him on the 'telephone of prayer' and tell him about their troubles." Were the social setting properly understood as determinative, Cone argued, then Martin Luther's wrangling over the "ubiquitous presence of Jesus Christ at the Lord's table" would give way to different and perhaps more urgent questions. "While not diminishing the importance of Luther's theological concern, I am sure that if he had been born a black slave his first question would not have been whether Jesus was at the Lord's Table but whether he was really present at the slave's cabin, whether slaves could expect Jesus to be with them as they tried to survive the cotton field, the whip, and the pistol."[58] It was this "slave cabin"

---

[58]James H. Cone, *God of the Oppressed* (Maryknoll, N.Y.: Orbis, 1997), p. 14.

view of Jesus that Black Theology under Cone's formative leadership attempted to construct. The tradition of black people superseded the tradition of Christian history, and the need for a "liberating presence in the lives of the poor in their fight for dignity and worth" replaced the need to arrive at intellectual statements of the person and work of Christ.[59] Not surprisingly, then, the christological conclusions of Black Theology were significantly different from those of the broader Western tradition.

Cone's Christology assumed the centrality of the incarnation and person of Christ as both an appropriate Christian starting place and a vital doctrine for emphasizing the importance of concrete historical settings for comprehending God's self-disclosure in Christ. He hypothesized that a proper appreciation of the person and work of Jesus depended upon understanding who he was in history, who he is to blacks in their social situation, and who he will be in the consummation of liberation hopes.

As for who Jesus was in history, Cone believed the incarnation "disclosed the divine will to be with humanity in our wretchedness" and bound God together with humanity in one reality.[60] Cone wrote: "Jesus' Jewishness therefore was essential to his person. He was not a 'universal' man but a particular Jew who came to fulfill God's will to liberate the oppressed. His Jewishness established the concreteness of his existence in history, without which Christology inevitably moves in the direction of docetism."[61] The incarnation of Jesus and the humanity it emphasized prevented any docetic error that separated divine spiritual salvation from earthly physical liberation—a mistake Cone felt privileged Western theologians made throughout the centuries because their soteriology prescribed their Christology. The historical reality of Jesus' pain and suffering with oppressed Israel warranted hope that he shared in the suffering of black people and hope in a fully liberated humanity through the crucifixion and resurrection.[62] The tendency of some theologians to emphasize only the divinity of Jesus in such a way as to reduce him to "an idea-principle in a theological system" found little room in Cone's view. Here, his theology departed from Garvey and Thurman before him.

---

[59] Ibid., p. xiii.
[60] Ibid., p. 33; see also p. 232 n. 38.
[61] Ibid., p. 109.
[62] Ibid., pp. 106-9.

Though Cone emphasized the humanity of Jesus in order to underscore his concrete identification with oppressed peoples, he realized that a historical remembrance of Jesus was insufficient for addressing who Jesus is for black people in their contemporary situation. If Jesus were to be relevant, he needed to transcend the confines of his own historical life to be present with blacks in their struggle. Cone interpreted the resurrection as that decisive moment in history when the divine One entered contemporary existence to liberate humanity from sin and death—the moment when he escaped temporal limitations to be present with the struggles of oppressed people at all times. Jesus' divinity entailed this transtemporal power, but traditional orthodox delineations of Jesus' Sonship or status in the Godhead remained spare in Cone's writings.[63] Cone could easily write that "God in Christ comes to the weak and the helpless, and becomes one with them," but he stopped well short of saying that Christ *is* God.[64] God in a sense revealed the "divinity" of Christ in the resurrection, but the resurrection and the "divinity" it revealed took on political rather than spiritual significance. The resurrection not only provided the poor and the helpless the ability and freedom to resist their tyranny, it ethically required such resistance.[65] To define who Jesus *is*, according to Cone, demanded an understanding of his messianic role as the "inaugurator" of a present new age of freedom for captives. Jesus embodied the promises of deliverance expressed through biblical prophecies of a messiah and a suffering Servant King. Moreover, he fulfilled those promises by inextricably identifying himself with the poor.[66]

Who Jesus *will be* pointed to the eschatological hope of his return to "consummate the liberation already happening in our present." Black Theology's Jesus of the future grounded the contemporary struggle in a confident hope that justice would prevail and that the fight must continue even when circumstances were dire. Glimpsing Jesus from only one standpoint was an incomplete examination. Cone claimed that, "We can truly know Jesus' past and its soteriological significance only if his past is seen in dialec-

---

[63]Ibid., pp. 110-15.
[64]Ibid., p. 70.
[65]Ibid., p. 115.
[66]Ibid., pp. 67-74. Cone depends on several passages of Scripture for developing this view: Ps 2:7; Is 29:18-21; 35:5; 42:1; 61:1-2; Lk 4:18-19; and the temptation narratives following the Lord's baptism in Lk 4:1-13 and Mt 4:1-11.

tical relation to his present presence and future coming."[67]

The dialectical relation envisioned between Jesus' past, present and future as aspects of his person required Cone to affirm the blackness of Jesus. Cone defended this conclusion against white theologians remonstrating against the "blackness" of Jesus as merely psychological and political concessions to the emergence of Black Power. Cone retorted that subjectivity pervaded all theological argumentation, including traditional theology. The test of the legitimacy of the "black Christ" was not an imagined "universality" or "objectivity," but whether any particularized conception pointed to the universal will of God to liberate the oppressed. Did the past and future comings of Jesus find present expression in the condition of black people? If so, Christ disclosed himself as "black" by participating in the struggles of black people. He revealed himself as "black" by coming as a Jew in first century Palestine. Affirming the "blackness" of Christ meant affirming that God never left the oppressed alone to bear their suffering; he entered into their suffering at the exodus, in the incarnation, and through the struggles of American blacks.[68] The inviolable political and experiential solidarity between Jesus and oppressed blacks proved for Cone the truth of Jesus' blackness. The fight of black Americans for freedom proved that his divine work was liberation.

END OF CENTURY, POSTMODERN ERA (1980-PRESENT)

At the close of the twentieth century, America moved into the Postmodern era. Post-Enlightenment ideals gained control of historical, cultural and religious interpretations. "Local narratives," or subjective approaches to relating truth, mutinied against modernist notions of absolute truth. Multicultural methods and stories opposed the "metanarratives" of world history, offering new prisms through which to examine human drama. Alongside cultural renditions emerged gendered versions of nearly every discipline. Feminist and womanist ideologies pressed into the theological fold. In addition, the decades at the close of the century were known as the era of greed, imbued as they were with rampant individualism and materialism.

In many respects, the theology of African Americans swam with the pre-

---

[67] Ibid., p. 120.
[68] Ibid., 122-26.

vailing cultural and intellectual tide. In the later years of the twentieth century, African American theology devolved into three broad divisions. Orthodox evangelical theologians—though not as strongly or self-consciously Reformed as Hammon and Haynes—continued in the familiar christological path treaded over 2,000 years of Christian history. Their views reigned among rank and file Christian pastors and laypeople in most churches. Meanwhile, theologically liberal writers expanded the corpus of Black Theology to reflect feminist and "womanist" themes and concerns.[69] Through the period, Black Theology principally dominated academic discourse and training. Finally, Charismatic and word-of-faith preachers broadcasted the expanded atonement tenets of Holiness-Pentecostal forerunner William J. Seymour with a "prosperity gospel" stressing physical healing as well as material and financial success. Belief in the "prosperity gospel" grew popular among megachurches and televangelists but made significant inroads into smaller congregations as well. While three divisions can be traced along very general lines, cross-fertilization of ideas occurred to some extent. Evangelical, liberal and Charismatic thinkers enjoyed an easy coexistence, a doctrinal détente, avoiding or ignoring any significant public debate or controversy like that triggered by the Black Power and Black Theology movements. However, despite the theological peace between different groups, African American theology drifted so far from the Reformed convictions of New England writers like Jupiter Hammon, Phillis Wheatley and Lemuel Haynes that at least one author felt the necessity of devoting an entire book to reconciling today's apparent contradiction of being both African American and theologically Reformed.[70]

---

[69]Novelist Alice Walker offered the term "womanist" or "womanism" as an alternative to the feminist ideology of many white women. The term is intended to gather together both the call for equality and justice for black women and to signal a unity between the sexes, particularly black men and black women, as they champion the causes of gender and racial equality. Some African-American women have adopted the term for its avoidance of male-female antipathy and its reliance on the experiences and wisdom of black women as a source for struggle. See, for example, Alice Walker, *In Search of Our Mothers' Gardens* (New York: Harcourt Brace Jovanovich, 1983). On using the experiences of black women as a source for doing theology, see, for example, Delores S. Williams, "Womanist Theology: Black Women's Voices," *Christianity and Crisis* 47 (March 2, 1987). The collection of essays on womanist theology in part 4 of James Cone and Gayraud Wilmore, eds., *Black Theology: A Documentary History, Volume Two: 1980-1992*, 2nd ed. (Maryknoll, N.Y.: Orbis, 1993) provide a useful overview of issues and themes in womanist theological writings.

[70]Anthony J. Carter, *On Being Black and Reformed: A New Perspective on the African American Christian Experience* (Phillipsburg, N.J.: P&R Publishing, 2003).

The black Christ in womanist terms. In the 1986 preface to the twentieth anniversary edition of *A Black Theology of Liberation,* James Cone acknowledged several shortcomings of his earlier work. Among them, Cone included the failure to seriously reflect on the problem of sexism in the black community and the unique perspective of African American women as the "most glaring limitation."[71] Reflecting on the development of Black Theology, Cone concluded, "we now must realize that our continued silence can only serve to alienate us further from our sisters. We have no other choice but to take a public stance for or against their liberation."[72] Fueled by their own experiences and a growing feminist orientation, some African American women concurred with Cone's self-critique. For example, Jacquelyn Grant issued a call for Black Theology to focus on the liberation of women in both the black community and the black church, where women represented fifty percent and seventy percent of the population, respectively. Grant proclaimed, "Black Theology cannot continue to treat black women as if they were invisible creatures who are on the outside looking into the black experience, the black church, and the black theological enterprise."[73] Frances Beale spoke of the "double jeopardy" of being black and female in America; while Theresa Hoover "one-upped" Beale by insisting, "To be a woman, black, and active in religious institutions in the American scene is to labor under *triple jeopardy*."[74] These women called for a reconceptualization of the black Christ that included, reflected and affirmed black women and their contributions in the struggle for liberation.

The first book-length critique of the black Christ as defined by black male theologians appeared in Kelly Brown Douglas's *The Black Christ.* Appreciative of Black Theology in general, Douglas, like other womanist writers, found the theology deficient for its omission of women. Black Theology, according to Douglas, presented a view of black life and culture that failed to be critical of negative

[71]See Cone's Preface to his 1986 edition of *A Black Theology of Liberation,* p. xv.
[72]Cone and Wilmore, *Black Theology,* p. 279.
[73]Jacquelyn Grant, "Black Theology and the Black Woman," in *Black Theology: A Documentary History, Volume One,* ed. James Cone and Gayraud Wilmore, 2nd ed. (Maryknoll, N.Y.: Orbis, 1993), pp. 323-38.
[74]See Frances Beale, "Double Jeopardy: To Be Black and Female," in *Black Theology: A Documentary History, Volume One,* ed. James Cone and Gayraud Wilmore, 2nd ed. (Maryknoll, N.Y.: Orbis, 1993), pp. 284-92; Theresa Hoover, "Black Women and the Churches: Triple Jeopardy," in *Black Theology: A Documentary History, Volume One,* ed. James Cone and Gayraud Wilmore, 2nd ed. (Maryknoll, N.Y.: Orbis, 1993), pp. 293-304.

practices and ideas in the culture; it affirmed "blackness" too indiscriminately and did not "compel black people to look at the ways in which they enslave themselves or perpetuate enslaving structures and systems."[75] Also, Black Theology failed to be "multi-dimensional," to consider the effects not only of racism but sexism, classism and "heterosexism" as well. Last, Black Theology failed to make inroads into the theology and praxis of the black church.[76]

Douglas called for a view of Christ that stressed both his physical blackness (as had Albert Cleage Jr.) and his existential blackness (as had James Cone). However, she extended the thought of Cleage and Cone and rejected the moderate tenets of reconciliation expressed by theologian J. Deotis Roberts.[77] Rejecting what she termed "slaveholding Christianity" because of its undue emphasis on the incarnation, which tended toward a salvific understanding that minimized the need to live and act against oppression, Douglas stressed the importance of Jesus' earthly ministry of healing and liberation. She argued for a "social-political analysis of wholeness," which she defined as a bidirectional focus on "racism, sexism, classism, and heterosexism not only as they impinge upon the black community, but also as they are nurtured within that community."[78] Douglas intended this social-political perspective to be a corrective for the omissions caused by Black Theology's unifocal concern for white racism. She also discerned the need for a "religio-cultural analysis" that nurtured a "spirituality of resistance" birthed and nurtured by black women throughout their history and that denounced negative elements of black culture.[79]

From the socio-political and religio-cultural viewpoints, Douglas affirmed the blackness of Christ and demanded that Christ be pictured with the face of black women. She reasoned that if Christ identified with the most oppressed people, then Christ must identify with and possibly even be a black woman because of their most victimized and deprived status. She wrote:

[A] womanist Black Christ will consistently lift up the presence of Christ in the faces of the poorest Black women. These women, as an icon of Christ, are important reminders of accountability. Any theology of "survival and liberation/

[75]Kelly Brown Douglas, *The Black Christ* (Maryknoll, N.Y.: Orbis, 1994), pp. 84-86.
[76]Ibid., pp. 86-88.
[77]See, for example, J. Deotis Roberts's works, *Liberation and Reconciliation: A Black Theology* (Philadelphia: Westminster Press, 1971), and *Black Political Theology* (Philadelphia: Westminster Press, 1974).
[78]Douglas, *The Black Christ*, p. 99.
[79]Ibid., pp. 104-6.

wholeness" that emerges from the Black community must be accountable to the least of these in that community. It is only in a commitment to insure the life and wholeness for the "least of these" that we can grasp the radicality of who the Black Christ is for all Black people.[80]

For Douglas and other womanist theologians, Christ was best revealed where the struggle for "wholeness" was most acute—and that was wherever black women lived.

SUMMARIZING THE DECLINE

Any discussion of the history of African American views of Jesus Christ must guard itself against the commonplace errors of either insisting that a particular idea is correct simply because it is older or that it is correct because it is new. Though history is a useful guide and offers clues for development and conservation, the age of an idea has little or nothing to do with its veracity. And while people naturally long for solutions and ideas appropriate for their time and setting, new custom-fitted ideas are not any more trustworthy for their newness or for their identification with a particular place and time. This truism certainly justifies a discriminating consumption of knowledge and ideas passed from generation to generation, especially ideas about the person and work of Jesus Christ.

The story of African American Christology is an object lesson in learning to examine and appropriate the old and the new. We opened this chapter with a brief statement on the historical consensus regarding the person and work of Jesus Christ as reflected in the creed of Nicaea and Chalcedon. That creed is the "old" idea that has guided Christian thinkers for nearly 1,700 years. It is the old idea that stood regnant at the dawning of the first African experiences with Christianity in the New World. And, it is the old idea that found itself intertwined with the people, forces and ideologies that justified subjugating Africans to the brutalities of slavery.

Little wonder, then, that African Americans throughout their nearly 400-year history have wrestled with how to understand old ideas regarding the nature and mission of Jesus. From the beginning, christological reactions toward Nicean/Chalcedonian orthodoxy among slaves ranged from ambiguity

---

[80]Ibid., pp. 108-9.

and ambivalence, on the one hand, to full articulation and adoption on the other. But in either case, African Americans felt the escalating pressure to identify and apply the teachings of Jesus to their condition as chattel and their aspirations as men. Over time, that pressure to apply Jesus to their situation resulted in an impulse to invent something "new." Until the generation following Emancipation and Reconstruction, the old orthodoxy stood strong, even if there were certain differences in ethical and political inferences drawn by African Americans and white Americans. But after Reconstruction, and with the rise of a new black consciousness and cultural ideology, a new christological orthodoxy gained footing. The new Christology of Garvey, Thurman, Cone and womanist writers like Kelly Brown Douglas deemed Nicaea and Chalcedon irrelevant to the aims of black people and proclaimed that Jesus was on the side of the poor and oppressed and that liberation was his work. These thinkers stressed Jesus' ethnicity and national origin rather than his divine nature. They underscored his earthly ministry more than his incarnation or resurrection. Consequently, two hundred years after Jupiter Hammon published his first works, the orthodoxy he drank as naturally as water evaporated into a misty silhouette of the Jesus he preached.

But does Christian theology, black or white, really leave room for an "out with the old, in with the new" attitude toward the doctrine of Christ? Is one left to simply choose or fashion an understanding of Jesus' life, ministry and being as one chooses? Are there no consequences for what position a person takes? Moreover, can any source for developing a Christology be used as if it is equal with or determinative of the meaning of any other source?

While all people are equal, made in the image of God, and therefore of infinite worth, not all ideas are true or worth believing. And if, as Jesus teaches, the critical question is "Who do you say that I am?" then the stakes for answering correctly are extremely high. In the High Priestly prayer of John 17, Jesus defines eternal life as knowledge of God the Father and of himself, whom the Father sent (Jn 17:3). Moreover, in his discussion with the Samarian woman at the well, Jesus makes it plain that accuracy in our knowledge of God is one of two determining factors in God-satisfying worship. The Father seeks those who will worship him in Spirit and in truth (Jn 4:21-24). All other worship violates the first and second commandments, which prohibit both the carving and the mental fabrication of idols to worship.[81]

The genius of Thurman and Cone lie in their insight that slave ambivalence toward an "academic" doctrine of Jesus Christ occurred because of their preoccupation with the relevance of Jesus for their present suffering. This led them to emphasize the concrete historical existence of Jesus as a disclosure of God's will to be with the oppressed and to include them in his plan of redemption. Thus emerged new boundaries for political and ethical discourse on the meaning of both the crucifixion and resurrection and the earthly ministry of Jesus. These writers were correct in their assertion that Western theology failed to address the gospel to the condition of the poor and oppressed. To the extent that Black Theology called attention to these concerns, it made an important advance beyond the old orthodoxy. However, this achievement in the doctrine of Christ came with significant problems outweighing any advance.

First, the Christology that evolved over the course of African American Christian history unnecessarily and dangerously ignored or rejected the biblical teaching and long-standing consensus that Jesus Christ is both fully man and fully God. Thurman, Cone and Douglas arrived at their conclusions by emphasizing the humanity of Jesus. This, they reasoned, yields greater hope for the afflicted. But one might ask, "Why does emphasizing the humanity of Jesus require the de-emphasis or denial of the deity of Jesus?" And, "would not coupling the humanity of Jesus with the deity of Christ, as orthodox Christology does, exponentially multiply the hope and certainty of liberation offered to the oppressed?" The price of liberation seems to be the deity of Jesus. A theology ceases to be Christian and biblical at the point that it relegates Jesus to ordinary human status. As Karl Barth proclaimed, "one cannot speak of God simply by speaking of man in a loud voice." In some quarters of African American Christianity, this is precisely the error that reigns.

Second, and following from the first point, the decline in African American understandings of the doctrine of Christ positions many unsuspecting and sincere people to fall into idolatry. God does not exist—and Jesus did not tabernacle among men, suffer the agony of crucifixion, and was not raised from the grave—to affirm the ethnic sense of identity and self-worth of any single

---

[81]See Ex 20:3-6. For an excellent discussion of the first and second commandments' prohibition of mental images, see J. I. Packer, *Knowing God* (Downers Grove, Ill.: InterVarsity Press, 1973), pp. 43-51.

people. Nor does God so identify with a people, even his sovereignly elected people Israel or the church, to the point that he becomes one with that people without regard for their holiness and proper worship. The Lord God proclaims through the prophet Isaiah, "For my thoughts are not your thoughts, neither are your ways my ways," and "As the heavens are higher than the earth, so are my ways higher than your ways and my thoughts than your thoughts" (Isaiah 55:8-9). The easy identification of God with the designs and intent of men obscures his holy transcendence and omniscience. The history of African American Christology is partly a history of selective Bible reading. The Christ that appears in the writings of many is an idol of their own making, a god graven with the tools of self-esteem and self-advancement. Unsuspecting Christians are vulnerable to imbibing idolatrous errors and offering to God fetid praise instead of worshiping him in Spirit and in truth. A cult of the group self or a materialistic bellhop God displaces true worship of the only true God and Jesus Christ whom he has sent.

Third, some depictions of Jesus set the affections of the would-be worshiper on "things below" and not "things above." Does the fact that Jesus was born a Jew during the Roman occupation of Israel really warrant identifying him as "black" in the sense that Black Theology prescribes? While Jesus was a Jew, and Jerusalem was controlled by the Roman Empire, Jesus never acted in a way that suggested a political liberation for his contemporaries—to the consternation and disappointment of many would-be followers of his time and ours (Jn 6:14-71). The Jesus of Scripture always sought to do the Father's will and to point men to spiritual realities beyond and above this life's circumstance. He did not come to "set the captives free" in any political or military sense. Neither does Jesus enter human history to purchase material possessions and opulent lifestyles for the "faithful." Jesus gives his life for a far more fundamental problem—the sin that ruins all of humankind and incurs the holy wrath of God.

There is a place in Christian theology—stemming from a deep reflection on the person and work of Christ—for radical jeremiads against bigotry, injustice and oppression of all kinds. The earliest African Americans understood this and, consequently, were able to hold both a conventional Christology and an active political praxis. The two are not mutually exclusive; and yet, the theological trajectory followed in the last seventy-five years seems to treat them as such. To the extent that African American thinkers obfuscated the centrality of Jesus' spiritual mission to purchase a special people for himself, they traded their heavenly birthright for a mess of socioeconomic pottage. This is no victimless crime. Materialism and black nationalism masquerading as Christology overthrow the faith of many—shrouding the cross of Jesus in the temporal affairs of this world, which in turn choke the seeds of the gospel.

5

"What Must I Do to Be Saved?"

African American Soteriology

Amazing grace! How sweet the sound, that saved a wretch like me!
I once was lost, but now am found, was blind, but now I see.

'Twas grace that taught my heart to fear, and grace my fears relieved;
How precious did that grace appear the hour I first believed!

Thro' many dangers, toils, and snares, I have already come;
'Tis grace hath bro't me safe thus far, and grace will lead me home.

The Lord has promisd good to me, His word my hope secures;
He will my shield and portion be as long as life endures.

When we've been there ten thousand years, bright shining as the sun,
We've no less days to sing God's praise than when we first begun.

Amazing Grace
JOHN NEWTON (1725-1807)

GENERAL INTRODUCTION AND CONTEXT

The doctrine of salvation is perhaps one of the most hotly debated subjects in the history of the church—and rightly so, since it is the subject that most specifically addresses the eternal state of all humanity. In that sense, the doctrine of salvation is the most pastorally pressing issue to be studied, understood, preached and applied.

From the time of the early church fathers, it was well understood that humanity needed a Savior and that sin ruptured the relationship between God

and man. "The church was cross-centered and Christ-centered in proclamation and ritual." Nevertheless, this early consensus did not produce a precise
doctrinal synthesis explaining the relationship between human nature and
God's grace in salvation through Christ.[1]

Perhaps the strongest early synthesis of the Bible's teachings regarding human nature and grace came during the dispute between Augustine and the Pe-
lagians. At issue was the question of whether humankind possessed the ability
to satisfy the just demands of God, and by implication how sin affected the
will and nature of man. First, the British monk Pelagius (c. 354-418) and his
followers held that Adam's sin was not reflected in any inherited guilt or original sin in men. Each person, according to Pelagius, was born into the same
state as Adam before the Fall and by voluntary acts of commission fell from
grace. Second, since men were not fallen in Adam, they were free to choose
between good and evil. Humanity's will was free and unrestrained, and the will
was one causal force in human action. Third, grace then was resistible by man
and was an illumination that influenced men to cooperate with God if they
chose. God's election of humankind in Pelagius's thought depended on his
knowledge of the sinner's actions if given grace. In other words, God elected
those whom he knew would respond to grace and cooperate with his will.

Augustine of Hippo (354-430) opposed Pelagius's teachings. He argued
that Adam's first sin corrupted the entire human race physically and morally.
The nature of man was so corrupt that they could only choose sin. The will of
humankind was free, but not in the sense Pelagius had defined it. Man's will
was free to make choices but only in conformity with his desires, which were
sinful. God's grace was necessary for revealing the beauty of Christ and for
strengthening humankind's will in order that they might turn to Christ for
forgiveness. In Augustine's view, this operation of God's grace was irresistible—though without coercion. Grace overcame humanity's absolute moral
inability and revealed God's initiative in drawing people to himself. Contrary
to Pelagius's contention, then, God's predestination was solely based upon his
sovereign choice and not his knowledge of the person's anticipated response to
grace. In A.D. 431, the Council of Ephesus condemned Pelagius's views of hu-

---

[1]John D. Hannah, *Our Legacy: The History of Christian Doctrine* (Colorado Springs: NavPress, 2001),
pp. 203-5, 209.

man ability and nature. And in A.D. 529 at the Synod of Orange, the church confirmed a moderate Augustinian understanding of the fallen nature of man and of grace, though it stopped short of Augustine's views on election and predestination.[2]

During the Middle Ages, through the influential writings of men like Peter Lombard (c. 1100-1160) and Thomas Aquinas (c. 1225-1274), the Roman Catholic church linked grace to the sacraments of the church. The Roman Catholic system taught that the grace was gradually infused in the person through participation in the sacraments, initially with baptism and then increasingly with the other sacraments. Leaders of the Protestant Reformation opposed the Roman Catholic view of justification as a gradual process of infusing grace into the person through the sacraments. The Reformed theological tradition—popularly beginning with Martin Luther (1483-1546) and associated with the thinking of Swiss Reformer John Calvin (1509-1564), hence the moniker "Calvinism"—advanced the so-called five *solas*. Salvation or justification, the reformers held, came by grace alone *(sola gracia)* through faith alone *(sola fide)* in Christ alone *(solus Christus)* for the glory of God alone *(soli Deo gloria)*. The authoritative basis for this teaching was Scripture alone *(sola scriptura)*, not a teaching magisterium or councils whom the reformers believed could and did err in such matters. The reformers sought to recover an Augustinian view of man corrupted in sin inherited from Adam and unable to choose anything but sin in matters of salvation. So, God's grace was essential to salvation as well as God's sovereign election. The five *solas* became the general framework for Protestant soteriology.

Later, however, a group of theologians in Holland, followers of Dutch theologian and professor Jacobus Arminius (1560-1609) known as the Remonstrants, objected to another five points that were emerging as the Reformed soteriological synthesis. These five points became known as the so-called five points of Calvinism.[3] The Remonstrants taught election on the basis of foreseen faith, a universal atonement, partial human depravity, resistible

---

[2]Ibid., pp. 211-16.
[3]The terms "Reformed" and "Calvinism" are often used as synonyms. Here, I've restricted the use of "Reformed" and "Reformed theology" to the broader Reformation movement that came to be characterized by the five solas. I've restricted the use of "Calvinism" to that particular soteriology characterized by the so-called T-U-L-I-P formulation.

grace and the possibility of lapse from grace. A national meeting at the Synod of Dordt (1618-1619) rejected the Remonstrants and systematized the Bible's teaching on salvation into five core doctrines commonly referred to by the acrostic T-U-L-I-P.[4]

The Synod of Dordt began its soteriology with its doctrine of man. First, they held that man was "totally depraved." As a fallen creature, sin corrupted him at the root of his being and bent him always toward sin. This corruption placed man at enmity with God, and made him morally incapable of choosing or meriting salvation under his own ability. Second, and as a logical consequence of man's depravity, the Reformers taught that salvation depended wholly on the free and sovereign election of God. God redeemed man in accord with his own free will apart from anything in man meriting or earning salvation. This second doctrine became known as "unconditional election." Third, "limited atonement" held that while Christ's sacrifice was sufficient for the whole world, it was efficient or effective only for those God elected. Since nobody could achieve salvation through merit or effort, and not all people were saved, it followed scripturally and logically that God applied the atonement of Christ only to the account of those elected. The fourth doctrine, "irresistible grace," flowed naturally from the doctrine of limited atonement. Irresistible grace posited that the sinner could not thwart God's purposes in redemption. The grace of regeneration implemented by the Holy Spirit was always effective for those called to salvation. Fifth, the Synod of Dordt's soteriology taught the "perseverance of the saints." God actively worked to preserve his people such that none called to and given eternal life would perish or fall away.

Both the "five *solas*" and the Synod of Dordt's doctrines of total (or radical) depravity, unconditional election, limited atonement, irresistible grace and perseverance (or preservation) of the saints provided the skeletal system for theology in the American colonies. Nearly all African American Christians inherited the "five *solas*" as a general Protestant framework over and against the Roman Catholic view of authority and justification and the Arminian view of

---

[4]For this summary of Reformed soteriology, I found the following sources useful: R. C. Sproul, *Grace Unknown: The Heart of Reformed Theology* (Grand Rapids: Baker Books, 1997); Hannah, *Our Legacy*, pp. 201-55. For original writings by early Reformers, John Calvin's *Institutes of the Christian Religion* and Martin Luther's *Bondage of the Will* are useful resources.

man and grace rejected at Dordt. African Americans gained exposure to these views of salvation through their earliest contact with Europeans in the colonies, especially in the North. Southern slave testimonies and northern writers reveal a "soft orthodoxy" consistent with the Reformation *solas*, with some even putting forth a stronger Calvinistic view of salvation owed largely to the influences of the Great Awakening and early Baptists in the South.[5]

EARLY SLAVERY ERA THROUGH ABOLITION ERA (1600-1865)

Evidence of African converts to Christianity date back to the early 1600s. Some records indicate that a William Tucker was baptized at Jamestown in 1624.[6] Slightly later, we have baptism and full church membership records for a slave held by a Puritan minister in Dorchester, Massachusetts.[7] Conversions began in the early colonies with a trickle, but increased among southern slaves as revival winds blew through the colonies in the mid-1700s. John Wesley (1703-1791) noted the conversion of some slaves during his ministry efforts in South Carolina and Georgia before leaving the area. George Whitefield toured the colonies and received a large, warm welcome from slaves who heard him preach.[8] John Marrant (1755-1791), author of one of the earliest slave narratives, heard Whitefield preach as a thirteen-year-old boy and fell under conviction of his sins.[9]

The earliest period of American slavery permitted very little in the way of African conversions to Christianity, particularly in the South where slaveholders feared that "Christianizing" the slave would either require his emancipation or make the newly converted slave unfit for slave labor. Such fears were

---

[5]Historian E. Brooks Holifield concluded that, "Among the few surviving theological essays written by black authors, statements of Calvinist thought remain prominent." See E. Brooks Holifield, *Theology in America: Christian Thought from the Age of the Puritans to the Civil War* (New Haven, Conn.: Yale University Press, 2003), p. 308.

[6]Compiled by Workers of the Writers' Program of the Work Projects Administration in the State of Virginia, *The Negro in Virginia* (Winston-Salem, N.C.: John F. Blair, 1994), p. 106.

[7]Mark Noll, *A History of Christianity in the United States and Canada* (Grand Rapids: Eerdmans, 1992), p. 79.

[8]Ibid., pp. 106-8. For brief accounts of their encounters with slaves, see representative excerpts from Wesley's and Whitefield's journals in *The African-American Archive: The History of the Black Experience Through Documents*, ed. Kai Wright (New York: Black Dog & Leventhal, 2001), pp. 29-31.

[9]John Marrant, *Narrative of the Lord's Wonderful Dealings with John Marrant, A Black*, in *Pioneers of the Black Atlantic: Five Slave Narratives from the Enlightenment, 1772-1815*, ed. Henry Louise Gates Jr. and William L. Andrews (Washington, D.C.: Counterpoint, 1998), pp. 66-67.

more concerned with the maintenance of the economic engine of slavery than with any ethical questions provoked by the contradiction of enslaving a brother in Christ. Early efforts among Anglican missionaries also proved ineffective at converting many Africans to the Christian faith because of their heavy emphasis on conversion through catechesis, which required literacy levels beyond that typically allowed of slaves. For most of the 1600s and early 1700s, although slaveholders had not brought Christianity more fully into the employ of the slave system as a method of justifying slavery and controlling slaves, the system of slavery went unchallenged by the church or society, and the prevailing sentiment regarded slaves as useful for physical labor and little else.[10] However, by the mid-1700s and 1800s, when many slaveholders themselves were converted to Christianity and developed concern for the spiritual salvation of their slaves, larger numbers of Africans were exposed to the preaching of the gospel and its saving message.[11]

Given these early conditions, there is little surprise that documents reflecting the theology of the earliest slaves do not exist. However, the popularity and success of ministers like Whitefield suggests at least an early exposure to Reformed soteriology. Historian Mark Noll observed, "The revival message of personal experience with God was a message that not only resonated with the American experiences of blacks but also echoed aspects of African religions. *Especially in the Calvinist overtones of the major revivalists of the period*, slaves heard the message that only God's grace mattered."[12]

The remainder of this chapter examines how African Americans understood the saving grace of God and the nature of man and his need for salvation.

Calvinistic soteriology in northern black writers. Jupiter Hammon: Spiritual liberty to the captives. With the publication of his first work on December 25, 1760, Jupiter Hammon became the "father of African American literature." A devout evangelical Christian, Hammon was likely converted during the Great

---

[10]A few early objections to slavery were launched in the 1680s by the Quaker and German Mennonite churches, which regarded slavery a violation of God's will for humanity. In 1706, Cotton Mather defended the humanity of Africans in a tract entitled "The Negro Christianized"; however, Mather failed to attack the system of slavery itself. See Noll, *History of Christianity*, pp. 77-78; Eugene D. Genovese, *Roll, Jordan, Roll: The World the Slaves Made* (New York: Vintage Books, 1976), pp. 183-93.

[11]Genovese, *Roll, Jordan, Roll*, pp. 188-93. Genovese suggests that the white Christian church did not become safely proslavery until about the 1840s.

[12]Noll, *History of Christianity*, p. 107, emphasis added.

Awakening, twenty-nine years following his birth in 1711.[13]

One historian summarized Hammon's theology as "incorporating themes from both revivalist Calvinism and an Anglican heritage that combined a moderate Calvinism with an emphasis on 'holy living.'"[14] As a northeastern Calvinist, Hammon believed in the radical depravity of man. And, perhaps more than any writer of his period, he saw the pervasiveness of sin and its effects on his people. While Hammon professed to have "never said nor done anything, neither directly nor indirectly, to promote or to prevent freedom" for the slave, he demonstrated resolute commitment to the idea that spiritual salvation outweighed temporal freedom:[15]

> My dear brethren, we are many of us seeking for a temporal freedom, and I pray that God would grant your desire. If we are slaves, it is by the permission of God. If we are free, it must be by the power of the most high God. Be not discouraged, but cheerfully perform the duties of the day, sensible that the same power that created the heavens and the earth and causeth the greater light to rule the day and the lesser to rule the night can cause a universal freedom. And I pray God may give you grace to seek that freedom which tendeth to everlasting life.[16]

He continued:

> My dear brethren, let not your hearts be set too much on the pleasure of this life. For if it were possible for one man to gain a thousand freedoms and not an interest in the merit of Christ, where must all the advantage be? "For what is a man profited if he should gain the whole world, and lose his own soul?"[17]

On one level, Hammon proved somewhat indifferent to physical freedom,

---

[13]Sondra O'Neale, *Jupiter Hammon and the Biblical Beginnings of African-American Literature* (Metuchen, N.J.: American Library Association, 1993), pp. 28-30.

[14]Holifield, *Theology in America*, p. 308.

[15]Jupiter Hammon, *A Winter Piece*, in Sondra O'Neale, *Jupiter Hammon and the Biblical Beginnings of African-American Literature* (Metuchen, N.J.: American Library Association, 1993), p. 103. Hammon was not the only early writer to hold this view. It also can be clearly seen in the preaching of Bishop Daniel A. Payne, a generation following Hammon. See, for example, Payne's famous sermon "Welcome to the Ransomed; or, Duties of the Colored Inhabitants of the District of Columbia" in *Bishop Daniel Alexander Payne: Sermons and Addresses: 1853-1891*, ed. Charles Killian (New York: Arno Press, 1972), pp. 7, 14-15. Hiram R. Revels, who would later serve as a U.S. Senator from reconstructed Mississippi, also maintained a similar posture when preaching to slaves. Genovese, *Roll, Jordan, Roll*, p. 263.

[16]Jupiter Hammon, *An Evening's Improvement*, in Sondra O'Neale, *Jupiter Hammon and the Biblical Beginnings of African-American Literature* (Metuchen, N.J.: American Library Association, 1993), pp. 172-73.

[17]Ibid., p. 173.

earning him the ire of some later critics.[18] However, his comments must be interpreted in the context of his concern for holiness and genuine conversion among the slaves. He began his position by acknowledging "that liberty is a great thing and worth seeking for if we can get it honestly and by our good conduct prevail on our masters to set us free," but finally concluded that physical freedom "is by no means the greatest thing we have to be concerned about. Getting our liberty in this world is nothing to our having the liberty of the children of God."[19]

Hammon believed regeneration or new birth was a prerequisite to saving faith due to man's moral inability. In his essay *An Evening's Improvement,* he saw in the raising of Lazarus (Jn 11:43-44) a parallel to the spiritual deadness and moral inability of all men. "Doth not the raising of Lazarus give us a sight of our own natures?" Hammon recognized the miraculous power required and concluded, "Is this not a simile of our deadness by nature? And there is *nothing short of the power of the most high God can raise us to life.*" Hammon continued, "it is only by the precious blood of Christ we can be saved, when we are made sensible of our own imperfections and are desirous to love and fear God; *this we cannot do of ourselves,* for this is the work of God's Holy Spirit. 'And He said, Therefore I said unto you that no man can come unto me, except it were given unto him of my Father' (Jn 6:65)."[20] For Hammon, as was typical of Augustinian, Reformed theology, the moral inability of man flowed naturally from man's complete depravity and spiritual deadness.

So, in Hammon's theology, the conversion of man from sinner to saint depends wholly on the work of God, by the agency of the Holy Spirit, on and in the heart of the unbeliever. "We must come to the divine fountain to turn us from sin to holiness and to give us grace to repent of our sins; *this none can do but God.*"[21] Lest his hearers miss the point that coming to this fountain is accomplished only after divine initiative is taken, Hammon added, "There must

---

[18]In the annals of African-American history and writing, Jupiter Hammon is not without his detractors and controversies. Critics find Hammon's writings too passive and "heavenly minded," by which they generally mean he shows too little protest against the major political and social issue of his day—slavery. Writers such as J. Saunders Redding and Benjamin Mays argue that Hammon's effect was to perhaps pacify the slave (O'Neale, *Jupiter Hammon and the Biblical Beginnings,* pp. 4-5).

[19]Jupiter Hammon, *An Address to the Negroes,* in Sondra O'Neale, *Jupiter Hammon and the Biblical Beginnings of African-American Literature* (Metuchen, N.J.: American Library Association, 1993), p. 236.

[20]Hammon, *Evening's Improvement,* pp. 166-67, emphasis added.

[21]Hammon, *Winter Piece,* p. 98, emphasis added.

be a principle of love and fear of God *implanted in our hearts* if we desire to come to the divine fountain."[22] Citing 1 Corinthians 3:6, Hammon concludes his sermon *A Winter Piece* and summarized his Reformed soteriological view by stating, "Here we see that if we are saved, it must be by the power of God's Holy Spirit."[23]

New birth. Hammon did not explicate the necessity and the effects of the new birth in as much detail as Haynes, although the two held the same position. Using 2 Corinthians 5:17 as his touchstone, Hammon simply defined the new birth or becoming a "new creature" as having "our minds turned from darkness to light, from sin to holiness, and to have a desire to serve God with our whole hearts and to follow his precepts."[24] This, in Hammon's view, was the radical and complete effect of the miraculous work of God when he saves his people. Spiritual regeneration was required in any true convert, even though he believed that people, especially his "brethren," were ignorant of it.[25]

Salvation to all. Just as he believed men were equal in their depravity, Hammon also held that the potential scope or reach of the gospel *appeal* was universal. Both whites and blacks, slave and free were potentially included in the redeemed. Unlike many who argued the African had no soul or no interest in the gospel, Hammon countered that it was the duty of all men, including the African, to repent and believe. Both his essays and poetry reflected this view. In *An Evening's Improvement*, for example, Hammon confidently asserts that, "if we love God, black as we be and despised as we are, God will love us."[26] The love of God overcame barriers of color or social rejection. Neither social symbol nor the prejudicial opinions of others limited the reach of God's love. To underscore that point, Hammon called upon Acts 10:34-35. "Then Peter opened his mouth, and said, 'Of a truth I perceive that God is no respecter of persons: But in every nation he that feareth him, and worketh righteousness, is accepted with him'" (KJV).

"Redemption now to everyone" declared Hammon in the opening verse of

---

[22]Ibid., p. 100, emphasis added.
[23]Ibid., p. 113.
[24]Hammon, *Winter Piece*, p. 103.
[25]Ibid., p. 105.
[26]Hammon, *Evening's Improvement*, p. 171.

An Evening Thought: Salvation by Christ, with Penitential Cries.[27] By depicting Jesus as a slave, Hammon pictured the slave as owning salvation through Christ:

> Dear Jesus by thy precious blood,
> The world redemption have:
> Salvation comes now from the Lord,
> He being thy Captive Slave[28]

In his poetry, Hammon inserted the African into the stream of redemption by making the Redeemer both the spiritual liberator and the slave. Ironically, the One who became captive provided the gift of redemption. The universal availability of salvation was evidenced in the protagonist's penitential cries or prayers:

> Dear Jesus let the nations cry,
> And all the people say,
> Salvation comes from Christ on high,
> Haste on tribunal day.[29]

The penitent expressed concern for all "nations" and "all the people," including all those with "dark benighted souls."[30] Some commentators see here a double reference to the African and to the sin-sick unrepentant. Whether this is the case is a matter of literary criticism, but there could be no doubt that Hammon saw the salvific call of God going forth to "Awake . . . every Nation."[31] His mission, as he saw it, was to proclaim spiritual liberty to the captives of American slavery through the gospel.

Lemuel Haynes. The structuring influence of Calvinism was particularly evident in Haynes's thoughts on salvation, where he held firmly to the doctrines of God's sovereign election, predestination and the radical corruption or fall of man. Haynes's understanding of salvation was perhaps best represented by a 1776 sermon on John 3:3. The sermon sets forth two themes prominent in

---

[27]Jupiter Hammon, *An Evening Thought: Salvation by Christ, with Penitential Cries,* in Sondra O'Neale, *Jupiter Hammon and the Biblical Beginnings of African-American Literature* (Metuchen, N.J.: American Library Association, 1993), p. 59.

[28]Ibid., p. 60.

[29]Ibid. See verse 9.

[30]Ibid., p. 61. See verse 12.

[31]Ibid. See verse 14.

Reformed and Calvinist theology: the total or radical depravity of man and man's need for a spiritual rebirth.

For Haynes, the state of humankind after the fall of Adam forecast the necessity of regeneration or spiritual rebirth. Haynes believed that from birth people are "haters of God – enemies to God – estranged from God."[32] He saw the human heart as hostile toward God and "all the Divine perfections." No peace existed between God and humanity because humans opposed the very nature and attributes ("Divine perfections") of God. Young Haynes wrote:

> We shall find them acting most freely and most voluntarily in these exercises [hating and opposing God]. There is no state or circumstance that they prefer to the present, unless it be one whereby they may dishonour God more, or carry on their war with heaven with a higher hand. They have no relish for divine things, but hate, and choose to remain enemies to all that is morally good.[33]

Reasoning from John 3 and Romans 8:7-8, Haynes concluded that "there is nothing truly spiritual or holy in the first birth" and that natural man cannot please God.[34]

From this description of the total depravity of man, Haynes argued for the necessity of the new birth. The necessity, Haynes thought, stemmed from consideration of two points. First, it was unreasonable to believe that God should "bring them into favour with himself, or be at peace with them, without regeneration."[35] Haynes found the prospect of such reconciliation inconsistent with the perfection and righteous judgment of God on guilty men. Second, Haynes believed that totally depraved, unregenerate humanity was unable to find happiness in the kingdom and presence of God. He wrote, "The very essence of religion consists in love to God; and a man is no further happy in the favour of God than he loves God. Therefore, to say we enjoy happiness in God, and at the same time hate God, is a plain contradiction."[36] Thus, both God and man were unable to find pleasure in the company of the other without a complete regeneration of corrupted man.

---

[32]Richard Newman, ed., *Black Preacher to White America: The Collected Writings of Lemuel Haynes, 1774-1833* (Brooklyn: Carlson, 1990), p. 32.
[33]Ibid.
[34]Ibid., p. 33.
[35]Ibid.
[36]Ibid.

The new birth was beyond the ability of natural man in Haynes's perspective, and required the agency of God himself to produce it. "This is the work of the Holy Spirit, who is represented in Scripture as emanating from the Father and the Son, yet co-equal with them both. It is God alone who slays the native enmity of the heart." Citing John 1:13, Ephesians 2:8, Philippians 2:13, and the writings of the Puritan Stephen Charnock (1628-1680), Haynes concluded, "man is entirely passive in this work, but it is wrought immediately by a Divine agency."[37]

As a consequence of this new birth, Haynes believed several changes would occur. First, faith—which he defined as "a believing of those truths that God has exhibited in his word *with a friendly heart*"—would naturally follow as previously hostile persons found fellowship with God. Second, the regenerate person would love God supremely, preferring holiness, the law of God, the gospel, the people of God and all godly things to his previous pursuit and disposition. Third, the spiritually reborn would repent of all his sin, hating sin when once he only loved it. Fourth, the regenerate would believe on the Lord Jesus Christ, knowing the truth of the gospel through his experience. Fifth, regenerate persons would attempt to obey God without blame. In total, then, Haynes believed that salvation was by regeneration and faith, producing in the spiritually reborn "the same kind of affections and dispositions as there are in God. He has a living principle within him, which is active and vigorous, springing up into everlasting life,"[38] a life wholly contrary to the life lived before conversion and genuine faith.

By the early 1800s, growing interest in the universal salvation of all men began to take root and spread in the New England area. During his ministry, Haynes ardently opposed both Arminian and universalist views of salvation. Sermon notes written in 1780 on Psalm 96:1, for example, revealed a consistent effort to defend the sovereignty of God in election against free will and theodicy-related objections.[39] Haynes regarded encroachments and abandonment of the sovereignty of God as evidence of low comprehension

---

[37]Ibid., p. 34.
[38]Ibid., p. 36, emphasis added.
[39]Lemuel Haynes, "Outline of a Sermon on Psalm 96:1," in *Black Preacher to White America*, ed. Richard Newman (Brooklin: Carlson, 1990), pp. 39-41. Haynes's view of the righteousness of God in face of injustice is reviewed in chapter 2.

of Scripture in the Christian church. In perhaps his most famous and most widely published sermon, "Universal Salvation," he offered a defense of Reformed soteriology by satirizing the nascent universalism of his day. In an extemporaneous satirical response to an address given by universalist preacher, Hosea Ballou (1771-1852), Haynes likened the doctrine of universal salvation to the original lie told in the garden of Eden and compared the universalist preacher to the serpent himself.[40] Correspondence between Ballou and Haynes revealed the personal sting of Haynes's satire, while the seventy published editions of his sermon circulating in America and Europe into the nineteenth century demonstrated the popularity of his address and defense.

Testifyin': salvation in slave testimonies. On the whole, enslaved Africans held a "soft Calvinism," a generally Reformed soteriology that followed the same general contours of the Reformation *solas* that defined the preceding two hundred years of American religious heritage.

The testimony of former slaves reveals four general themes regarding salvation in their beliefs and experience. These themes suggest a widely accepted point of view among slaves about how a person came to be saved. Recorded testimonies of ex-slaves emphasize: (1) a person must die and be born again to be saved; (2) God is sovereign in election and salvation; (3) salvation is attained only through the grace of God; and (4) assurance of salvation is a labor, a struggle sometimes taking years to realize.

You must die. Frequently—sometimes through visions, sometimes through dogmatic statements—slave testimonies underscored the slaves' belief that a death was necessary before new spiritual life were possible. For example, in a testimony Johnson entitled "The Inside Voice Never Leaves Me Lonely," an ex-slave reported:

> I saw in a vision, myself in two bodies, a little body and an old body. My old body was dangling over hell and destruction. A voice said to me, "My little one, I have cleansed you of all iniquity. By grace are you saved and it is not of yourself but the gift of God. Weep not, for you are a new child. Abide in me and you need never fear." I looked in the distance and saw the rejoicing and singing.

---

[40]Lemuel Haynes, "Universal Salvation" (1805), in *Black Preacher to White America,* ed. Richard Newman (Brooklyn: Carlson, 1990), pp. 105-11.

I know that I have been dug up and made alive and my soul made satisfied.[41]

Another slave reported a more vivid experience:

One Thursday morning, the sun was shining bright. I was chopping corn in the garden, when a voice "hollered," and said, *"Oh, Nancy, you got to die and can't live." I started to run because it scared me but I got weak and felt myself dying from my feet to my head. I fell and said, "Lord, I haven't done nothing to nobody." As I got weaker and colder I cried, "I am dying; I am dying; I am dying. Lord, have mercy and save my soul."* As quick as a flash I felt a change.

When I know anything I was in hell and there I stayed until I got orders to leave. There was a deep pit and on the other side a man was sitting. His eyes were like fire, his hair like lamb's wool and his feet like brass. He said nothing to me but just sat looking to the far corner of the world. A voice came to me saying, "This is heaven, the place you have been seeking for. Do as they do." Then I began to shout, too. A voice said, "I am almighty God. I will be closer to you than a brother. My hand spans the world. Look to Me for I am wider than all creation, higher than the heavens and deeper down than hell. I call whomsoever I will and they shall hear my voice. Amen."

I started to shouting in the spirit and haven't stopped yet. *I died the sinner death and ain't got to die no more.* I am fixed up for the building.[42]

After hearing the voice of God at nine years of age, another former slave recounted his conversion:

I was killed dead by the power of God one evening about four o'clock. I don't remember what I was doing but I do know that the sun was shining bright and that all at once I fell to the floor as somebody struck by lightning. I couldn't move or speak but in my heart I was trying to say, *"Lord, have mercy, I am dying."*[43]

A number of slaves reported hearing a voice, or the voice of God, instructing them that they must die before living again. In a testimony entitled, "The Gospel Train," one former slave relayed his testimony of dying as follows:

[41]Clifton H. Johnson, ed., *God Struck Me Dead: Religious Conversion Experiences and Autobiographies of Ex-Slaves* (Cleveland: United Church Press, 1969), p. 48, emphasis added.
[42]Clifton Johnson, ed., "I Ain't Got to Die No More," in *God Struck Me Dead: Religious Conversion Experiences and Autobiographies of Ex-Slaves* (Cleveland: United Church Press, 1969), pp. 55-56, emphasis added.
[43]Clifton Johnson, ed., "I Came to Myself Shouting," in *God Struck Me Dead: Religious Conversion Experiences and Autobiographies of Ex-Slaves* (Cleveland: United Church Press, 1969), p. 30, emphasis added.

When I first heard the voice He said to me, "You got to die to live again." When I died I was as wide awake as I am now. I felt the flesh trembling on my bones and I died from my feet up. I heard my tongue as it clicked and seemed to be fastened to the roof of my mouth so I couldn't speak.[44]

In all of these accounts, dying was portrayed as a sensible experience. The convert was fully aware of visions, her or his own body, and a resultant change or rebirth. This act of dying was most often associated with a dramatic awareness of one's personal sinfulness and impending judgment. The unrepentant sinner saw her or himself in eternal peril, often unable to offer any defense or effort to overcome this death. Dying was a necessary prerequisite to spiritual life. One slave recounted, "A voice spoke to me one day and He called me by name saying, 'You got to die and can't live!'"[45] In many respects, and despite the fact that biblical texts were not cited explicitly, these experiences of death were analogous to the Bible's insistence that one must be born again and that one must die to self, sin and the world.[46]

Sovereignty of God in election and salvation. Slaves during the abolition era also held to a view of God's sovereignty in election and salvation. This, too, indicated Reformed theology's impact on religious thinking in early America and on converted slaves who participated in that heritage. Many slaves clearly understood God carried out his saving work according to his own free choosing and will. That is, slaves generally understood that God was choosing them and that they were not themselves choosing God or being chosen because of their own merit.

For example, one slave told of his attempt to influence God to save him. "He [God] spoke to me once after I prayed and prayed trying to hurry him and get a religion. He said, 'I am a time-God. Behold, I work after the counsel of my own will and in due time I will visit whomsoever I will.'"[47] Another convert relayed a similar story. "I began to pray for my soul more and more and began to hurry God. He gave me the gift in His own time. He was drawing

---

[44]Johnson, *God Struck Me Dead,* p. 36.

[45]Clifton Johnson, ed., "To Hell With a Prayer in My Mouth," in *God Struck Me Dead: Religious Conversion Experiences and Autobiographies of Ex-Slaves* (Cleveland: United Church Press, 1969), p. 93.

[46]See for example Jn 3:1-8 for Jesus' remarks to Nicodemus regarding the new birth.

[47]Clifton Johnson, ed., "Hooked in the Heart," in *God Struck Me Dead: Religious Conversion Experiences and Autobiographies of Ex-Slaves* (Cleveland: United Church Press, 1969), p. 7.

me all the time but I didn't know it."[48] These two records describe the slaves' view of God as one who brought salvation in his own timing and according to his own will. The saving act of God, then, was not motivated by anything other than his own decision and sometimes was hidden from the awareness of men ("He was drawing me all the time but I didn't know it"). One interviewee commented, "God has his own time and way of taking hold of his people and his works are more than we read and think about."[49]

Some testimonies also provide a clear statement of election. For example, in a testimony entitled "I Came from Heaven and Now Return," Johnson recorded:

I was born a slave and lived through some very hard times. If it had not been for my God, I don't know what I would have done. Through His mercy I was lifted up. My soul began singing and *I was told that I was one of the elected children* and that I would live as long as God lives.[50]

But perhaps the clearest statement regarding God's sovereignty in election and salvation is found in the prologue to Johnson's collection, titled "A Man Is a Man." Here, Johnson's interviewee explained how one finds God:

All the reading in the world will not help you. Unless God opens your understanding and reveals His mighty works to you, you are dead. Thus, if you are dead you have no part with Him. We judge a tree by the fruit it bears. A good tree cannot bring forth corrupt fruit. We must get right on the inside before we can get right on the outside and we only reach this stage when God, through His mercy, has compassion on us and frees our souls from Hell, for we are conceived in iniquity and born in sin.

How can we find God? *God has a chosen people. He has always had a chosen people and He calls whomsoever He wills.* Any child who has been born of the spirit, knows it for he has felt His power, tasted His love and seen the travail of his soul.[51]

This former slave's statement rivaled the eloquence and force of any preacher

---

[48]Clifton Johnson, ed., "To Hell with a Prayer in My Mouth," in *God Struck Me Dead: Religious Conversion Experiences and Autobiographies of Ex-Slaves* (Cleveland: United Church Press, 1969), p. 41.

[49]Clifton Johnson, ed., "I Came from Heaven and Now Return," in *God Struck Me Dead: Religious Conversion Experiences and Autobiographies of Ex-Slaves* (Cleveland: United Church Press, 1969), p. 25.

[50]Ibid., p. 23, emphasis added.

[51]Clifton Johnson, ed., "A Man in a Man," in *God Struck Me Dead: Religious Conversion Experiences and Autobiographies of Ex-Slaves* (Cleveland: United Church Press, 1969), p. 13.

during his lifetime or before. Like Haynes and Hammon, he saw the desperate spiritual plight of slaves as death and alienation from God. Further, the internal change or conversion preceded the external evidences of good deeds and a moral life, because man was "conceived in iniquity and born in sin." The cure could only be the sovereign choosing of God to grant mercy and to "free our souls from Hell."

Salvation by God's grace. Since salvation came to those sovereignly elected by God, Christian slaves understood that salvation could only be procured at the gracious hand of God. In this, they were astonishingly consistent with the orthodoxy of their time. The credit for redemption was due only to God and wholly unearned by man. "It is no wisdom of ours nor any righteousness of ourselves but the goodness and mercies of God. It is not religion but the grace of God that saves us and grace is a gift from God."[52]

In words reminiscent of the apostle Paul,[53] one slave posited that the election of God both originated in eternity past and worked in complete contradiction to human merit and effort. He described his conversion thus:

> After I passed through this experience [a vision of Jesus and the city] I lost all worldly cares. The things I used to enjoy don't interest me now. I am a new creature in Jesus, the workmanship of His hand saved from the foundation of the world. *I was a chosen vessel before the wind ever blew or before the sun ever shined.*
>
> *Religion is not a work but a gift from God. We are saved by grace and it is not of ourselves but the gift of God.*[54]

Assurance of salvation delayed. Another defining feature of many of the existing slave conversion testimonies is the view that assurance of salvation is often delayed, being obtained only after much pleading and struggle with God. Such a view was consistent with the earlier Puritan view that the diligent "use of means"—prayer, Bible reading, listening to the preached word, attending to the sacraments—was typical and essential in acquiring assurance of salvation. For example, one slave testified, "from this time on [after hearing a voice at nine

---

[52]Clifton Johnson, ed., "Voice Like the Coming of a Dove," in *God Struck Me Dead: Religious Conversion Experiences and Autobiographies of Ex-Slaves* (Cleveland: United Church Press, 1969), p. 16.
[53]Compare the slave's testimony to Paul's words in Rom 3:19-28; Gal 3; Eph 1–2.
[54]Clifton Johnson, ed., "Before the Wind Ever Blew," in *God Struck Me Dead: Religious Conversion Experiences and Autobiographies of Ex-Slaves* (Cleveland: United Church Press, 1969), p. 57, emphasis added.

years old] I got very sorrowful and tried to pray until He freed my soul. I was almost grown when he finished his work with me."[55]

Olaudah Equiano (c. 1745-1797) recorded his struggle to gain assurance of true conversion. Over the course of several months, he sought out a number of ministers and counselors about how he could be sure that his sins were forgiven and that he

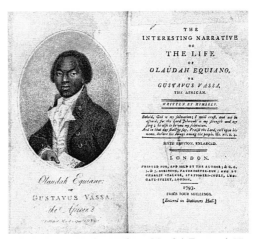

Frontispiece and title page from Olaudah Equiano's *The Interesting Narrative of the Life of Olauda Equiano, or Gustavas Vassa, the African*

would enter the kingdom of heaven. "I thought if I sinned, after having life and death set evidently before me, I should certainly go to hell."[56] One minister recommended Equiano "read the scriptures, and hear the word preached; not to neglect fervent prayer to God."[57] Taking the ministers advice, and following several months of doubt and despair, Equiano recounted the long-awaited experience of genuine conversion:

> In this deep consternation the Lord was pleased to break in upon my soul with his bright beams of heavenly light; and in an instant, as it were, removing the veil, and letting light into a dark place (Is 25:7). I saw clearly, with the eye of faith, the crucified Saviour bleeding on the cross on Mount Calvary: the Scriptures became an unsealed book; I saw myself a condemned criminal under the law, which came with its full force to my conscience and when "the commandment came, sin revived, and I died." I saw the Lord Jesus Christ in his humiliation, loaded, and bearing my reproach, sin, and shame.[58]

Or consider the example of former slave Richard Allen, a founding member

---

[55]Clifton Johnson, ed., "I Came to Myself Shouting," in *God Struck Me Dead: Religious Conversion Experiences and Autobiographies of Ex-Slaves* (Cleveland: United Church Press, 1969), p. 30.

[56]Olaudah Equiano, *The Interesting Narrative of the Life of Olaudah Equiano, or Gustavus Vassa, the African*, in *My Soul Has Grown Deep: Classics of Early African-American Literature*, ed. John Edgar Wideman (Philadelphia: Running Press, 2001), pp. 324-25.

[57]Ibid., p. 324.

[58]Ibid, p. 326.

and the first bishop of the African Methodist Episcopal church:

> I was awakened and brought to see myself poor, wretched and undone, and
> without the mercy of God must be lost. Shortly after I obtained mercy
> through the blood of Christ, and was constrained to exhort my old compan-
> ions to seek the Lord. I went rejoicing for several days, and was happy in the
> Lord, in conversing with many old experienced Christians. I was brought un-
> der doubts, and was tempted to believe I was deceived, and was constrained
> to seek the Lord afresh. I went with my head bowed down for many days. My
> sins were a heavy burden. I was tempted to believe there was no mercy for me.
> I cried to the Lord both night and day. One night I thought hell would be my
> portion. I cried unto Him who delighteth to hear the prayers of a poor sinner;
> and all of a sudden my dungeon shook, my chains flew off, and glory to God,
> I cried. My soul was filled. I cried, enough for me—the Saviour died. *Now my
> confidence was strengthened that the Lord, for Christ's sake, had heard my prayers,
> and pardoned all my sins.* I was constrained to go from house to house, exhort-
> ing my old companions, and telling to all around what a dear Saviour I had
> found.[59]

Though Methodist and Wesleyan in his polity and theology, Allen recounted
his conversion experience in terms characteristic of earlier Puritan and Reformed writers.

Bishop Richard Allen

Slave conversion testimonies present a
relatively clear and sophisticated soteriology—including themes consistent with
the biblical record and contemporary
northern Calvinists, laced with African
distinctives like visions and dreams. Absent from these testimonies is anything
resembling the "free will religion" of Pelagius, Arminius or the revivalist campaigns in the late 1800s. The generally
Reformed theology and soft Calvinism of
these conversion accounts shine through

---

[59]Richard Allen, *The Life, Experience, and Gospel Labours of the Rt. Rev. Richard Allen*, in *My Soul Has
Grown Deep: Classics of Early African-American Literature*, ed. John Edgar Wideman (Philadelphia:
Running Press, 2001), p. 23, emphasis added.

despite the lukewarm reception given to many white preachers, ostensibly the most likely purveyors of Calvinism—especially any doctrine of predestination misused to support existing racial inequities in social, economic, and political contexts. This suggests that the Christian slave convert considered the basic framework of Reformed theology sufficiently true to beckon subscription.

RECONSTRUCTION, "JIM CROW" SEGREGATION, GREAT MIGRATION AND THE "NEW NEGRO" MOVEMENT (1865-1929)

If evangelical Protestantism, characterized by the remnants of formal Calvinism in the North and a generally Reformed theology and personal conversionism in the South, defined the years leading up to Abolitionism, the Civil War and Emancipation, then Wesleyan theology defined the years following. Reformed soteriology survived in some quarters among pastors like Joseph Baysmore (1823-?) from Weldon, North Carolina,[60] but the theological tide turned swiftly toward a Wesleyan-Arminian understanding of conversion and salvation largely as a result of the evangelistic fervor and reform attempts of Anglican clergyman John Wesley (1703-1791). The movement founded by Wesley, commonly called Methodism, began its organizational life in the United States in Baltimore, Maryland. In December 1784, American Methodist preachers at Wesley's instruction formed the Methodist Episcopal Church and elected as their first bishops Francis Asbury (1745-1816) and Thomas Coke (1747-1814). The new church recorded twenty thousand members at its founding, two thousand of whom were African American,[61] including such notable converts as Sojourner Truth (1797-1883).[62]

---

[60]Baysmore preached as an ardent advocate of Calvinism or a reformational understanding of salvation. His surviving sermons reveal a polemical zeal for key Reformed doctrines like predestination and opposition to hyper-Calvinism in his day. See Joseph Baysmore, *"Falling from Grace," "Baptism," and "Predestination;" Sermons by Elder Joseph Baysmore, of Weldon, N.C. to which is Added His Lecture on Humanity* (Raleigh, N.C.: Edwards, Broughton & Co., 1878); and *A Historical Sketch of the First Colored Baptist Church Weldon, N.C., With the Life and Labor of Elder Joseph Baysmore, with Four Collected Sermons, First: The Harmony of the Law and Gospel. Second: Subject of the Pure in Heart. Third: How We Were Made Sinners and How We Were Redeemed from Sin and Made Heirs of God by His Love. Fourth: The Confirmation of Christian Faith* (Weldon, N.C.: Harell's Printing House, 1887). Electronic editions of both works are available from the Documenting the American South project at the University of North Carolina at Chapel Hill.

[61]Charles Yrigoyen Jr., "Methodism, North America," in *The Encyclopedia of Protestantism, Volume 3,* ed. Hans J. Hillerbrand (New York: Routledge, 2004), pp. 1223-26.

[62]Nell Irvin Painter, *Sojourner Truth: A Life, A Symbol* (New York: W. W. Norton, 1996), chap. 4.

Wesley received his theological training first at the hands of his parents, Samuel Wesley, rector at Epworth, and Susanna Annesley, daughter of a Dissenting minister. He attended Charterhouse School in London and later received a B.A. degree at Christ Church, Oxford. Wesley's "basic theological framework continued to reflect his Church of England heritage" and included "both sacramentalism and evangelism, free will and free grace, faith and good works, without any inconsistency."[63] Wesley and his movement freely cobbled together Christian ideas from diverse traditions. As one recent historian of Methodism, David Hempton, comments:

> [Wesley] read and was influenced by a bewildering array of Christian traditions: the church fathers, monastic piety, and ancient liturgies; continental mystics such as Jeanne-Marie Guyon, François Fénelon, Claude Fleury, Marquis de Renty, Brother Lawrence, and Antoninette Bourignon; Byzantine traditions of spirituality approached through Macarius and Gregory of Nyssa; the English and Scottish Puritan divines; the Moravians and other channels of central European Pietism; his mother and through her to Pascal; classics of devotional spirituality including Thomas à Kempis, Jeremy Taylor, and William Law; and the canon of Anglican writers from Hooker to the seventeenth- and eighteenth-century High Churchmen. Writers on each of these traditions are prone to compete for the preeminent influence over Wesley, but the truth of the matter is that Wesley's eclecticism is itself preeminent.[64]

Hempton continues with an attempt at summarizing Wesley's theology with more precision than the phrase "Church of England heritage."

> The attempt to boil Wesley's theology down to a simple formula, such as the much-peddled quadrilateral of scripture, reason, tradition, and experience, spectacularly misses the point. A forensic appeal to geometrical precision, of all the approaches to Wesley's theology, is the one least likely to capture its essence. If Wesley's theology must be reduced to a model, one that offers better explanatory power than the quadrilateral is to see it more as a moving vortex, fueled by scripture and divine love, shaped by experience, reason, and tradition, and moving dynamically toward holiness or Christian perfection. Any model that lacks dy-

---

[63]R.P. Heitzenrater, "John Wesley," in *Biographical Dictionary of Evangelicals*, ed. Timothy Larsen (Downers Grove, Ill.: InterVarsity Press, 2003), p. 714.
[64]David Hempton, *Methodism: Empire of the Spirit* (New Haven, Conn.: Yale University Press, 2005), pp. 56-57.

namic movement toward holiness and its growth within individuals and its dissemination throughout the world is clearly inadequate.[65]

Wesley opposed the Calvinist view of God's sovereignty in election. He "could not conceive of a God who had determined everything in advance or of human spirituality that was mere acquiescence."[66] In Wesley's theology, God's prevenient grace made human beings genuinely free to either accept or deny God's saving grace, which pardoned sins and granted new life by faith in Christ's atonement.

Wesley's soteriology bore similarities and significant differences from that of Augustine and Calvin. Similar to the Reformers, Wesley maintained the total depravity of man and recognized the universal and systemic effect of sin on humanity. Unlike Calvin and Augustine, however, Wesley differed in his view of prevenient grace. Augustine and Calvin limited prevenient grace to the elect. Along with Arminius and others, Wesley saw God's prevenient grace operating on all humanity.

Wesleyanism, the movement acquiring its name from John Wesley, struggled to maintain some of the mediating theological tensions that Wesley himself fought to maintain. For example, one writer comparing Augustinian soteriology with Wesleyanism's view of human nature and free will wrote:

> Arminian Wesleyanism affirms the Augustinian understanding of divine sovereignty, original sin, and total depravity. However, it rejects the conclusion that these doctrines must result in a doctrine of individual predestination. In that sense Wesleyanism may fairly be identified as semi Augustinianism. Likewise, Arminian Wesleyanism embraces the Pelagian regard for free will, but utterly rejects the Pelagian denial of original sin. Therefore, because Wesleyanism simultaneously embraces divine sovereignty, human depravity, and human free well, it may accurately be stated that Wesleyanism is neither purely Augustinian or Pelagian, but is in fact both semi-Augustinian and semi-Pelagian.[67]

This "semi-Augustinian, semi-Pelagian" view came to characterize the theological tendencies of many African Americans in the latter half of the 1800s.

If Wesley was semi-Pelagian in his view of the human will, then Charles

---

[65]Ibid., p. 57.
[66]Ibid.
[67]Daniel L. Burnett, "Wesleyanism," in *Encyclopedia of Protestantism*, vol. 3, ed. Hans J. Hillerbrand (New York: Routledge, 2004), p. 1994.

Grandison Finney (1792-1875), the best-known revivalist of the Second Great Awakening, was fully Pelagian. Finney, perhaps the most significant white evangelical of his era and arguably "ranked with Andrew Jackson, Abraham Lincoln, and Andrew Carnegie as one of the most important public figures in nineteenth-century America,"[68] pushed beyond Wesley's understanding of the necessity of prevenient grace to assert that no preparatory grace was needed in choosing God, that implicit in God's command to repent was the ability to do so *at once*. He noted:

> The sinner has all the faculties and natural abilities requisite to render perfect obedience to God. All he needs is to be induced to use these powers and attributes as he ought. . . . Regeneration then is a radical change of the ultimate intention, and of course, of the end or object of life. . . . Regeneration . . . must consist in a change in attitude of the will, or a change in its ultimate choice . . . to the interests of His kingdom.[69]

Finney pioneered revival methods consistent with his view of human freedom in salvation and profoundly changed the practice of camp meetings even today. The Methodism that Wesley pioneered and the revival methods that Finney adapted greatly affected American theology and society. Two commentators on Methodism's impact concluded, "Methodism rivals Puritanism in its force and intensity, its ability to mobilize followers, to generate new modes of communication and organization, and to instill habits of industry, sobriety, and mutual accountability."[70]

Following the Civil War, predominantly Methodist churchmen lamented the economically and spiritually impoverished condition of the South and launched a reclamation effort aimed at reviving religion in the region. One writer observed:

> In the dark days following the war, the impoverished states of the defeated Confederacy turned to religion for solace. During 1865-1867, "a sound of revival"

---

[68]Noll, *History of Christianity in the United States and Canada*, pp. 174-78. Noll suggests that Finney is as pervasive and significant in his influence on American society as any industrialist or politician of his period.
[69]Charles G. Finney, *Systematic Theology* (1846; reprint, Minneapolis: Bethany, 1976), p. 285.
[70]Nathan O. Hatch and John H. Wigger, eds., *Methodism and the Shaping of American Culture* (Nashville: Kingswood Books, 2001), p. 11; cited in Charles Yrigoyen Jr., "Methodism, North America" in *The Encyclopedia of Protestantism*, vol. 3, ed. Hans J. Hillerbrand (New York: Routledge, 2004), p. 1223.

was heard from one border to the other. The journals of Methodism teemed with news of great evangelistic efforts. The bishops of the Methodist Episcopal Church, South, meeting in General Conference in 1866, called for a return to Wesleyan principles as an answer to the post-war moral crisis. . . . In 1870, the bishops of the Southern church again called for a re-emphasis on sanctification: "Nothing is so much needed at the present time throughout all these lands as a general and powerful revival of scriptural holiness."[71]

The call for religious reform resulted in a short-lived southern revival and the birth of the Holiness movement. It also signaled a wider infusion of Wesleyan theology across the South and into African American churches. Arthur Paris recognized this period of African American theological history as "basically Wesleyan" and "predominantly Methodist." He wrote, "the shape of Black religious practice, with its emphasis on 'enthusiasm' and biblical literalism, had been set long ago as a result of the evangelization of Blacks during the Methodist and Baptist revivals that began in the mid-eighteenth century."[72] The Wesleyan impulse among African Americans found its earliest defenders in John Jea (b. 1773) and Richard Allen (1760-1831). The theology spread with the tireless efforts of circuit riders and black preachers of Methodism and the revivalism of Charles Finney, and gained its first institutional expression with the founding of the African Methodist Episcopal Church in 1816.

While many African Americans like Richard Allen accepted Methodist doctrine without edit, the rise of the Holiness and Pentecostal movements brought the first significant African American innovation with the Wesleyan framework. This innovation opened up a second stream of soteriological thought, one consistently anti-Calvinist in tone and Wesleyan/Arminian in content.

William Seymour and the "full gospel" of Azusa Street. Among African Americans, and to a great extent the larger Pentecostal world of the early 1900s, William Seymour stands out as the father of the Pentecostal movement. Seymour saw the Pentecostal movement and the Azusa Street revival as a continuation of God's reforming activity in the church:

---

[71]Vinson Synan, *Holiness-Pentecostal Movement*, p. 20, as quoted in Arthur E. Paris, *Black Pentecostalism*, p. 17.

[72]Arthur E. Paris, *Black Pentecostalism: Southern Religion in an Urban World* (Amherst: University of Massachusetts Press, 1982), pp. 16-17.

All along the ages men have been preaching a partial Gospel. A part of the Gospel remained when the world went into the dark ages. God has from time to time raised up men to bring back the truth to the church. He raised up Luther to bring back to the world the doctrine of justification by faith. He raised up another reformer in John Wesley to establish Bible holiness in the church. Then he raised up Dr. Cullis who brought back to the world the wonderful doctrine of divine healing. Now He is bringing back the Pentecostal Baptism to the church.[73]

According to Seymour, that such restoration was needed indicated that the church had entered the latter day apostasy, with "the precious truths" hidden by the traditions of the elders.[74]

The rise of Pentecostalism brought with it a conscious anti-Calvinist—if not consciously Arminian—soteriological tradition. Following the theological course laid by Wesley and other Methodist leaders, and in the spirit of John Jea, Seymour and other Pentecostal leaders rejected Calvinistic soteriology. "We believe in *a real salvation* that gives you the witness by the Spirit. Calvin taught a salvation that if you said you had it, you did not have it; and if you had it, you did not know it; and if you lost it, you could not get it again. Wesley taught that if you had it you would know it, and if you lost it, you could get it again."[75] Seymour understood the Wesleyan system of salvation to be superior in terms of the assurance it offered true believers and the possibility of salvation it offered even to the apostate. Calvinism, he thought, offered neither.

And implicit in this negative view of Calvinistic soteriology and positive view of Wesleyanism was a high view of the moral ability of man as a result of prevenient grace. Where the Reformed Hammon and Haynes and generally Reformed southern slaves saw men enslaved by sinful desires unable to incline themselves toward God without divine intervention in giving them a new birth, Seymour saw them as morally free enough to choose salvation and able to "get it again" should they lose it. Moreover, concluded Seymour:

If your heart is open to the Blood of Christ He will save you. *All He wants is a repentant heart that has Godly sorrow for sin*, and He will wash you. Though your sins be red like crimson, they shall be as wool. O the promises of God are sure

---

[73]William Seymour, "The Pentecostal Baptism Restored," *Apostolic Faith* 1, no. 2 (October 1906): 1.
[74]Ibid., p. 2.
[75]"Everywhere Preaching the Word," *Apostolic Faith* 2, no. 10 (September 1907): 1.

and steadfast, and though the heaven and earth pass away, the promises of Jesus will never pass away. As long as there is breath and life in your body, you can look up to Jesus and He will save you, but if there is no repentance in your heart you would have no desire to be saved. But, beloved, *if there is one particle of desire in your heart to look to God*, you have not sinned away your day of grace.[76]

Such language as "an open heart" or "one particle of desire in your heart" would have been unthinkable in the Calvinistic systems of Haynes and Hammon. They would have objected not only to the idea that man could possibly have "a repentant heart [with] Godly sorrow for sin," but would have been repulsed by the idea that the "particle of desire" is the *determinative element* in salvation. In other words, Haynes and Hammon would have regarded Seymour's depiction of conversion as a violation of the Bible's entire teaching on redemption—distorting the fallen depravity of man, diminishing Christ's atoning work on the cross for the elect and contradicting a Calvinistic view of God's sovereignty in election.

Seymour's three-stage view of the converted Christian life. Seymour's contribution to African American perspectives on salvation did not lie merely in a rejection of the Calvinism of Haynes and Hammon or the mere assertion of a more positive view of human nature. Seymour expanded the Wesleyan doctrines of salvation and sanctification to include three distinct phases, two of which belonged to Wesley's view, and a third unique to Seymour's brand of Pentecostalism.[77] This three-stage view Seymour held to be the "full gospel."

The statement of faith frequently printed in the movement's official organ, *Apostolic Faith*, stated Seymour's soteriology succinctly. First, "Justification is that act of God's free grace by which we receive remission of sins (Acts 10:42, 43; Rom 3:25)." Contrary to the Reformed view where regeneration precedes justification, in Seymour's system justification was simultaneous with regeneration. Justification required repentance from sins and faith toward the Lord Jesus. Once justified, the pardoned sinner became a child of God.[78]

Second, sanctification was the second and last work of grace. At this point, Seymour's soteriology was consistent with his understanding of Wesley's teachings. Appealing to various passages of Scripture, Seymour taught,

---

[76]*Apostolic Faith* 2, no. 10 (September 1907): 1, emphasis added.

[77]Strong, *They Walked in the Spirit*, pp. 40-41.

[78]William Seymour, "Receive Ye the Holy Ghost," *Apostolic Faith* 2, no. 1 (January 1907): 2.

"Sanctification is that act of God's free grace by which He makes us holy."[79] However, Seymour's conception of justification differed from Wesley's in one important respect. Wesley taught that God's prevenient grace "provided for the forgiveness of original sin" and that "the guilt of Adam's sin . . . was universally pardoned through God's prevenient grace."[80] According to Seymour, sanctification *removed* original sin from the sinner. "Sanctification takes out the disobedience, rebellion and resistance out of our hearts and gives us a pure, clean heart that our Christ may come and dwell in. Amen. Sanctification is the second work of grace that deals with our original sin. Sanctification destroys the root and breed of sin and makes us holy."[81] To state the matter more clearly, Seymour later wrote, "sanctification . . . *frees us from original sin—the sin that we were born with, which we inherited from our father Adam.* We were not responsible for that sin until we received light, for we could not repent of a sin that we did not commit."[82] Seymour contended that, "it is His will for every soul to be saved from *all sin, actual and original.* We get our actual sins cleansed away through the Blood of Jesus Christ at the cross; but *our original sin* we get cleansed on the cross. It must be a real death to the old man."[83]

The "cross" that Seymour believed cleansed original sin was not that of Calvary but that of experiential holiness, "the death of the old man." Consequently, Seymour's doctrine of sanctification, *though a work of God's grace,* depended essentially on the believer's ability to crucify sin after the atoning work of Christ, making Christ's sacrifice only effectual for sins actually committed by a person but insufficient with regard to the sins inherited from Adam. Dealing with those sins required a second cross, as it were, a cross of the individual's making and execution.

Third, and distinct from sanctification in Seymour's system, was the baptism with the Holy Ghost. While Reformed theologians held that at the moment of saving conversion a person was justified, sanctified and baptized with the Holy Ghost, some Pentecostals insisted that such a baptism was included

---

[79]The Apostolic Faith Mission Statement of Faith, *Apostolic Faith* 2, no. 6 (September 1907): 1; Seymour referred to passages like Jn 17:15, 17; 1 Thess 4:3; 5:23; Heb 2:11; 12:14; 13:12.

[80]Burnett, "Wesleyanism," p. 1993.

[81]"Type of Pentecost, II Chronicles 5," *Apostolic Faith* 2, no. 3 (April 1907): 3.

[82]William J. Seymour, "Letter to One Seeking the Holy Ghost," *Apostolic Faith* 2, no. 5 (June-September 1907): 2.

[83]William Seymour, "Sanctified on the Cross," *Apostolic Faith* 3, no. 2 (May 1908): 2.

only in the second work of grace, sanctification. For Seymour, however, the second work of grace and the baptism with the Holy Ghost were separate stages of the Christian life with two distinct effects. While sanctification removed original sin in the converted, baptism with the Holy Spirit was a gift of power upon the sanctified life signified by the same evidence the disciples received on the Day of Pentecost (Acts 2:3-4)—speaking in new tongues. The miraculous gift of speaking in unknown tongues demonstrated that a "personal Pentecost" had come to the believer.[84] However, it was not a "salvation of tongues"; rather, the baptism of the Holy Ghost was an effusion of power to witness, ineffable joy in the heart of the believer and abounding love. For example, Antoinette Moomau's personal testimony, printed in the *Apostolic Faith*, concluded, "the baptism of the Spirit means to me what I never dreamed it could this side of Heaven: victory, glory in my soul, perfect peace, rest, liberty, nearness of Christ, deadness to this old world, and power in witnessing."[85]

One edition of the *Apostolic Faith* summarized Seymour's doctrine of salvation thus: "God stands today to *save* every sinner, to *sanctify* every believer, and to *baptize* every sanctified believer with the Holy Ghost."[86] According to Seymour, this threefold view of salvation was pictured in the Old Testament. For example, the doctrine was discernible in the contents of the Ark of the Covenant, where Aaron's staff represented justification, the pot of manna sanctification, and the tablets of stone the baptism of the Holy Ghost. In addition, the two works of grace were "plainly shown in the tabernacle by the two altars—the brazen altar and the golden altar."[87] Seymour also saw this system pictured in the New Testament as well, where he interpreted Paul's analogy of the church as the body of Christ as a picture of unity between justified, sanctified and Holy Ghost baptized believers.[88]

Losing salvation. Although Seymour seems to have given far more attention to the benefits of sanctification and baptism with the Holy Spirit, he also ventured something else that no well-known African American preacher had before him—the idea that salvation, from justification to baptism with the Holy

---

[84]"The True Pentecost," *Apostolic Faith* 1, no. 4 (December 1906): 2.

[85]Antoinette Moomau, "China Missionary Receives Pentecost," *Apostolic Faith* 2, no. 7 (October-December 1907): 3.

[86]*Apostolic Faith* 2, no. 4 (June-September 1907): 1, emphasis added.

[87]"Baptism with the Holy Ghost Foreshadowed," *Apostolic Faith* 1, no. 4 (December 1906): 2.

[88]"The True Pentecost," *Apostolic Faith* 1, no. 4 (December 1906): 2.

Ghost, could be lost by the believer. Though Seymour taught that the Spirit sealed the believer unto the day of redemption, he also, quite contradictorily, argued, "Your life must measure with the fruits of the Spirit. If you get angry, or speak evil, or backbite, I care not how many tongues you have, you have not the baptism with the Holy Spirit. *You have lost your salvation.* You need the blood in your soul."[89] Arminian Wesleyanism maintained that one could renounce faith and so be lost, but he did not believe one could forfeit salvation through unknown sin or specific acts of known sin.[90] Comparing the sin of men with that of fallen angels, Seymour bluntly wrote, "Just as angels could not remain in the kingdom of God when they sinned, so *people cannot live in the kingdom of God, His church, if they sin.* The only way to remain in unity with Christ and His Spirit flowing in our souls is to be obedient subjects. *Obedience keeps us in the body of Christ* and His love flowing like an ocean."[91]

Moreover, Seymour believed that just as the Holy Spirit brought people to repentance and faith, the Holy Spirit also removed people from the church. "They remain members as long as they live free from sin. When they commence sinning, the Holy Ghost, the chairman and bishop, the presiding elder, turns them out, and they know when they are turned out of this church."[92] To prevent this, the justified sinner must "seek at once the cleansing Blood [of sanctification] *or lose all your salvation.*"[93] For, "if Jesus who was God Himself, heeded the Holy Ghost to empower Him for His ministry and His miracles, how much more do we children need the Holy Ghost today."[94]

Seymour's soteriological emphasis was not without opposition. From the start, many opponents black and white, Pentecostal and non-Pentecostal rejected his three-stage view of salvation and Wesleyan teachings regarding perfection and sanctification. For example, former Azusa Street devotee William H. Durham (1873-1912) defected from the doctrine he learned at Azusa Street to promote his "Finished Work" view of the atonement, where sanctification was accomplished in conversion because Christ's crucifixion eliminated

---

[89]"To the Baptized Saints," *Apostolic Faith* 2, no. 5 (June-September 1907): 2, emphasis added.
[90]Burnett, "Wesleyanism," p. 1994.
[91]William Seymour, "Sanctified on the Cross," *Apostolic Faith* 3:2 (May 1908): 2, emphasis added.
[92]William Seymour, "The Holy Spirit Bishop of the Church," *Apostolic Faith* 2, no. 5 (June-September 1907): 3.
[93]*Apostolic Faith* 2, no. 6 (September 1907): 2, emphasis added.
[94]"The Baptism of the Holy Ghost," *Apostolic Faith* 3, no. 2 (May 1908): 3.

the need for a "second blessing" or "second change."[95] Also, in an 1899 address before the Arkansas Baptist Convention, Elias C. Morris (1855-1922) offered an exposition of the doctrine of sanctification as a response to "wantonly perverted and misunderstood" teachings. Morris defined sanctification as a progressive work of the Holy Spirit *beginning* with regeneration but not accomplished at conversion as Durham would later teach, and he believed that the need for growth in sanctification ruled out sinless perfection.[96]

Despite wrangling over conversion and sanctification and some retorts against new evangelistic methods, the Wesleyan/Arminian theological tradition took firm and sprawling root in African American churches as the country moved from its Calvinistic heritage to a doctrinally broader Protestant evangelicalism.[97]

DEPRESSION AND WORLD WAR II (1930-1949)

By the early 1900s, quarters of American Christianity were leaning toward theological liberalism. Founded upon Enlightenment convictions from the eighteenth century, early twentieth century liberalism heralded optimistic views of man's moral capacity and rejected as *passé* the old orthodoxy of radical depravity and original sin. Among white Christians, men like Lyman Abbot (1835-1922), pastor at New York's Plymouth Congregational Church, advanced evolutionary perspectives on salvation, arguing, "Every man is two men—a divine man and a human man, an earthly man and a super-earthly man; he is linked to the lower, out of which he is emerging; he is linked to the upper toward which he is tending." University of Chicago Divinity School professor Shailer Matthews (1863-1941) proclaimed that "salvation centers

[95]Thomas G. Farkas, *William H. Durham and the Sanctification Controversy in Early Pentecostalism, 1906-1916* (Doctoral diss., The Southern Baptist Theological Seminary, 1993); William H. Durham, "The Finished Work of Calvary—It Makes Plain the Great Work of Redemption," *Pentecostal Testimony* 2, no. 2 (May 1912); William H. Durham, "The Great Battle of 1911," *Pentecostal Testimony* 2, no. 6 (January 1912); Paris, *Black Pentecostalism*, pp. 21-24.

[96]Elias Camp Morris, "Sanctification," *Sermons, Addresses and Reminiscences and Important Correspondence, with a Picture Gallery of Eminent Ministers and Scholars* (Nashville: National Baptist Publishing Board, 1901), pp. 32-35. It should be noted that Morris's critique of perfectionism revealed a misunderstanding of what Wesley meant by perfection. Wesley did not mean the absence of ignorance, mistakes, confusion or improper judgments, temptation or the need for growth. He saw Christian perfection as a freedom from the bondage of sin and freedom to love God due to the cleansing of original sin from the life of the believer, a life marked by no self-conscious acts of sin.

[97]Noll, *History of Christianity*, pp. 232-35.

about God in a man, not a man made into a God."[98] Among African Americans, progressive theological ideas made their way into African American expressions of Christianity through the works of men like Howard Thurman.

The modernistic liberalism and universalism of Howard Thurman. If Calvinism and a generally Reformed theology represent the first stream of African American soteriology and Weslyan/Arminian perspectives are the second, then the modernistic liberalism of Howard Thurman opens the third stream. Thurman biographer Luther Smith defined "modernistic liberalism" as a methodology that avoided appeals to biblical authority or tradition and sought empirical verification for faith claims. To this modernistic liberalism, Thurman appended an "evangelical liberalism" by holding a "religious teleology in which Christianity wins the world to profess Jesus Christ as Lord" by winning society to "the way" of Jesus.[99] Thurman was reportedly disinterested in converting individuals to Christianity from other religions. Instead, he favored a universalism that equated all religious truth and valued all religious traditions.

Thurman's philosophy of conversion, where it could be called "conversion," had more to do with a subjective encounter with the divine than with embracing Christ as Savior and Lord. In *Disciplines of the Spirit* (1963), Thurman detailed his understanding of religious "commitment," which was the clearest proxy for the Christian idea of conversion. He adopted the proposition of German mystic Meister Eckhart (1260-1328) who insisted that, "to the extent that a man rids himself of creatureliness, to that extent God *must* enter his life. When creatureliness gives way, God comes in automatically."[100] "Commitment" signaled the incoming presence of God to meet with the creature.

Thurman assumed a rather Pelagian ability of the individual to make such a surrender. Any hindrances to such surrender had to be eliminated or cleared. "The commitment is a self-conscious act of will by which (one) affirms his identification with what he is committed to." He understood that Christianity placed an "ever central, inescapable demand of surrender" upon the adherent, without

---

[98]Lyman Abbot, *The Theology of an Evolutionist* (New York: Outlook, 1925), p. 48; Shailer Matthews, *The Faith of Modernism* (1924; reprint, New York: AMS, 1969), p. 124; cited in Hannah, *Our Legacy*, p. 244.

[99]Luther E. Smith Jr., *Howard Thurman: The Mystic as Prophet* (Richmond, Ind.: Friends United Press, 1991), pp. 92-93.

[100]Howard Thurman, *Disciplines of the Spirit* (Richmond, Ind.: Friends United Press, 1977), p. 16, italics original.

exception and without the need for "any special talent, gift, or endowment."[101]

> The demand is direct and simple: Surrender your inner consent to God—this is
> your sovereign right—this is your birthright privilege. And a man can do it di-
> rectly and in his own name. For this he needs no special sponsorship. He yields
> *his* heart to God and in so doing experiences for the first time a sense of coming
> home and of being at home.[102]

Returning "home" to God was a "sovereign right" of all *people*—not God—
and did not require the mediating propitiation of Jesus' sacrifice. Thurman
sought to preserve the autonomy of individuals in conversion because to deny
a person's self-rule would be to deny one's personality. At this point, he distinguished his views from both Calvinism and Arminianism, opting for a fully
Pelagian understanding of human will. Previous generations recognized that
the corruptions of human nature disassociated man and God; but that notion
vanished in the thought of Thurman.

"Commitment" in Thurman's theology was analogous to Protestant Christianity's view of conversion and was evident in his comparison of the two.
Thurman saw Christian conversion as a defining moment when a person felt
the conviction of sin, renounced his past life and accepted a new way of life
through an encounter with Christ. "The conversion experience" was "the moment when at the depths of his being a man says 'Yes' to the will and the rule
of God in his life—the moment when he is cleansed, his life redeemed from
his old ways, and his feet set on a new path."[103]

Likewise, "commitment" provided a total reintegration of the self and re-
orientation toward something "outside the self, almost independent of it, to
which one can now refer when one's way is lost."[104] Whether instantaneous or
gradual, the realization of commitment released new creative energies for living a new life. The key was to remain open to the "inflow" or the "invasion of
the Spirit of God" by "yielding the real citadel" of the personality. By yielding,
the communicant discovered answers to the critical questions of personality
and existence: Who am I? What do I want? And how will I get what I want?[105]

---

[101]Ibid., pp. 17, 19-20.
[102]Ibid., p. 20, italics original.
[103]Ibid., pp. 23-24.
[104]Ibid., p. 24; see also *Creative Encounter*, pp. 72-80.
[105]Ibid., pp. 26-35.

So, "conversion" in Thurman's soteriology focused not on historical formulations of forgiveness of sin and redemption from God's wrath, but on self-fulfillment. Sin was not transgression against an external, universal law[106] but doing anything that goes against one's own values, to corrupt one's will by choosing against life.[107] Though Christian views of the cross offered some comfort in suffering,[108] the sacrifice of Jesus on the cross was not a necessary atonement for sins. For that, a person only had to open up to the truth that resided in him, to pray and seek the level of commitment that provided coherence to life.[109]

The mystical universalism of Howard Thurman might be summed up in his rather poetic description of the inward spiritual journey of every person:

> There is in every one of us an inward sea. In that sea there is an island; and on that island there is a temple. In that temple there is an altar; and on that altar burns a flame. Each one of us, whether we bow our knee at an altar external to ourselves or not, is committed to the journey that will lead him to the exploration of his inward sea, to locate his inward island, to find the temple, and to meet, at the altar in that temple, the God of his life. Before that altar, impurities of life are burned away; before that altar, all the deepest intent of your spirit stands naked and revealed; before that altar, you hear the voice of God, giving lift to your spirit, forgiveness of your sins, renewal of your commitment. As you leave that altar within your temple, on your island, in your inward sea, all the world becomes different and you know that, whatever awaits you, nothing that life can do will destroy you.[110]

CIVIL RIGHTS ERA (1950-1979)

With the dawning of the Civil Rights era, the theological notion of salvation took on a decidedly temporal character. Many eschewed the "otherworldly" view of salvation believed to characterize orthodox and historical African

---

[106]Howard Thurman, *Temptations of Jesus* (Richmond, Ind.: Friends United Press, 1978), p. 23.

[107]Thurman, *Disciplines of the Spirit*, pp. 58-60. In his discussion on page 60, Thurman identified this form of sin as "the unpardonable sin" that Jesus mentioned in His rebuke of Jewish religious leaders who insisted that He cast out demons by the power of the devil (Mt 12:31). Thurman interpreted this passage to mean that "the man who calls a good thing bad, deliberately" committed "the unpardonable sin because it is a sin against the Spirit of Truth." The Truth Thurman seemed to have in mind was not the Holy Spirit, also called the Spirit of Truth in Jn 16:13, but the correctness of following the dictates of personal principle. In this way, he spiritualized the text to support his philosophy.

[108]Ibid., pp. 77-78.

[109]Ibid., p. 103.

[110]Howard Thurman, *The Growing Edge* (Richmond, Ind.: Friends United Press, 1956), pp. 43-44.

American Christianity for a view seeking the political, economic and social "salvation" of blacks in America. This newfound emphasis—with roots dating back to the African American church's involvement in the abolitionist movement and the black nationalist tones of Marcus Garvey and others—marked a decisive shift from the more conservative biblical, theological, spiritual and ultimately eschatological view of salvation understood by Hammon, Haynes and other African American forerunners.

This new wave of black theologians swam in the third stream of African American theology opened up by liberal thinkers like Howard Thurman. Black theologians and preachers of the 1960s era were theological heirs of the liberal tradition that came to prominence in seminaries and universities around the country. Most theologically conservative seminaries adopted the racist segregationist policies and attitudes of the time. Because liberal seminaries and universities were more likely to admit and train African Americans, and the ethos of the Civil Rights movement was more compatible with theological liberalism than with its conservative counterpart, African American exposure to and adoption of liberal intellectual viewpoints was nearly guaranteed.

James H. Cone—the cross as liberation. The rise of Black Power militancy during the 1960s presented a new problem to black Christians committed to the faith. Militant voices denounced Christianity as "the white man's religion" and an insidious "ideological justification of black passivity."[111] In response, the liberation theology of James Cone insisted that salvation was not merely spiritual, but temporal and physical in nature. Cone insisted on a view of salvation that emphasized human liberation from oppressive structures. He argued, "The biblical God is the God whose salvation is liberation."

The cross of Christ signaled the divine affirmation of the liberation struggle, not the penal substitutionary atonement central to western Christianity's theological system. "The pain of the cross was God suffering for and with us so that our humanity can be liberated for freedom in the divine struggle against oppression."[112] The fundamental problem facing humanity was not sin

---

[111]James H. Cone, *God of the Oppressed* (Maryknoll, N.Y.: Orbis, 1997), p. 172.

[112]Ibid., p. 128; see also pp. 150-69 for Cone's discussion of suffering in light of the cross and resurrection of Jesus Christ. He concludes that, "the cross and resurrection of Jesus are God's decisive acts against injustice, against the humiliation and suffering of the little ones. Indeed, it is because God is disclosed as the Oppressed One in Jesus that the oppressed now know that their suffering is not only wrong but has been overcome" (p. 168).

and broken fellowship with God in the traditional sense, but the tyrannical powers of the ruling class. This was Cone's starting point and it shaped the individual and corporate dimensions of his soteriology.

Individually, Cone affirmed that fellowship with God was central—it was the beginning and the end of liberation. Personal conversion, or "a radical, transforming encounter with the One the people believe to be the foundation of their existence," resulted in a death to the old life and initiation into a new life of communion with God chiefly through prayer. Cone defined this liberation as "knowledge of self," a "vocation to affirm who I am created to be."[113] Individual conversion or liberation formed a "vertical sense of personal relationship with the God of Jesus" and indicated the beginning of black attempts "to take their history in their own hands on the basis of the gift of freedom made possible in and through divine fellowship." Individual liberation came "logically prior to the other components of liberation," but corporate expressions of liberation were important as well.[114]

Cone argued that, "authentic liberation of self is attainable only in the context of an oppressed community in the struggle of freedom."[115] Moreover, the concrete historical reality of the oppressed community was inseparable from the spiritual aims of God. By emphasizing the earthly ministry of Jesus Christ, Cone's soteriology attempted a serious reappraisal of the relationship between salvation and earthly pursuits of freedom and wholeness. He wrote:

> The historical character of liberation as an essential ingredient in salvation is also found in the New Testament. Jesus' message centered on the proclamation of liberation for the poor, and his exorcisms clearly illustrated that he viewed his ministry as an engagement in battle with the powers of evil that hold people in captivity. The healing of the sick, feeding the hungry, and giving sight to the blind mean that *Jesus did not regard salvation as an abstract idea or a feeling in the heart. Salvation is the granting of physical wholeness in the concreteness of pain and suffering.*
>
> Liberation then cannot be separated from the historical struggle of freedom in this world.[116]

---

[113]Ibid., p. 134.
[114]Ibid., p. 132.
[115]Ibid., p. 135.
[116]Ibid., p. 140, emphasis added.

For Cone, liberation and salvation were largely synonymous with self-determination in history. Consequently, "sanctification" became "the subjective appropriation of divine liberation." "Justification" became "the removal of oppressed black people from the control of white power, thereby making it possible for the enslaved to be free." "Reconciliation" with God entailed God's intrusion into human history to destroy servitude and white definitions of blackness objectively and black participation in the plan of God subjectively.[117]

Though Cone's soteriology emphasized human liberation and struggle in specific historical contexts, he attempted to temper his reliance on human struggle for temporal freedom with an eschatological expectation. He recognized a "not yet" aspect of salvation to be accomplished ultimately through the will and work of God.[118] This caveat notwithstanding, Black Theology practically equated the truths of biblical redemption and salvation in Christ to a divine edict condemning white oppression and sanctioning black resistance.

END OF CENTURY, POSTMODERN ERA (1980-PRESENT)

Eventually the flames and heat of the Civil Rights and Black Power era cooled as significant legal and social advances were achieved, and the momentum of radicalism faltered as a result of government opposition and internal disintegration. In the wake of these movements, strident individualism replaced group consciousness and solidarity. The 1980s ushered in the "me mentality" of popular psychology and the crass greed that accompanied newfound economic opportunities. Materialism swept up both white and African American culture.

Christians were not immune to these changes. Many believers became increasingly self-focused as they searched for meaning in one emotional worship experience or spiritual guru after another. In time, materialistic pleas for prosperity, health and wealth became the loudest appeals in popular Christian circles. Various adjectives reflecting the mood of the period adorned the term "gospel." "Full" gospel, "prosperity" gospel, and "health and wealth" gospel challenged the biblical gospel of Jesus Christ for supremacy on television and radio outlets.

As the culture moved toward individualism and materialism, an Arminian

---

[117]Ibid., pp. 214, 217.
[118]Ibid., pp. 145-49.

consensus further entrenched itself in African American views of soteriology. By the end of the twentieth century, Calvinistic tendencies were nearly extinct, surviving almost solely in the most self-consciously Reformed circles. This is not to say, however, that no significant soteriological differences existed within Wesleyan/Arminian frameworks. Persons holding common understandings of sin and the freedom of human will in conversion could nonetheless differ on major salvation-related doctrines like justification. Two of the most popular African American preachers of the late twentieth century, Tony Evans and Creflo Dollar Jr. (1962-), espoused similar understandings of the gospel and conversion but wildly different definitions of the justification of God that followed conversion.

Arminian orthodoxy and word-of-faith excess. Both Evans, pastor of Oak Cliff Bible Fellowship in Dallas, Texas, and Dollar, pastor of World Changers Church International in Atlanta, Georgia, hold to the Arminian conception of conversion. They both hold that man is born in sin, commits acts of sin, and is in need of a savior to rescue him from the wrath of God. They both hold that Jesus Christ is that Savior, who died on the cross to atone for the sins of the world. And, they agree that man is saved from the penalty of sin and eternal condemnation when he repents of sin and trusts in Jesus Christ as Lord and Savior. Both pastors also teach that, as a consequence of placing faith in Jesus, the repentant sinner is then justified by God. However, their understandings of justification are drastically different.

Tony Evans and Arminian orthodoxy. Though not Calvinistic in his doctrine of salvation, Evans's view of justification squared well with the broadest historically Christian teachings of both Calvinistic and non-Calvinistic Protestant tradition. Like most churchmen before him, Evans understood justification as "a judicial act by which God declares righteous those who believe in Jesus Christ." Justification was the "favorable verdict" that God rendered or declared upon those who renounced sin and trusted in the propitiating sacrifice of Jesus.[119] God's imputation of Christ's righteousness to the believer made such a verdict possible. Evans taught that, because the Scriptures depicted Christians as "being 'clothed . . . with Christ' (Gal 3:27) and 'hidden

---

[119]Tony Evans, *Totally Saved: Understanding, Experiencing and Enjoying the Greatness of Your Salvation* (Chicago: Moody Press, 2002), p. 33.

with Christ' (Col 3:3) . . . when God looks at us He sees not merely justified sinners, but His own dear Son." Consequently, "those who belong to Christ now stand in the same relationship to God as Jesus Himself."[120] Though there was a real change in the status of the sinner before God, that change depended wholly on the identification of the sinner with Christ's righteousness, a foreign righteousness provided through faith.

Though Evans saw justification as declarative or forensic, it was nonetheless real, demonstrating itself in "changes in our attitudes and behavior that are visible in the sight of others."[121] Evans insisted that the visible fruit of justification was a life of ethical virtue. A life of love and good works confirmed the presence of genuine saving faith and justification. Moreover, justification produced benefits in the life of a believer: peace with God, unlimited access to God through his Son, lasting hope and restored fellowship with God.[122]

Creflo Dollar and the "righteousness" that produces prosperity. One of the most popular African American televangelists of the late twentieth century is Creflo Dollar of Atlanta-based Creflo Dollar Ministries and World Changers Ministries International. As a member of word-of-faith Christianity, Creflo Dollar's soteriology was one part Wesleyan/Arminian and one part Pentecostal. On the surface, his view of man, sin and salvation shared much with that of William Seymour and other forerunners of the Pentecostal and Charismatic movement. However, Dollar's soteriology represented a far-reaching departure from the Arminian preachers before him despite reliance on the same passages of Scripture other Pentecostals and Arminians used to support their positions.[123]

Dollar's understanding of salvation begins with a distinction between "belief" or "mental acceptance of something as truth, though absolute certainty may be absent," and "faith" or "*acting* on what you believe."[124] This distinction lay at the heart of Dollar's theology and, in his view, explained the difference between those who prosper in God's blessing and the mere "wishers" who did

---

[120]Ibid., p. 38.

[121]Ibid., p. 39.

[122]Ibid., pp. 42-46.

[123]For example, both Evans and Dollar develop their doctrines of justification by commenting primarily on Rom 3—5 and 2 Cor 5:21.

[124]Creflo A. Dollar, *Not Guilty: Experience God's Gift of Acceptance and Freedom* (Tulsa, Ok.: Harrison House, 2002), pp. 8-9, emphasis added.

not act in faith and consequently did not receive healing, financial freedom or the blessings of righteousness in God's sight.

Righteousness or the doctrine of justification—understood historically as the forensic declaration of right standing before God secured through faith in Jesus Christ—depended in Dollar's soteriology on the distinction between faith and belief. Righteousness was available to all Christians, but only those who behave in ways corresponding to their belief (i.e., exercise faith) appropriated the righteousness available to them.[125] Both Evans and Dollar posited some concept of "benefits" derived from justification. However, while Evans tended to construe those benefits in terms of one's relationship to God, Dollar thought of the benefits primarily in terms of earthly or temporal advantages. So, while both defined justification as "right standing before God," Dollar stressed that, "I am righteous; therefore I can be healed. I am righteous; therefore, I have angelic protection. I am righteous; therefore, I will always triumph in Christ Jesus." Dollar continued with the claim that, "Every promise in the Bible hinges on my acceptance of the righteousness of God. By simply realizing His righteousness in me, the wrong in my life can be fixed. If I am poor, I have a right to prosperity. If I am sick, I have a right to be healed. If I am in bondage, I have a right to be delivered. Everything can be received through God's righteousness in me."[126]

Dollar's conception of righteousness included certain entitlements that never appeared in Reformed or evangelical Protestant theology in centuries past. Those who were justified possessed certain powers and privileges, but the powers and privileges of righteousness were often unrealized because Christians lacked the requisite faith to produce benefits. Dollar explained:

> The reason so many believers do not operate *at the same level of power as Jesus did while on earth* is that they do not accept the certainty of faith he has. He not only had the right to perform those miracles, but he could not be persuaded otherwise. When Jesus spoke the Word in fearless confidence he expected something to happen.
>
> Likewise, when our faith is mixed with fearless confidence in knowing we are the righteousness of God in Christ, we can confront debt and declare it to leave, and then live as though we are free from debt.

---

[125]Ibid., pp. 13-16.
[126]Ibid., p. 19.

People stand around you wondering why you think things are supposed to happen just the way you say. All you have to do is tell them that you have fearless confidence in knowing that *you are the righteousness of God.*

Just as Jesus did, we have to know that *as sons and daughters of God, we are righteous.* Like Jesus, we must have fearless confidence born of absolute faith in the Word of our Father, believing that it would be as He said it would.[127]

Instead of the orthodox understanding of justification or being declared righteous through faith in the sacrifice of Jesus Christ, righteousness became a *power* equal to Jesus' power. Moreover, instead of being *declared* righteous as in Evans's Arminian orthodoxy, the Christian was supposed to *be* the righteousness of God.

Assuming that Christians "*stand as equals with Jesus,*" Dollar contended that, "When you stand in the righteousness of God, *you stand in everything He is,* everything He has, and in the very same anointing He possesses!"[128] Alluding to 2 Corinthians 5:21, Dollar hinted at a "sons of God" theology that teaches the deification of the believer. Rather than the biblical picture of being "clothed with Christ" or being "united with Christ," Dollar pushed 2 Corinthians 5:21 beyond vicarious identification with Christ to an essential transformation of the believer in this life.

SUMMARIZING THE DECLINE

Three theological streams flowed through the doctrine of salvation in African American history. The first stream was the Calvinism adopted by the earliest generation of northern writers, preachers and thinkers and the broadly Reformed thinking of African Americans in the plantation South. Their convictions included the doctrines of radical depravity, sovereign election, the necessity of regeneration and a general denial of free will. God was the author and administrator of salvation.

The slave's adherence to the sovereign election of God in salvation is amazing given the perversion of the doctrines of election and predestination in support of slavery and the triumphalistic political theology of the day. Some writers of African American religious history assert that black Christians rejected

---

[127]Ibid., pp. 17-18, emphasis added.
[128]Ibid., p. 103, emphasis added.

predestination and election as incompatible with their lived experience in slavery, their hope of freedom in this life, and their view of God as just and benevolent. For example, Genovese asserts that "predestinarian doctrine did not appear in black religion" and "only rarely did Orthodox Calvinism come from the mouths of black preachers, and even in those cases its uses remain in doubt."[129] However, as demonstrated from the writings of Hammon and Haynes and the slave testimonies of conversion presented herein, orthodox Calvinism provided some of the foundational structuring elements of African American soteriological thought.

The Wesleyan/Arminian tradition, sparked among African Americans by the labors of Methodist churchmen, was the second stream of thought. Institutionalized by Richard Allen and the African Methodist Episcopal Church, Arminian soteriology with its higher view of human moral ability and freedom spread in African American faith communities during the 1800s, from the Second Great Awakening through the early 1900s. Holiness and Pentecostal revivals in the late 1800s and early 1900s represented flash floods of Arminianism and helped establish this soteriological view as the dominant perspective among African Americans into the present.

The transition to a predominantly Arminian soteriology represented a break from the earlier Augustinian and Reformed theology and led to a weakening of African American theology. Consistent with heightened optimism about man's moral ability (detailed in the previous chapter), later generations of African Americans appear to have downplayed the sovereign election of God and elevated the importance of human freedom in salvation. While taking seriously the biblical commands to repent and believe, this position failed to adequately address those passages of Scripture that plainly teach both man's moral inability and God's sovereignty in conversion.[130]

For example, though Seymour's statement of the basic requirements of the gospel was evangelical enough—repent from sin and believe on Jesus Christ and you shall be saved—his view of spiritual life once inside the family of God was totally heterodox. Where earlier writers viewed grace as the saving and preserving power of God toward the believer, Seymour's Pentecostalism held

---

[129]Genovese, *Roll, Jordan, Roll*, p. 243.
[130]See, for example, Jn 1:12-13; 6:65; 8:34; Rom 9:8-24; Eph 1:3-12; 2:1-10; 2 Tim 1:9.

that obedience and works preserved the believer. Where salvation was once impossible even to achieve in the power of the human heart/soul, it was now not only achievable but *ultimately maintained* by human effort. Worse, and perhaps predictable once human actions became the standard for the saint's preservation in Christ, eternal life could be lost as a consequence of the very sins for which Christ died. In the final analysis, faith in Jesus made salvation *possible*—it did not rest completely on the accomplishment and merit of the Savior but on the merits of the saved.

The worst part of the decline came, not with the move to Wesleyan/ Arminianism, which retained significant elements of orthodox doctrine found in the broader Reformation, but with the distortions of theological liberalism and word-of-faith and prosperity "gospel" excesses on the other. Theologically liberal streams opened up in the mid-1900s in the mainstream ideas of the Civil Rights movement and the revolutionary propositions of Black Theology. Black Theology achieved some academic success and reputation, and the iconic stature of theologically liberal leaders like Dr. Martin Luther King Jr. helped shape much of the church's social ethics. However, African Americans remained largely evangelical in their view of Scripture and conversion.

Word-of-faith messengers, while keeping orthodox enough statements regarding man and sin, obscured the gospel with a focus on material temporal blessings. For example, Creflo Dollar's doctrine of justification reproduces the very errors that divided Protestants and Roman Catholics for nearly five centuries. The difference between being *called* righteous and being *made* righteous, or between having a radically corrupted sin nature or being free from Adam's sin, are enormous and determine whether a view of the gospel and conversion is biblical or heretical.

6

"Gettin' in de Spirit"

Pneumatology in the African American Experience

And we believe in the Holy Spirit, the Lord and giver of life,

Who proceeds from the Father and the Son, Who is worshiped and glorified

together with the Father and Son, and Who spoke through the Prophets.

<small>FROM THE NICENE-CONSTANTINOPOLITAN CREED (A.D. 381)</small>

GENERAL INTRODUCTION AND CONTEXT

Most of the ink spilled in church history debating the nature of God has centered on the doctrine of the Trinity, especially the person and work of Jesus Christ and his relationship to the Father. The Nicene Creed, discussed in the previous chapter, illustrated the rapt attention paid to Jesus as the central figure of Christianity. The vast majority of the Creed devoted attention to the doctrine of Jesus Christ, with only two lines describing the early church's teaching on God the Father and the Holy Spirit.

Not withstanding Nicaea's silence regarding the *person* of the Holy Spirit, writings from church leaders in the second and third century developed a somewhat clearer understanding of the *work* of the Holy Spirit. For example, Novatian (c. 200-c. 258) of Rome wrote a treatise called *On the Trinity* in which he identified the role of the Spirit in inspiring the prophets and apostles in their missions, the indwelling ministry of the Spirit in the New Testament, the Spirit's guarding and guiding action in the church and the Paraclete who abides with the saints. Novatian wrote:

> This is He who in the apostles gives testimony to Christ; in the martyrs shows
> forth the constant faithfulness of religion; in virgins restrains the admirable conti-
> nency of their sealed chastity; in others, guards the laws of the Lord's doctrine in-

corrupt and uncontaminated; destroys heretics, corrects the perverse, condemns infidels, makes known pretenders; moreover, rebukes the wicked, keeps the Church uncorrupt and inviolate, in the sanctity of a perpetual virginity and truth.[1]

But despite the early church's progressing delineation of the Holy Spirit's ministry, there remained confusion about the relationship of the Spirit to the Godhead. Gregory of Nazianzus (c. 330-c. 390) conceded that a fair amount of ambiguity existed among the early church regarding the person of the Holy Spirit with some thinking of him as "an activity, some as a creature, some as God; and some . . . uncertain which to call him."[2] Justin Martyr (c. 100-c. 165) and Theophilus (later second century) of Antioch seemingly confused the Spirit with Christ the Word, and sometimes placed the Spirit below angels in priority. Others understood there to be three distinct persons in the Godhead but did not enunciate their equality or their relationship to one another. For its part, the first ecumenical Council at Nicaea simply issued the unadorned pronouncement "And [we believe] in the Holy Spirit."

Not surprisingly, then, early ambiguity in the years following Nicaea only prompted questions regarding the relationship of the Spirit to the Father and the Son. The Council of Constantinople (A.D. 381) affirmed the Nicene Council and clarified the consensus for the Eastern churches—the council determined that the Holy Spirit is equal to the Father and the Son and is the third person in the Trinity. Figures like Hilary of Poitiers (c. 315-368) and Augustine (354-430) reiterated the Council of Constantinople for the churches in the West.[3] Despite the schism between the Western and Eastern churches in the *filioque* controversy (A.D. 867-1054),[4] which at its root was an

---

[1] Novatian (c. 257) *Treatise Concerning the Trinity.* In Alexander Roberts and James Donaldson, eds., *Ante-Nicene Fathers, Volume 5, Hippolytus, Cyprian, Caius, Novatian, Appendix* (Peabody, Mass.: Hendrickson, 1999), p. 641.

[2] Cited in Jaroslav Pelikan, *The Christian Tradition: A History of the Development of Doctrine, Volume 1: The Emergence of the Catholic Tradition (100-600)* (Chicago: University of Chicago Press, 1971), p. 213.

[3] John D. Hannah, *Our Legacy: The History of Christian Doctrine* (Colorado Springs: NavPress, 2001), pp. 74-75, 80-81, 84-89.

[4] The *filioque* controversy involved a disputed amendment to the Constantinopolitan Creed addressing the Holy Spirit. To the Constantinopolitan statement that the Spirit proceeds from the Father, the provincial council at Toledo added three words: "and the Son." The strife erupted when the patriarch of Constantinople, Photius (c. 810-895) accused Pope Nicholas I of Rome (c. 819-867) of teaching heresy that destroyed the unity of the Godhead by insisting on two sources for the Holy Spirit. See Hannah, *Our Legacy*, pp. 87-88.

argument over theological accuracy and authority, the deity of the Holy Spirit as a consubstantial member of the Trinity survived as the orthodox doctrine of Christians everywhere and persisted as such throughout the medieval, Reformation and early modern periods.[5]

The doctrine of the Holy Spirit was well established at the founding of the New World and the birth of the new Republic, where in one sense, the doctrine receded to the background importance it maintained during the ecumenical debates from Nicaea to Constantinople. While other matters took center stage, European theologians in the colonies largely assumed historical orthodoxy for the person and work of the Holy Spirit or pneumatology.

However, among African Christians, the Holy Spirit figured more prominently in theological and doctrinal developments. Almost from the onset, particularly in the theological musings of enslaved Africans in the South, there appeared an emphasis on the Spirit's role in salvation and worship. And three decades after Emancipation, African Americans led the charge to reassert and defend the ongoing activity of the Holy Spirit in dispensing spiritual gifts. The doctrine of the Holy Spirit animated African American worship, revivals and theology in a distinctive manner, calling attention to the immediacy of divine-human interactions. The present chapter explores the development of pneumatology among African Americans.

EARLY SLAVERY ERA THROUGH ABOLITION ERA (1600-1865)

Northern writers: The tacit presence of the Spirit. Little novelty in ideas regarding the Holy Spirit existed in the early writings of African Americans in the North. As they had with most other doctrines, these writers followed the pattern traced out by the Reformers and other Protestant thinkers. As might be expected then, the pneumatology of northern black writers provided ambient background music but rarely played a spotlight solo in theological debate.

Jupiter Hammon's sermon *A Winter Piece* typified the northern penchant for nearly tacit acknowledgement of the deity and work of the Holy Spirit. Hammon, preaching on the salvation promised to those who "come to Christ laboring and heavy-laden," briefly mentioned the work of the Spirit in conversion with no reference to the Holy Spirit's person. He asserted, "Now, in order

---

[5]Hannah, *Our Legacy*, pp. 86-89.

to see God, we must have a saving change wrought in our hearts, *which is the work of God's Holy Spirit, which we are to ask for.*"[6] Without elaboration or defense, Hammon simply stated that the Spirit indeed had the power to change hearts and "guide you in the right way to eternal life."[7] Usually careful to cite and expound Scripture, Hammon glided over this supposition as though general knowledge made further comment unnecessary. His Reformed leanings made this omission all the more remarkable, since Calvinists often took pains to explain their convictions about the moral inability and ruin of man as a central tenet in their soteriological system.

A Winter Piece, a sermon that included major themes like sin, the moral corruption of man, repentance and regeneration, displayed a striking silence on the doctrine of the Holy Spirit. A mere two lines were devoted explicitly to the subject of the Holy Spirit. And yet, as though the entire work were an exposition of his pneumatology, Hammon ended the sermon with the curious declaration, "Here we see that if we are saved, it must be by the power of God's Holy Spirit."[8]

In short, Hammon's beliefs regarding the Holy Spirit were articulated in two ideas—conversion was the domain of the Holy Spirit and the Holy Spirit influenced and guided the sinner in seeking God.[9] Beyond this, it is uncertain whether Hammon knew little more about the doctrine of the Holy Spirit or whether he simply took for granted the orthodoxy prevalent in his day.

Lemuel Haynes's doctrine of the Spirit followed that of Hammon's. With slightly more detail, Haynes's pneumatology also proceeded from his understanding of the nature of man and regeneration. Disclosing his doctrine of the Spirit in one paragraph, Haynes reasoned:

If we consider that state that mankind are in by nature, as has been described

---

[6]Jupiter Hammon, "A Winter Piece," in Sondra O'Neale, *Jupiter Hammon and the Biblical Beginnings of African-American Literature* (Metuchen, N.J.: American Library Association, 1993), p. 98, emphasis added.

[7]Ibid.

[8]Ibid., p. 113.

[9]See also Jupiter Hammon, "An Evening's Improvement," in Sondra O'Neale, *Jupiter Hammon and the Biblical Beginnings of African-American Literature* (Metuchen, N.J.: American Library Association, 1993), pp. 167, 171. As in "A Winter Piece," Hammon only mentions the work and role of the Holy Spirit in two sentences. He refers to the Spirit making men "sensible of our own imperfections and desirous to love and fear God" and "the influence of the Holy Spirit to guide us through this howling wilderness and sea of trouble to the mansions of glory."

above, we need not stand long to know who to attribute this work to. It is a work too great to attribute to men or angels to accomplish. None but He who, by one word's speaking, spake all nature into existence, can triumph over the opposition of the heart. *This is the work of the Holy Spirit, who is represented in Scripture as emanating from the Father and the Son, yet co-equal with them both.* It is God alone that slays the native enmity of the heart—that takes away those evil dispositions that govern the man—takes away the heart of stone and gives a soft heart—and makes him that was a hater of God, an enemy to God, to become friendly to his divine character.[10]

Haynes understood the Holy Spirit in terms consonant with the early church, which argued for the Holy Spirit's deity based upon the divine works he performed.[11] He accepted the trinitarian conclusion that the Spirit was coequal with the Father and the Son. The Scriptures, he argued, demanded this doctrinal position. Since only God could convert, renew and sanctify a Christian, the Holy Spirit then must be God because these are the works ascribed to him in the Scriptures. It was "God the Holy Ghost" that applied "the purchase or merit of Christ's blood to [the Christian's] soul for justification before God."[12]

Though he described the Spirit as "*emanating* from the Father and the Son," nothing in Lemuel Haynes's writings revealed a concern for the *filioque* controversy. Rather, his teachings on the Trinity evidenced a soteriological orientation consistent with that of Jupiter Hammon and other evangelistic writers of the North. The primary way, then, of understanding the Holy Spirit was through his work in salvation. Only God conquered the human heart and re-created man through the new birth—actions performed by the Holy Spirit.

Southern writers: The ubiquitous Spirit in slave testimonies and song. If the Holy Spirit was little mentioned in the writings of northern blacks during the antebellum period, he was nearly everywhere present in the understanding of blacks in the south. The richest sources for African American views on the Spirit were perhaps the slave testimonies and songs, where the slaves commu-

---

[10]Lemuel Haynes, "A Sermon on John 3:3," in *Black Preacher to White America: The Collected Writings of Lemuel Haynes, 1774-1833,* ed. Richard Newman (Brooklyn: Carlson, 1990), p. 34.
[11]For a history of the development of the doctrine of the Holy Spirit, see, for example, Pelikan, *Christian Tradition, Volume 1,* pp. 211-25. On pages 215-16, Pelikan summarizes the soteriological arguments of Didymus, Cyril, Athanasius, and Basil in favor of the deity of the Holy Spirit.
[12]Lemuel Haynes, "On Baptism," in *Black Preacher to White America: The Collected Writings of Lemuel Haynes, 1774-1833,* ed. Richard Newman (Brooklyn: Carlson, 1990), p. 243.

nicated their thoughts on the attributes and roles of the Holy Spirit.

If one were to summarize the slave's view of the Spirit in one word, perhaps "perceptible" would be a good candidate. Enslaved Africans seemed primarily to think of the Spirit's presence and involvement with humanity as sensible, perceptible phenomena. One ex-slave recalled how slaves often concluded religious worship services with the following Canticle:

> Jest befo' day, I feels' 'im. Jest befo' day, I feels 'im.
> My sister, I feels 'im. My sister, I feels 'im.
> All night long I've been feelin' 'im.
> Jest befo' day I feels 'im. Jest befo' day I feels 'im.
> The sperit, I feels 'im. The sperit, I feels 'im.[13]

The pervasiveness of the Spirit in the sensory experience of the slaves was matched only by the pervasiveness of the song's constant refrain, "I feels 'im." The slave's personal experience of "feeling" the Spirit empirically verified the reality of the Spirit's existence and work; he had ways of "moving" people that were observable to the spectator and participant alike. Immanent and omnipresent described the person of the Holy Spirit in the Christian folk theology of African American southerners before the Civil War and Emancipation.

Slaves believed the Spirit exercised a direct agency with them, and in ways distinct from the experiences of white people. One white clergyman in 1832 noted painfully that, "Many of the blacks look upon white people as *merely* taught by the Book; they consider themselves *instructed by the inspiration of the Spirit.*"[14] Minerva Grubbs verified this preacher's observation as she described slave worship: "dey would git to singin', prayin', an' a-shoutin'. When de overseer hear 'em, he alwa's go make 'em be quiet lak. *You see, de white folks don't git in de spirit. Dey don't shout, pray, hum, an' sing all through de services, lak us do.*"[15] Some slaves attributed the difference between white and black encounters

---

[13] *The American Slave: A Composite Autobiography*, 41 vols., ed. George P. Rawick (Westport, Conn.: Greenwood, 1977), Supplement 1, 3:259; cited in Will Coleman, "Coming' through 'Ligion: Metaphor in Non-Christian and Christian Experiences with the Spirit(s) in African American Slave Narratives," in *Cut Loose Your Stammering Tongue: Black Theology in the Slave Narrative*, ed. Dwight N. Hopkins and George C. L. Cummings, 2nd ed. (Louisville, Ky.: Westminster John Knox Press, 2003), p. 59.

[14] Cited in Eugene D. Genovese, *Roll, Jordan, Roll: The World the Slaves Made* (New York: Vintage Books, 1976), p. 214, emphasis added.

[15] James Mellon, ed., *Bullwhip Days: The Slaves Remember* (New York: Grove Press, 1988), p. 85, emphasis added.

with the Spirit to a difference in religious sincerity. Former slave Dinah Cunningham speculated, "Well, maybe us does love the Lord just a little bit better, and what's in our mouth is in our hearts."[16] A sincere faith allowed one to "git in de Spirit" as Minerva Grubb saw it. It seems Grubb and others thought the hypocrisy of slaveholding white Christians placed such experiences with the Spirit beyond the pneumatic reach of whites. But for the masses of slave faithful, vocalizations, shouting and emotional exhortation accompanied genuine spiritual rebirth.[17]

In the view of slaves, if the primary attributes of the Holy Spirit were his immanence and omnipresence, the *work* of the Spirit consisted primarily of his animating worship and converting sinners. The presence of the Holy Spirit was the defining factor in true worship; his absence left a lamentable hole. Consequently, slaves sought their own worship venues and meetings in order to commune with God by his Spirit. One emancipated slave described the slaves' preference for spiritual meetings that reflected their worship preferences. "We used to steal off to de woods and have church, *like de Spirit moved us*—sing and pray to our own liking and soul satisfaction—and we sure did have good meetings, honey—baptise in the river like God said. *We had dem spirit-filled meetings at night on de bank of de river and God met us dere.*"[18]

The presence of the Holy Spirit indicated the presence of God, who allowed identification with him in song and prayer to the slave's "own liking and soul satisfaction." In separate religious gatherings, "African Americans were creating a religious culture of their own through the appropriation and transformation of the worship service."[19] "Dem spirit-filled meetings" provided an emotional catharsis and spiritual freedom for the slave who felt religiously repressed in white services.

However, the work of the Spirit in worship was not limited to mere emotional release. Some slaves recognized that in the supernatural acts of God—of which they included certain experiences reminiscent of African worship patterns like trances and shouting—there existed opportunity for resistance.

---

[16] Ibid., p. 187.

[17] Sylvia R. Frey and Betty Wood, *Come Shouting to Zion: African American Protestantism in the American South and British Caribbean to 1830* (Chapel Hill: University of North Carolina Press, 1988), pp. 122-24.

[18] Mellon, *Bullwhip Days*, pp. 194-95, emphasis added.

[19] Frey and Wood, *Come Shouting to Zion*, p. 122.

One slavery survivor recalled:

> Dey singin' an shoutin' till de break of day. Some goin' into trances an' some
> speakin' what dey called strange tongues, *dis wuz a good chance for de slaves to run
> away,* for wen' dey would rise up from dey trance some would run like de debbil
> wuz after him, an jes keep runnin' until he run clear off. So de w'ite folks den
> puts de trusty niggers to guard de door or de way dey leaves hit in de arbor, but
> hit is hard to make de trusty catch dem *for dey think hit de Holy Ghost dat is makin'
> dem run,* so dey is afraid to stop dem, *claimin' dey can't stop de Holy Ghost.*[20]

According to this witness, some slaves believed the Holy Ghost exerted influence beyond human interference. He stirred the worshiper to both religious
ecstasy and temporal rebellion. Moreover, their belief in the omnipotence of
the Holy Spirit offered justification for both the runaway's rebellion and the
"trusty" slave's inefficacy at preventing unwanted escape.

As important as the Holy Spirit was to slave worship experiences and resistance, slaves also considered the third person in the Trinity central to spiritual
conversion. Conversion necessitated the presence and work of the Spirit. That
work sometimes exceeded the slave's expressive ability but not their experiential recognition that the Divine was operating. "Many of the old Negroes were
ignorant, they could neither read nor write. They knew that the entrance of
'the Spirit of God' made a difference in their lives but they did not know how
to express it only in their limited way."[21] Most often the "difference" made by
the Spirit was the spiritual rebirth and awakening of faith in the slave. Such
conversions or rebirths occurred instantaneously in many cases and depended
solely on the immediate power of the Spirit and not the knowledge of the individual. In one sense, then, the slaves' view of the Spirit democratized a faith
that had been controlled by literacy requirements and restrictions imposed by
white missionaries like those of the Society for the Propagation of the Gospel
with their catechetical approaches to slave evangelization.

In the slave's theological outlook, the Holy Spirit gave "that old time 'li-

---

[20]George C. L. Cummings, "The Slave Narrative as a Source of Black Theological Discourse," in *Cut
Loose Your Stammering Tongue: Black Theology in the Slave Narrative,* ed. Dwight N. Hopkins and
George C. L. Cummings, 2nd ed. (Louisville, Ky.: Westminster John Knox Press, 2003), pp. 37-38,
emphasis added.
[21]George P. Rawick, ed., *The American Slave,* Supplement 1, 5:127; cited in Cummings, "Slave Narrative as a Source of Black Theological Discourse," p. 34.

gion" to the exuberant congregant. The slave was said to have "got religion" when the Holy Ghost changed his heart.

> I heard them get up with a powerful force of the Spirit, slappin' they hands and walkin' round the place. They'd shout "I got the glory. I got that old time 'ligion in my heart." I seen some powerful "figurations" of the Spirit in dem days.[22]

The most powerful and celebrated manifestation of the Spirit occurred in the conversion of the sinner to faith. As has been pointed out elsewhere, evangelical doctrines involving the Spirit's activity in conversion overlapped comfortably with traditional West and West Central African religious beliefs about communication with spirits in religious rituals.[23]

At the close of the antebellum era, African Americans North and South shared a major emphasis on the work of the Holy Spirit in quickening those "dead in trespasses and sins." They accepted the theological orthodoxy fashioned before them, particularly in the North where African American writers and preachers rarely mentioned the Holy Spirit in their discourses. And though slaves in the South readily accepted the triune nature of God, their main concern regarding the Holy Spirit was not his person but his presence and work among them in their worship and in producing spiritual change. The Holy Spirit seemed uniquely present among them in their religious exercises, where freedom of expression and emotion evidenced his approving participation. The slave's conception of the Holy Spirit laid the foundation for later Pentecostal fervor and pneumatology emphasizing miraculous gifts.

RECONSTRUCTION, "JIM CROW" SEGREGATION, GREAT MIGRATION AND THE "NEW NEGRO" MOVEMENT (1865-1929)

Until the establishment and control of a significant number of independent black churches and denominations, African doctrinal distinctives regarding the person and the work of the Holy Spirit developed primarily in the context of "hush arbors" and camp meetings where either egalitarian or quasi-independent modes of religious expression predominated. Camp meetings and revivals permitted unbounded exercises of the Spirit, detached as they

---

[22]Rawick, *The American Slave*, Supplement 1, 4:170; cited in Cummings, "Slave Narrative as a Source of Black Theological Discourse," p. 34.
[23]See, for example, Frey and Wood, *Come Shouting to Zion*, pp. 100-101.

were from the confines of ecclesiastical structure and hierarchy. But with the rise of the African Methodist Episcopal (AME) Church, the first independent African American denomination, and the spread of independent black Baptist churches, the organizational context changed significantly. Many African American leaders needed or desired more precision in theological matters, including the need to define more carefully the person and work of the Holy Spirit lest their efforts at institutionalization become "organized chaos."

Two categories of thinking emerged in the late nineteenth and early twentieth centuries. One category featured orthodox formulations made slightly more explicit and heightened reticence toward the freewheeling pneumatology of the slave quarters. Adherents of this category preferred more order in worship and often considered "gettin' happy" emotionalism a sign of sub-Christian behavior. The other category placed significantly more emphasis on the present-day manifestations of the Holy Spirit through supernatural gifts and miracles. This group held that the Spirit needed more freedom to move among his people, not less. In both cases, leaders reacted to southern folk rituals that dominated African American religious practice and popular theology. Bishop Daniel A. Payne typified the more cautious approach to the doctrine of the Holy Spirit, while William J. Seymour represented those who favored a fully blown Charismatic view.

The Spirit goes to church: The pneumatology of Bishop Daniel Alexander Payne. With the growth of independent African Baptist churches in the late 1700s and early 1800s and the rise of African Methodism in the years following the founding of Bethel AME Church in Philadelphia in 1816, the pneumatology that had been such a significant part of the "hush arbors" came indoors to the institutional church. African Methodist Episcopal founder Richard Allen left little evidence of his views on the Holy Spirit; so, defining the relationship between the church and the Spirit remained a task for a later bishop of the young denomination, Bishop Daniel Alexander Payne.

Opposing folk views of the Spirit. Some of the strongest statements Bishop Payne made regarding the Spirit were his denouncements of the popular practice of "praying and singing bands."[24] Payne championed the cause of educa-

---

[24] A generation earlier, other elite blacks like Andrew Bryan and Henry Evans, early leaders in the independent African Baptist church movement, also rejected such practices as improper for true worship. See Frey and Wood, *Come Shouting to Zion*, p. 181 n. 149.

tion among church leaders and laypeople alike. Without in any way intending offense, he considered the original founders and leaders of the AME church "unlearned" and "illiterate men," with the exception of Daniel Coker.[25] He maintained that, "An educated ministry is more highly appreciated by an educated laity, and hence always better supported. They act and react upon each other."[26] So, any practice that weakened this ideal drew the ire of the Bishop. The "Bands" were one such practice. In his autobiography, Payne described the practices and the challenges they presented to his pneumatology:

> I attended a "bush meeting," where I went to please the pastor whose circuit I was visiting. After the sermon they formed a ring, and with coats off sung, clapped their hands and stamped their feet in a most ridiculous and heathenish way. I requested the pastor to go and stop their dancing. At his request they stopped their dancing and clapping of hands, but remained singing and rocking their bodies to and fro. This they did for about fifteen minutes. I then went, and taking their leader by the arm requested him to desist and to sit down and sing in a rational manner. *I told him it was a heathenish way to worship and disgraceful to themselves, the race, and the Christian name.* In that instance they broke up their ring; but would not sit down, and walked sullenly away.[27]

Later, Payne attempted to instruct the leader of the bands in what he considered a more appropriate form of worship. Their exchange revolved around their differing views of the Holy Spirit, with the band leader expressing an understanding consistent with that developed in the "hush arbors" of the antebellum period and Payne conforming to a more orthodox position. Payne recalled the discussion:

> He said: "Sinners won't get converted unless there is a ring." Said I: "You might sing till you fell dead, and you would fail to convert a single sinner, because *nothing but the Spirit of God and the word of God can convert sinners.*" He replied: "The Spirit of God works upon people in different ways. At camp-meeting there must be a ring here, a ring there, a ring over yonder or sinners will not get converted." This was his idea, and it is also that of many others.[28]

---

[25]Daniel Alexander Payne, *Recollections of Seventy Years* (Nashville: AME Sunday School Union, 1888), p. 137.
[26]Ibid., pp. 220-21.
[27]Ibid., pp. 253-54, emphasis added.
[28]Ibid., p. 254.

Despite recalcitrant reactions, Payne crusaded against these practices and attempted reforms. The exchange with the bandleader revealed at least one reason for doing so: Bishop Payne held the traditional view that the Spirit of God worked effectually where the word of God was presented. In Payne's estimation, the use of "heathenish" and "disgraceful" rituals was not related to a true manifestation of the Spirit or proper worship of God, but revealed "that with the most stupid and headstrong it is an incurable religious disease" that probably deserved excommunication of the adherent.[29] True conversions, which were the province of the Holy Spirit, required order, decorum and the preaching of the Word.

The Spirit in the church and in Christ. In contradiction to the folk theology of his day, Payne insisted on more traditional understandings of the person and work of the Holy Spirit. While he regularly opened his addresses with an invocation of each person of the Trinity, indicating his subscription to the deity of the Spirit, most of Payne's comments focused on the Holy Spirit's work. For example, in his famous 1862 sermon delivered in celebration of the termination of slavery in the District of Columbia, Bishop Payne identified the Holy Spirit as the One who commits a congregation to a pastor's care, and he argued that just government and rulers were contingent upon the wise guidance inculcated by the Spirit.[30] Moreover, the Spirit of God inspired individuals for certain special tasks.[31]

However, Bishop Payne's pneumatology centered primarily on the role of the Holy Spirit in the life of the church and in the life of Jesus Christ. Regarding the Spirit's role in the church, Payne wrote that the Holy Spirit "lives, works, and moves in this temple by a direct agency." In the church, the "Comforter" or the "spirit of holiness and the spirit of truth" cooperated with the officers of the church in the work of the Christian ministry.[32] According to

[29]Ibid., pp. 255-57.
[30]Daniel A. Payne, "Welcome to the Ransomed; or, Duties of the Colored Inhabitants of the District of Columbia," in *Daniel A. Payne: Sermons and Addresses: 1853-1891*, ed. Charles Killian (New York: Arno Press, 1972), pp. 5, 12.
[31]Daniel A. Payne, *Recollection of Seventy Years*, pp. 223-24. For example, Bishop Payne asserted that, "individuals were moved by the Spirit of God" to support the founding of Wilberforce and other individuals, like Daniel Coker, to start schools for instructing youth. He saw his own mission to educate his people as a divine call from God.
[32]Daniel A. Payne, "The Quadrennial Sermon," in *Sermons Delivered by Bishop Daniel A. Payne Before the General Conference of the A.M.E. Church*, ed. C. S. Smith (Nashville: Publishing House AME Sunday School Union, 1888), p. 9; reprinted in Killian, *Daniel A. Payne.*

Payne, the Spirit instilled order and recoiled at practices like the ring shout. The growth of the church required order and organization.[33]

But by far, the majority of Payne's writings on the Spirit addressed the unique role the Spirit played in the life and ministry of Jesus Christ. On May 24, 1888, Payne delivered a sermon in honor of the ordination of Benjamin W. Arnett, Wesley J. Gaines, Benjamin T. Tanner and Abram Grant as AME bishops. Payne chose Isaiah 11:1-10 as his text, which outlined a "golden chain of the manhood of Jesus." Payne implored the newly elected bishops to "Let Jesus be your Teacher, your Guide, and your Counsel in every question concerning duty and character." He argued that Jesus was the perfect model of ministry for the new leaders because of the unique endowment of the Holy Spirit upon him. He interpreted the text's assertion, "The Spirit of the Lord shall rest upon him," as indicating that Jesus was "spiritual minded in all his feelings, all his thoughts, all the activities of the intellect, all the emotions and affections of the heart, and in the movements of the will," placing him "in perfect harmony and oneness with the spirit of the Father."[34] The Holy Spirit gave Jesus power from his birth and remained with him until his death. "All the powers of [Jesus'] soul and body were animated by the Spirit of the Lord," contended Payne.[35] Such animation by the Spirit made Jesus perfect in all his judgments and powerful in all his endeavors to serve God.

Daniel Payne's pneumatology was ultimately christological and ecclesiological in orientation. The distinguishing marks of the Spirit were to be found in the unique ministry he performed in the life of Christ and in the ordering of the church, and not in the "heathenish" antics of camp meetings. In making this case, Payne attempted to erect a wall against cultural preconditions that shaped theological positions. Theology defined appropriate "Christian culture." Culture was not to shape theology. The Bishop opposed the preservation of folk tradition at the expense of biblical orthodoxy.

William J. Seymour: Pentecostalism and the gifts of the Spirit. Despite his

---

[33]See, for example, Payne, "Organization Essential to Success for Quarto-Centennial of African Methodism in the South," in Killian, *Daniel A. Payne.*

[34]Payne, "The Ordination Sermon," in Smith, *Sermons Delivered by Bishop Daniel A. Payne Before the General Conference of the A.M.E. Church,* pp. 45-46; reprinted in *Daniel A. Payne: Sermons and Addresses: 1853-1891,* ed. Charles Killian (New York: Arno Press, 1972).

[35]Ibid., p. 53.

zealous efforts, Daniel Payne admitted that the masses of African Americans continued in "Spirit-inspired" practices like the ring shout and singing bands. The convergence of remnant African cultural patterns with African American adaptations of Christianity proved too strong to be easily reformed by a handful of men. In addition, some preachers and leaders intentionally and successfully propagated a doctrine of the Spirit that sanctioned what Payne and some others viewed as unbiblical excesses. One such man was William J. Seymour (1870-1922), leader of the Azusa Street revival of 1906-1909.

William Seymour, having received some instruction from Reverend Charles Fox Parham (1873-1929), a former Methodist Episcopal pastor and founder of the Bethel Bible College in Topeka, Kansas, set out to convince the world that the gifts of the Spirit were still active. While Parham claimed credit for "discovering" the Pentecostal phenomena at his Kansas Bible college, Seymour catapulted the doctrine and practice to worldwide significance. Seymour's doctrine of the Spirit featured a passing focus on the orthodox roles of the Spirit in conversion, but emphasized the Spirit's ministry of dispensing spiritual gifts like prophecy, healing and

Photograph of a "ring shout," a traditional spiritual ritual involving patterned and sometimes frenzied "dances" in response to preaching and singing.

some "gifts" not listed in the Bible like writing and singing in unknown tongues. Seymour's pneumatology was soteriological and ecclesiological, where Payne's had been christological and ecclesiological.[36]

The Spirit, tongues and missionary witness. While Seymour taught that all the gifts of the Spirit were operational in the church in all ages, *glossolalia* or speaking in tongues was the most controversial aspect of Seymour's doctrine of the Holy Spirit. The teaching—which maintained that speaking in un-

---

[36]Douglas M. Strong, *They Walked in the Spirit: Personal Faith and Social Action in America* (Louisville, Ky.: Westminster John Knox Press, 1997), p. 36. Strong organized the views of Seymour and early Pentecostals along three chief characteristics of the Spirit's presence and work: *glossolalia* or speaking in unknown tongues, empowerment for Christian witness and unity of believers across all categories of class, gender and race.

known tongues provided the "initial evidence" of baptism in the Holy Spirit—forced Seymour out of the Nazarene Church.[37] Most churches and denominations denounced the view as heretical and shunned early Pentecostals. Newspapers joined the rebuke as well. For example, the headlines of a first-page article in the April 19, 1906, edition of the *Los Angeles Times* disparaged the doctrine and the upstart movement when it read: "Weird Babel of Tongues, New Sect of Fanatics Is Breaking Loose, Wild Scene Last Night on Azusa Street, Gurgle of Wordless Talk by a Sister." Apparently, the worship experience at Azusa Street resembled that of the camp meetings and revivals of the preceding century, replete with trances, exuberant and ecstatic praise, shouting and being "slain in the Spirit." Such worship drew ridicule and opposition from many. Opposition notwithstanding, however, Seymour and his followers continued promoting their movement and their doctrine of the Holy Spirit.

Seymour taught that the gifts of the Spirit, including tongues, were available to all believers and normative for the church. Sprinkled throughout the issues of the *Apostolic Faith* were testimonies of not only "old men and old women but boys and girls" receiving the baptism of the Holy Ghost. According to the paper, "The gift of languages is given with the commission, 'Go ye into all the world and preach the gospel to every creature.'" The paper continued, "the Holy Ghost speaks all the languages of the world through His children" for the purpose of furthering missionary activity and authenticating the truth of the gospel message. Moreover, Seymour intertwined the normative experience of the Spirit, especially baptism with the Holy Spirit and glossolalia, with missiological fervor. The paper reported that "one young man was converted, sanctified, and baptized with the Holy Ghost, and spoke with tongues . . . was also healed from consumption" and "received many tongues, also the gift of prophecy, and writing in a number of foreign languages, and has a call to a foreign field."[38] Absence of the power conferred by Spirit baptism rendered witnessing for the truth of the gospel impossible according to Seymour.

---

[37]Vinson Synan, "Frank Bartleman and Azusa Street," in Frank Bartlemen, *Azusa Street: The Roots of Modern-Day Pentecost. An Eyewitness Account by Frank Bartleman, a Leader in the 1907 Azusa Street Visitation* (Plainfield, N.J.: Logos International, 1980), p. xvii.
[38]*Apostolic Faith* 1, no. 1 (September 1906): 1.

In defending their doctrine of the baptism of the Holy Ghost with the evidence of speaking in tongues, writers at the *Apostolic Faith* employed both their reading of Scripture and examples of revival in church history. Seymour concluded from Peter's sermon in Acts 2:14-39 that the promise of Holy Spirit baptism remained in effect "until Jerusalem comes."[39] In a short article titled "The Promise Still Good," one writer responded to the doctrine's cessationist attackers who appealed to 1 Corinthians 13:8, which reads "charity never faileth: Whether there be prophecies they shall fail; *whether there be tongues, they shall cease*; whether there be knowledge, it shall vanish away." The writers replied that, read in the context of verses nine and ten, Paul's argument in 1 Corinthians actually required the continuation of tongues until the return of Jesus Christ. They wagered the truth of their interpretation on the facts of history:

> At the beginning of the Eighteenth century, among the French Protestants, there were wonderful manifestations of the Spirit power accompanied by the Gift of Tongues. The early Quakers received the same powerful religious stimulus and had the Gift of Tongues. The Irvingite church, about 1830, had the baptism with the Holy Ghost, and spoke in other tongues. In the Swedish revival in 1841-43 there were the same manifestations of the Spirit and also the Gift of Tongues. In the Irish revival of 1859 there is the record of the power of the Spirit in winning souls and the speaking in tongues by Spirit filled men and women.[40]

The combination of biblical exegesis and historical evidence were meant to convince all who would believe that the Spirit of God still moved in the church and in the hearts of the willing. If Payne looked to annihilate such practices, Seymour sought to give them biblical and historical justification.

The Spirit, the church and spiritual equality. Seymour's doctrine of the Holy Spirit also accented the role of the Spirit in the church. Payne remonstrated against proto-Pentecostal exhibitions by arguing for order in the church as one of the Spirit's primary ecclesiological effects. Seymour taught that the Spirit was the "bishop of the church," presiding over the entire life of the church to give her power, not order. Churches organized and operating apart from the su-

[39]Seymour, "River of Living Water," *Apostolic Faith* (November 1906): 2.
[40]Ibid.

perintending presence of the Spirit were without divine sanction or power. "No religious assembly [was] legal without His presence and His transaction."[41]

Moreover, the ineffectiveness of churches found its origin in the lack of Spirit-given power.

> Sinners have gone to the meeting house, heard a nice, fine, eloquent oration on Jesus, or on some particular church, or on some noted man. The people have been made glad to go because they have seen great wealth, they have seen people in the very latest styles, in different costumes, and loaded down with jewelry, decorated from head to foot with diamonds, gold and silver. The music in the church has been sweet, and it is found that a good many of the church people seem to be full of love, but there has always been a lack of power. We wonder why sinners are not being converted, and why it is that the church is always making improvements, and failing to do the work that Christ called her to do. It is because men have taken the place of Christ and the Holy Spirit.[42]

Outward adornments and mere oratory vainly masqueraded as spiritual power in William Seymour's estimation. Schemes and tactics fueled by the wisdom and strength of men were impotent. Real power came from the indwelling Spirit that oversaw the church and converted sinners.

That same power also "credentialed" people for the work of the ministry. As Bishop of the church universal, the Holy Spirit anointed people for service and gave them authority to witness for the Lord to the ends of the earth. The Holy Spirit distributed these "credentials" when he baptized the saints "with fire" followed by signs and miracles. Seymour contended,

> Instead of new preachers from the theological schools and academies, the same old preachers, baptized with the Holy Ghost and fire, the same old deacons, the same old plain church buildings will do. When the Holy Ghost comes in He will cleanse out the dead forms and ceremonies, and will give life and power to His ministers and preachers, in the same old church buildings. But without the Holy Ghost they are simply tombstones.[43]

According to Seymour, wherever the Holy Spirit ruled, spiritual fruit followed. Consequently, any church that labored without the fruit of conversion,

[41]Seymour, "The Holy Bishop of the Church," *Apostolic Faith* (June-September 1907): 2.
[42]Ibid.
[43]Ibid.

peace and love was a dead church, not having the life of the Spirit.

One sign that the power of the Spirit was active in the church was the mark of unity in the church.[44] Borrowing the apostle Paul's metaphor of the body to describe the unity that Christians should share, Seymour called believers to "stand as assemblies and missions all in perfect harmony." He believed that "God [was] uniting His people, baptizing them by one Spirit into one body." The outpouring of the Spirit reconciled believers across racial, ethnic and class divisions. Seymour wrote:

> The work began among the colored people. God baptized several sanctified wash women with the Holy Ghost, who have been much used of Him. The first white woman to receive the Pentecost and the gift of tongues in Los Angeles was Mrs. Evans. . . . Since then multitudes have come. God makes no difference in nationality, Ethiopians, Chinese, Indians, Mexicans, and other nationalities worship together.[45]

The formative role that women played in the revival and the rapid spread across racial castes testified to the Spirit's power in the movement even from the outset according to Seymour.

Powered by the teaching of Seymour, the Azusa Street revival reached some measure of egalitarian success early in the movement. He proclaimed:

> It is the privilege of all members of the bride of Christ to prophesy, which means testify or preach. . . . [W]hen our Lord poured out Pentecost, He brought all those faithful women with the other disciples into the upper room, and God baptized them all in the same room and made no difference. All the women received the anointed oil of the Holy Ghost and were able to preach the same as the men. . . . It is the same Holy Spirit in the woman as in the man.[46]

The revival temporarily razed barriers against women and African Americans desirous of exercising authority in the church or preaching from the pulpit. Because the same Holy Spirit indwelled and empowered women and men, Seymour reasoned, unfettered access to the same ecclesial privileges was therefore required. Equal participation by all demonstrated the ruling presence and power of the Holy Ghost in the church.

---

[44]Ibid.
[45]Cited in Strong, *They Walked in the Spirit*, p. 46.
[46]Ibid.

Producing such distinction-abolishing unity in the church was "the office work" of the Holy Spirit according to Seymour. The Holy Ghost made all believers one in fulfillment of Jesus' prayer for unity in John 17. As Seymour saw it, this grand work of the Spirit needed to be welcomed in the church. The church required the Holy Spirit's power, offered first at Pentecost but no less available to all saints of every age.

DEPRESSION AND WORLD WAR II (1930-1949) AND CIVIL RIGHTS ERA (1950-1979)

African American views on the Holy Spirit remained essentially unchanged through the Great Depression, World War II and the Civil Rights era. Regional differences in attitudes toward "moves of the Spirit" defined most local congregations, with northern and Methodist churches exhibiting cooler attitudes akin to Bishop Payne's and Baptist churches in the South preferring "spirited" worship in both Pentecostal and non-Pentecostal congregations. The Great Migration helped to change this general distribution and the character of worship in many northern denominations and churches, but the basic poles typified by Payne and Seymour remained intact throughout the period.[47]

END OF CENTURY, POSTMODERN ERA (1980-PRESENT)

During the 1980s and 1990s, popular fascination with self-improvement influenced the way Americans thought about nearly every arena of personal endeavor. Books featuring self-help techniques and theories mushroomed in retail sales throughout the period as individuals sought panaceas to inadequacies in self-esteem, personal fulfillment, meaningful relationships, and material success. The self-help rage made inroads into Christian churches and affected the theological leanings of many. Perhaps the clearest example of this effect was the rise in popularity of the so-called health and wealth gospel associated with many word-of-faith and Charismatic personalities who re-conceptualized the doctrine of the Holy Spirit in ways that harmonized with the cultural ethos.

---

[47]For a good treatment of the Great Migration's impact on the character of worship in northern denominations and congregations, see James N. Gregory, *The Southern Diaspora: How the Great Migration of Black and White Southerners Transformed America* (Chapel Hill: University of North Carolina Press, 2005), pp. 197-235.

T. D. Jakes: Power from the Holy Spirit our helper. One of the most significant leaders shaping the idea of the Holy Spirit during the latter decades of
the twentieth century was Bishop T. D. Jakes of Potter's House Ministries in
Dallas, Texas.[48] An heir to the Pentecostal legacy of Azusa Street and William
Seymour and adherent to the Oneness theology that denies the orthodox understanding of the Trinity, Bishop Jakes downplayed traditional formulations
of the Godhead.[49] Despite his theologically heretical view of the Trinity, however, he resorted to trinitarian language when referring to the person of the
Holy Spirit. For example, the Holy Spirit *simultaneously* pleaded with the believer to accept God's will *while* Jesus the mediator interceded with the Father
on behalf of the Christian[50]—a doctrinal conclusion inconsistent with the se-
rial "manifestations" implied by most Oneness schemes. Elsewhere, referring
to the coming of the Comforter to replace Jesus, Jakes discussed the Spirit as
"another one just like [Jesus]" in ways that seemingly precluded a Sabellian interpretation.[51] But consistent with a Oneness understanding, Jakes avoided
deifying the Holy Spirit or discussing his person in ways that suggested his
distinctness as a person in the Trinity. Instead of dwelling on what he called
the "mystery" of the Trinity, the Bishop placed greater emphasis on the con-
soling and empowering work of the Spirit.

Bishop Jakes accepted the biblical language describing the Holy Spirit as
the Helper of the faithful. Generally, Jakes taught, the Holy Spirit helped the
believers by guiding them, assuring them of their adoption in God's family,
empowering them to witness, aiding in prayer and bearing spiritual fruit.[52] In
addition, the Spirit of God came as in John 16:8-11 to "reprove the world of
sin, and of righteousness, and of judgment."

But perhaps most significantly in Jakes's theology, the Holy Spirit relayed

---

[48]Along with Bishop Jakes several other prominent televangelists popularized the "prosperity gospel"
message that significantly altered the historical understandings of the work and person of the Holy
Spirit. Among them were pastors Creflo Dollar Jr. and Dr. Frederick K. C. Price. A number of lesser
known African American preachers and pastors also carried the message, while white leaders like
Benny Hinn, Kenneth Copeland, Kenneth Hagin and Rod Parsley took the message to predominantly white audiences.
[49]See chapter 2 for a review of Bishop Jakes's Oneness theology.
[50]T. D. Jakes, *Anointing Fall on Me: Accessing the Power of the Holy Spirit* (Lanham, Md.: Pneuma Life,
1997), p. 52.
[51]Ibid., p. 74
[52]Ibid., pp. 8-9.

the word of God and the will of heaven to the believer. Jakes interpreted the words of Jesus to his disciples in John 16:13 as a normative promise of Spirit-led guidance and truth available to all believers of all times.[53] According to Jakes, the work of the Holy Spirit included dispensing continuing revelation to Christians for their benefit and success in life. He summarized the revealing work of the Spirit thus:

> The Holy Ghost speaks for a variety of reasons. His word may be for you or someone else. He may testify to your spirit of God's faithfulness. He may give you direction. He may lead you to obey God's will for your life. He may speak into your spirit His special choice of companionship for marriage, ministry, or business. The Holy Ghost may be trying to close doors that are right but not timely for us. Finally, the Holy Ghost may speak a word of warning.
>
> God is trying to intervene in your life. He may use you to intervene in the life of someone else who may not be answering His call. Whatever the case, you can be confident that it is right because our *parakletos*, the Holy Ghost, only speaks the counsel that He has heard in Heaven.[54]

Such guidance, contended Jakes, became available only when the faithful were baptized with the filling of the Holy Ghost.

Bishop Jakes and other Pentecostals distinguished "receiving" the Holy Ghost at salvation from a subsequent "filling" of the Holy Ghost accompanied by the Pentecostal gift of speaking in tongues. Jakes believed, "You can be saved but not necessarily filled or baptized with the Holy Ghost. We receive the Holy Ghost as a mark of identity when we are saved, but another experience—the baptism in the Holy Ghost—awaits us."[55] Being "filled with the Holy Ghost" was not merited by the believer, rather it was a gift of God's grace made possible by Jesus' intercessory prayer on behalf of the saints, genuine conversion and the believer's "asking, seeking and knocking" for the gift.[56] Here, Jakes's doctrine diverged from Seymour's who emphasized sanctification or holiness as a prerequisite for being filled with the Spirit and at times exhorted Christians to prayerfully tarry for the gift. As if speaking to Seymour or others holding his doctrinal position, Jakes argued, "Many

---

[53]Ibid., pp. 53-54.
[54]Ibid., p. 91.
[55]Ibid., pp. 11-12.
[56]Ibid., pp. 17-19.

have made the baptism of the Holy Ghost and the Spirit-filled life so difficult when actually it is quite simple. Many have taught that if you wait long enough, if you pray hard enough, if you lift your hands, sell out, hold on or hold out that you will receive the Holy Ghost. While their intentions may be good, their approach is not scriptural."[57]

The condition of holiness was ambiguously related to being filled with the Spirit in Jakes's theology. On the one hand, he concluded that "the prayers of Jesus, the pleading of the blood in His Passover, and anticipation of the power of Pentecost" made a person "a worthy candidate." But on the other hand, the supplicant "must sweep [her] house" or "purge [himself] of anything that isn't of God."[58] Moreover, in contradiction to the slaves' view of the Spirit's irresistible omnipotence in possessing his devotees, Jakes espoused the possibility of hindering, resisting and denying the Spirit.[59]

Consistent with the self-help atmosphere of the 1980s and 1990s, Jakes believed that the ministry of the Spirit was to "impact lives" in ways that produced material and social success. Again, his understanding of the mission of the Holy Spirit in empowering people differed from earlier Pentecostal forbears. Seymour had linked the filling of the Spirit and the gift of tongues with missionary objectives; Jakes saw the Spirit as enabling people to "reach their potential." Statements like, "In order to fulfill everything that a sovereign God has ordained for your life, *you must use the power of the Holy Ghost to reach your potential and destiny,*" demonstrated the influence of the self-help zeitgeist of the 1980s on his theology.[60] What had been power for the spread of the gospel through the agency of God the Holy Spirit became power for the actualization of human potential and desires.

The gift of tongues in Jakes's theology became a primarily private and therapeutic activity to achieve intimacy with God. Jakes theorized that two types of tongues existed, a private prayer language and an utterance for the public assembly of the church.[61] While tongues were available to all believers, understanding of the spiritual language was at times obstructed in the life of

[57]Ibid., p. 18.
[58]Ibid., pp. 19, 21.
[59]Ibid., p. 18.
[60]Ibid., p. 69, emphasis added.
[61]Ibid., pp. 39-40.

a believer.[62] Bishop Jakes defended the contemporary practice of speaking in tongues by using arguments advanced by Seymour from 1 Corinthians 13 and by offering his own interpretations of Scripture to support the practice.[63] But on the whole, Jakes promulgated a doctrine of the Holy Spirit and a view of the divine gift of tongues that subjugated the gift to the whims of human needs. He encouraged his readers to speak in tongues because doing so "confused Satan," improved access to "what you need," produced results, improved knowledge of spiritual things and relieved anxiety.[64] Preoccupation with self, success and psychological well-being characterized Jakes's pneumatology and reduced the Holy Spirit to an ever-present "backup" for our worldly difficulties.

SUMMARIZING THE DECLINE

We began this chapter with a brief overview of the early church's teaching on the Holy Spirit in the ecumenical creeds of the first five centuries. The church fathers made rather brief, unadorned statements about the Holy Spirit, in large measure because of ongoing and more virulent debates about the nature of Jesus. Consequently, unlike the more refined orthodoxy defining God the Father or God the Son, African Americans inherited from their Western brethren less theological material from which to begin construction of a doctrine of the Holy Spirit.

In the vacuum left by their Christian forebears, African Americans developed a pneumatology that combined remnants of African beliefs concerning the spirit world and some teachings from Scripture, especially those associating miraculous gifts with the work of the Holy Spirit. The result was a doctrine of the Holy Spirit more inclusive of cultural patterns and ideas than either what was known in the Scriptures or by the early church fathers. Some, like Bishop Daniel A. Payne of the African Methodist Episcopal Church, expressed disdain for the development and practice. Others, like William J. Seymour, promoted the doctrine and practice as biblical and necessary to the Christian life.

---

[62]Ibid., pp. 82-83.
[63]Ibid., pp. 35-39. For an example of bizarre interpretations, see his use of Jas 3:2-8, where the writer warns of the unruly and evil acts of an unbridled, unholy tongue. Jakes misinterprets this Scripture by concluding that God "took the most difficult, uncontrollable member of our bodies and caused it to yield to divinely inspired speech," though the passage makes no reference to the gift of tongues.
[64]Ibid., pp. 46-62.

While most everyone will admit to some excesses and errors of one sort or another where the Holy Spirit is concerned, the greatest devolution and errors belong to the word-of-faith and Charismatic excesses of preachers like Bishop T. D. Jakes of Potter's House Ministries in Dallas, Texas. Bishop Jakes's conception of the Holy Spirit essentially reduced the third person of the Trinity to a self-help force in this therapeutic age. This is in addition to his denial of the Trinity in the form of Oneness Pentecostal views of the Godhead. In its worst form, the word-of-faith and Charismatic errors of teachers like T. D. Jakes and others displaces the Holy Spirit's central role in pointing people to Jesus Christ and the gospel.

The comparative silence of the early church on the doctrine of the Holy Spirit is understandable. The Holy Spirit, the third and most enigmatic person in the Trinity, defies precise definition in many ways. Moreover, the Scripture teaches that his mission is not to draw attention to himself, but to focus the world on the Son (Jn 15:26; 16:13-15). All that he does is meant to reveal or affirm more about Jesus. So, the construction of a doctrine that focuses on the Holy Spirit in isolation of the Son is bound to be fraught with complications and risk serious error or excesses. The history of pneumatology among African Americans records both precision and error as some have wrestled with the mercurial nature of the Spirit.

Perhaps the wisest course is to first establish some criteria for evaluating theology in this area, rather than commencing with evaluations based upon personal preferences. Three are offered here.

First, we should make every effort to measure our pneumatology by as thorough an understanding of the Bible's teachings as possible. The Bible assigns the Holy Spirit all the prerogatives of deity. He is an agent in creation (Gen 1:2), sovereignly produces a new birth in fallen humanity (Jn 3:5-8), knows the mind of God (1 Cor 2:7-16), sovereignly distributes spiritual gifts in the church (1 Cor 12:4-11), and convicts the world of sin, righteousness and judgment (Jn 16:8-11). Whatever else might be said about the person and work of the Holy Spirit, if our theology is to be biblically accurate, it must be said that the Spirit is God, one with the Father and the Son. Most of all, teachings that contradict the Scriptures are to be rejected. The Oneness Pentecostal denial of three persons in the Godhead is one such example.

Second, it is essential to ask "Does my doctrine of the Holy Spirit point me to Jesus Christ?" This criterion follows directly from Jesus' teaching on the role of the Holy Spirit. "When the Counselor [the Holy Spirit] comes, whom I will send to you from the Father, the Spirit of truth who goes out from the Father, he will testify about me" (Jn 15:26). The mission of the Holy Spirit is to "bring glory to [Jesus] by taking from what is [his] and making it known" to his disciples (Jn 16:14). Any doctrine of the Holy Spirit, his gifts and role in the church that does not make clear that he came to bring Jesus more glory and to make Jesus known ought to be roundly rejected as contrary to the teachings of Jesus and abandoned by the church.

Third, it seems prudent to admit that not every African cultural retention that influences or finds some compatibility with Christianity is worthy of the name "Christian." There may very well be certain commonalities between African dance and ritual trances and supernatural occurrences in the biblical record, for example, but similarities in and of themselves do not warrant the continued observance of practices that may not be properly biblical. Discernment is needed. And courage to modify practices may be required. In many cases, our theology may be shaped more by historical and cultural practice than by Scripture. While history and culture may not always be at odds with Scripture, a vigilant guard against inappropriate theological conclusions drawn from history and culture must be maintained.

Afterword

When I sat down to write a book, I wanted to write something about the African American church—something about its current state and ideas for improving its health. As I drafted outlines for that project and considered topics for each chapter, it became increasingly clear to me that I needed to know something more about the theological ideas and changes that have resulted in the contemporary church. The church as it is today is a product of the many saints and sinners that have gone before, from the first converts to Christianity in the 1600s to today's televangelists and megachurch pastors. Proposals for the future depend largely on an accurate understanding of the past. So, I set aside the first book idea and the current work was born.

The African American church has grown through several distinct periods of history and adapted to the various social contexts in which it found itself. In many respects, these changing contexts have worked to shape African American theology as well. On the one hand, that theology sustained a community of faith and practice in the face of tremendous odds. But on the other hand, those changes threatened and weakened the biblical integrity of the church's understanding of God.

At the start of this work, I assumed that not much material would be available from early African American history and that the material available would be rather crude given the effects of slavery on the intellectual production of African people. I was wrong on both fronts! What I found was a significant stockpile of theological reflection and application from men and women whose minds were sharp toward God even if they were blunted by oppression in other areas. Slavery had not shackled their pursuit of God. Speaking to me were men and women who had wrestled with the deep truths of Scripture and arrived at a self-conscious Reformed theology—a theology that I share.

What emerged, then, was a story line. From the earliest period of African American writing to the present, a clear and distinct theological decline could be traced. The rich God-centered treasure troves of Lemuel Haynes, Phillis Wheatley and others were plundered, wasted and forsaken until the fool's gold of much of contemporary African American theology and preaching were all that remained. This is not to say that the decline was always steady or precipitous, or that those who participated in the weakening of African American doctrine did so intentionally. I assume the sincerity of the men and women highlighted in this book, and I believe most of them were earnestly attempting to apply the teachings of Christianity to the pressing social problems of their day. But sincerity and truth are not synonyms. Theological errors and, in some cases, heresies have opened up fault lines that threaten to quake and destroy the souls of those inside a crumbling church. Faulty theology is not a victimless crime.

And, to be clear, the doctrines surveyed in these pages are not minor tenets better left to individual preferences and whims. These doctrines strike at the heart of what it means to be Christian, what it means to be saved from the wrath of God to come, what it means to know God and Jesus Christ whom he has sent. They define whether or not one can sensibly and credibly claim to be a disciple of Jesus Christ. If one is a disciple, then she or he must *at least* believe the things that Jesus believed and taught. And in far too many instances, the voice of Jesus is muffled and muted in the African American context such that following him as a disciple is nearly impossible.

And yet, the gates of hell shall not prevail against the Lord's church. The Lord has a remnant of believers who love the Truth, who hold fast to the faith once and for all delivered to the saints, who long to see the faithful turn from old wives tales and empty philosophies to embrace the eternal Word. They do not labor in vain, for those who hunger and thirst after righteousness will be filled.

There are a number of dangers associated with writing a book like this. First, there is the risk of painting too broadly or with one color. The vast history surveyed here is nuanced and complex, and deserves better craftsmanship than I have delivered. I pray that others will successfully tell the story better than I could.

Second, there is the danger of appearing uncharitable. I think the topics treated in this book are eternally important, and so I address them as forthrightly as possible. In doing so, I desperately wish not to appear unloving or unkind. The critiques and evaluations in the book are aimed at the ideas and their consequences, and not the particular people included. If it appears so, I pray that the reader will charge the error to my head and not my heart.

Third, there is the danger of biting off more than you can chew. I am acutely aware of succumbing to this temptation. There is far more I would like to include. Outlines for chapters on ecclesiology and eschatology are left on the cutting room floor. Several important figures, many of them women, are silent in this volume. Should the Lord tarry and give me favor, perhaps future efforts will correct for these important omissions.

Fourth, historical surveys of this sort are generally filled with diagnoses but short on prescriptions. This volume suffers in this respect as well, though in the comments that follow I hope to at least sketch one perspective on the way forward.

RECENTER THE BIBLE

Most theological difficulties stem from root deficiencies in comprehending the nature and content of the Bible. Though African Americans are predominantly evangelical in their attitudes toward the Bible—that is, we believe it to be the "Word of God" in some sense—we are no longer centered upon the Bible in faith and practice.

Our forefathers understood that the contents of the Scriptures were powerful because they contain the message of God to his people. Reading the Bible was the dying ambition of many slaves. Its words were manna from heaven for a starving soul. *Inerrant* and *inspired* were not common parlance, but the *ideas* these words represent were once commonly held. It was the perspective of our earliest leaders and thinkers. And, more importantly, Jesus and his disciples held and taught this high view of Scripture.[1]

Today, we need desperately to recenter the Bible in the life and practice of the church. We need to read the Bible, sing the Bible, preach the Bible, pray the Bible, think the Bible and live the Bible. More liberal and postmodern respondents may recoil at this plea, charging such Christians with "bibliolatry"

---

[1]See, for example, Mt 22:29-32, 43-44; Mk 12:36; 1 Thess 2:13; 2 Tim 3:16; Heb 1:1-2; 2 Pet 1:20-21.

and fundamentalist backwardness. But it must necessarily be God who dictates how acceptable worship is given and how his subjects are to live. And he does that through his Word, to which we are to submit and by which we are to fashion our lives. There are no answers to the identity of God and his requirements for his people outside the Bible. Therefore, outside the Bible there is only idolatry.

Recentering the African American church on the Bible suggests a (re?)discovery of the "regulative principle," where God's Word is seen as the norm for regulating the faith and practice of the church.[2] It demands the recovery of a literary hermeneutic, by which I mean the literal interpretation of Scripture in accord with the genre of Scripture studied and taught. Recentering the church on the Bible requires the best "expository preaching" possible, where the meaning of a passage of Scripture is "exposed" and the main point of the text is the main point of the sermon.[3] These are the kinds of principles that will make God's voice central and audible to his people.

By no means does the Bible answer all of the difficult questions and challenges of faith and life. However, it answers the truly fundamental questions concerning God, meaning, purpose, salvation and hope. Apart from it, we will wander blindly in the dark wilderness of idolatry and pragmatism for untold generations.

REEXALT GOD

One tragic result of the theological decline among African Americans—and the evangelical church in general—is a decline in our estimation of God. It is ironic that of all the people one might expect to hold a low view of God because of their circumstances, the African slave actually held the highest view. Despite all the suffering and oppression of slavery, slaves maintained a view of God that emphasized his sovereignty and his goodness. They were committed to the biblical revelation that exalted God in all of his perfections.

Over time, God became smaller and smaller in the teaching of many Af-

---

[2]Philip Graham Ryken, Derek W. H. Thomas and J. Ligon Duncan, eds., *Give Praise to God: A Vision for Reforming Worship* (Phillipsburg, N.J.: P&R Publishing, 2003); D. G. Hart and John R. Muether, *With Reverence and Awe: Returning to the Basics of Reformed Worship* (Phillipsburg, N.J.: P&R Publishing, 2002).
[3]Mark Dever, *Nine Marks of a Healthy Church* (Wheaton, Ill.: Crossway Books, 2004), see chap. 1.

rican Americans. Sovereignty, the crowning attribute of God, received quick dismissal as some reasoned from their own philosophies that God could not be both good and the ultimate ruler if evil existed. Surprisingly, this view did not catch hold until African Americans were free from chattel bondage, until God intervened in history to prove his goodness by delivering us. And not surprisingly, as our estimation of God shriveled, what we deemed within the scope of God's concern and rule also diminished. When once we acknowledged that he orchestrated all events for his glory, we now assume he exists merely to bless us with worldly riches. Once African Americans proclaimed God sovereign in the salvation of sinners, now he is relegated to one choice among many in a postmodern buffet of divine options. African Americans were once a zealously missionary people because they believed in that biblical God whose kingdom advanced inexorably toward worldwide dominance. Now, God appears as a bellhop who enthusiastically hustles to earn the "tip" of our tithes in exchange for bringing us whatever we name and claim.

If ever we needed a God-sized view of God it is now. If ever we needed to behold the resplendent glories of Jesus Christ who saves sinners by his blood it is now. Local deities bound by the will of man must be shattered for the idols they are! We must return to our first love. We must exalt the God of Abraham, Isaac and Jacob, the God of wrath, abounding grace, love and redemption, the one true God in whom all things consist. In our preaching and our living, we need to raise our gaze to him who rules heaven and earth in unapproachable glory. God made us for his own glory. He redeemed us for his glory. And he rules all things for his glory. May all those who love God seek to once again live for his glory in all things among all people.

RECOVER THE GOSPEL

Recentering the Word of God in the life of his people will help tremendously in recovering the gospel of Jesus Christ. Today, there are a number of false gospels—which really are not gospels at all—masquerading as the biblical gospel. These impostor gospels threaten the eternal souls of those who believe them and those who preach them. The apostle Paul was willing to confront all false teachers with the truth of Jesus Christ, and to even correct fellow apostles when they erred in their application of the gospel.[4] The good news about the birth, death and resurrection of Jesus Christ is worth fighting for; without it, we all perish.

We must return to making the biblical gospel the foundation for our Christian fellowship and our social ethics. That gospel holds that man is ruined in sin, estranged from God and in profound danger of eternal torment and condemnation in hell. But, God, who made man in his own image for eternal fellowship with him, has acted in history to redeem man from sin and his wrath to come. God the Father sent God the Son to live the perfect life of worship and obedience to God that we could not and would not live. Jesus volunteered to both live that life and to pay the penalty of death that we owed for our sin. He suffered on Calvary's cross, died a criminal's death as a substitutionary propitiation and atonement for our sins. Three days later, he was raised from the dead victorious over sin, death and the grave. Now, all who repent of their sins and believe on Jesus will be saved from the just penalty of their sins, justified before God and given a new life with God. This is the message of Christianity, the message that should dominate all Christian preaching.

Along with recovering the gospel, there is a significant need to recover a biblical understanding of conversion. Because the gospel is unclear in many circles, conversion is also unclear. And where the gospel is unclear, the souls of men dangle above perdition without the one message that can rescue them from falling into the depths of hell. In our effort to lead God's people, we need to prayerfully and carefully teach our people how the Bible describes conversion. Then, we need to encourage our people to examine their lives for evidence of saving grace and spiritual fruit confirming their conversion. In too many places, an unregenerate membership and leadership strangle the local church with unbelief and unredeemed living. Plumbing the depths of the gospel, including the imperative to live changed and holy lives, will work a profound and lasting effect in individuals, in families, in the church and in society.

REVITALIZE THE CHURCH

We are now living in a generation of African Americans who are significantly unchurched. For three centuries, the black church stood as the central institu-

---

[4]See Gal 2, for example.

tion of black life. Its relevance was unquestioned and its moral and spiritual capital unparalleled. Now, the church is largely viewed as irrelevant by vast numbers of mostly young African Americans, despite concerted efforts to make the church a multipurpose human service organization with housing, child care, after school, health care, economic development and other social service programs. It seems the more the church does the less relevant it becomes.

The reason for this state of affairs is that the unbelieving world tacitly understands that the primary reason for the church's existence is not temporal. Though the world is wracked with pain and suffering, it intuitively grasps the fact that the answers it longs for are transcendent, not earthly. So, the more the church appeals to the world's felt needs and physical deprivations, the more irrelevant it becomes to those who lack a true and saving knowledge of Jesus Christ.

The church needs to be revitalized with a sound theology and a praxis governed by the Word of God. Historically, theology was the domain of the church, as those called to serve Christ in the ministry of Word and sacrament committed their lives to the study of the Scriptures. The advent of modern seminaries displaced the church as the theology-generating institution of Christian life. With this transition, theological ideas became the elite province of academicians and individuals with essentially no accountability to living congregations and ecclesiastical bodies. Today, many rogue speculations infiltrate and corrupt the church's teachings and lead to extra- and nonbiblical abuses. When combined with the marketing muscle of the digital age and popular publishing, these ideas create a bewildering maze of concepts that exclude the average churchgoer from the esoteric theology club. Consequently, rigorous knowledge of God as he revealed himself in the Scriptures evades both pulpit and pew.

Pastors must be trained in sound doctrine and practice. This does not necessarily mean seminary training, but it should always include training in a local church learning from and serving alongside faithful pastors. As the church once again becomes the main training center for affirming and issuing the call to prospective pastors who labor to preach the entire counsel of God, revitalization of the church will occur. As the gospel—and the real Jesus of the gospel—recaptures the message and mind of the church, revitalization of the church will inevitably occur. When we once again stand in awe of God, we will find ourselves in a great company of saints rekindled with passion for the glory of God and the purity of his people, the church.

My prayer is that the Lord of lords and King of kings will be pleased to revive us, to turn today's watered-down "faith" back into the enduring faith once for all delivered to the saints, and give us a holy zeal for his glory above all things.

Bibliography

Allen, William Francis, Charles Pickard Ware and Lucy McKim, eds. *Slave Songs in the United States*. New York: A. Simpson, 1867.

Andrews, Dale P. *Practical Theology for Black Churches: Bridging Black Theology and African American Folk Religion*. Louisville, Ky.: Westminster John Knox Press, 2002.

Bailey, Richard A., and Gregory A. Wills, eds. *The Salvation of Souls: Nine Previously Unpublished Sermons on the Call of Ministry and the Gospel by Jonathan Edwards*. Wheaton, Ill.: Crossway Books, 2002.

Bartleman, Frank. *Azusa Street: The Roots of Modern-day Pentecost, An Eyewitness Account by Frank Bartleman, A Leader in the 1907 Visitation*. Plainfield, N.J.: Logos International, 1980.

Bay, Mia. *The White Image in the Black Mind: African-American Ideas About White People, 1830-1925*. New York: Oxford University Press, 2000.

Baysmore, Joseph. *"Falling from Grace," "Baptism," and "Predestination;" Sermons by Elder Joseph Baysmore, of Weldon, N.C. to Which Is Added His Lecture on Humanity*. Raleigh, N.C.: Edwards, Broughton, 1878.

————. *A Historical Sketch of the First Colored Baptist Church Weldon, N.C., with the Life and Labor of Elder Joseph Baysmore, with Four Collected Sermons, First: The Harmony of the Law and Gospel. Second: Subject of the Pure in Heart. Third: How We Were Made Sinners and How We Were Redeemed from Sin and Made Heirs of God by His Love. Fourth: The Confirmation of Christian Faith*. Weldon, N.C.: Harell's Printing House, 1887.

Blassingame, John, ed. *Slave Testimony: Two Centuries of Letters, Speeches, Interviews, and Autobiographies*. Baton Rouge: Louisiana State University Press, 1977.

Carter, Lawrence Edward, Jr., ed. *Walking Integrity: Benjamin Elijah Mays, Mentor to Martin Luther King, Jr.* Macon, Ga.: Mercer University Press, 1998.

Clemmons, Ithiel C. *Bishop C. H. Mason and the Roots of the Church of God in Christ, Centennial Edition*. Bakersfield, Calif.: Pneuma Life Publishing, 1996.

Colston, Freddie C., ed. *Dr. Benjamim E. Mays Speaks: Representative Speeches of a Great American Orator*. Lanham, Md.: University Press of America, 2002.

Cone, James H. *Black Theology and Black Power*. Maryknoll, N.Y.: Orbis, 1997. (First published in 1969 by Harper & Row.)

———. *A Black Theology of Liberation, Twentieth Anniversary Edition*. Maryknoll, N.Y.: Orbis, 2003. (First published in 1970 by J. B. Lippincott Company.)

———. *God of the Oppressed*. Maryknoll, N.Y.: Orbis, 1997. (First published in 1975 by Seabury.)

———. *Risks of Faith: The Emergence of a Black Theology of Liberation, 1968-1998*. Boston: Beacon, 1999.

Cone, James, and Gayraud Wilmore, eds. *Black Theology: A Documentary History, Volume One: 1966-1979*. 2nd ed. Maryknoll, N.Y.: Orbis, 1979.

Cone, James, and Gayraud Wilmore, eds. *Black Theology: A Documentary History, Volume Two: 1980-1992*. 2nd ed. Maryknoll, N.Y.: Orbis, 1993.

Dixie, Quinton Hosford, and Cornel West, eds. *The Courage to Hope: From Black Suffering to Human Redemption*. Boston: Beacon, 1999.

Equiano, Olaudah. *The Interesting Narrative of the Life of Olaudah Equiano, or Gustavas Vassa, the African*. In *Pioneers of the Black Atlantic: Five Slave Narratives from the Enlightenment, 1772-1815*. Edited by Henry Louis Gates Jr. and William L. Andrews. Washington, D.C.: Civitas, 1998.

Evans, James H. *We Have Been Believers: An African-American Systematic Theology*. Minneapolis: Fortress, 1992.

Evans, Tony. *Totally Saved: Understanding, Experiencing and Enjoying the Greatness of Your Salvation*. Chicago: Moody Press, 2002.

Ferry, Henry J. *Francis James Grimké: Portrait of a Black Puritan*. Ph.D. dissertation, Yale University, 1970.

Fields, Bruce L. *Introducing Black Theology: Three Crucial Questions for the Evangelical Church*. Grand Rapids: Baker Academic, 2001.

Foner, Eric. *Reconstruction: America's Unfinished Revolution*. New York: Harper & Row, 1998.

Frey, Sylvia R., and Betty Wood. *Come Shouting to Zion: African American Protestantism in the American South and British Caribbean to 1830*. Chapel Hill: University of North Carolina Press, 1998.

Gates, Henry Louise, Jr., and William L. Andrews, eds. *Pioneers of the Black Atlantic: Five Slave Narratives from the Enlightenment, 1772-1815*. Washington, D.C.: Civitas, 1998.

Genovese, Eugene D. *Roll, Jordan, Roll: The World the Slaves Made*. New York: Vintage Books, 1976.

George, Carol V. R. *Segregated Sabbaths: Richard Allen and the Rise of Independent Black Churches, 1760-1840*. New York: Oxford University Press, 1973.

Goff, James R., Jr., and Grant Wacker, eds. *Portraits of a Generation: Early Pentecostal*

Leaders. Fayetteville: University of Arkansas Press, 2002.

Gregory, James N. *The Southern Diaspora: How the Great Migrations of Black and White Southerners Transformed America.* Chapel Hill: University of North Carolina Press, 2005.

Hannah, John D. *Our Legacy: The History of Christian Doctrine.* Colorado Springs: NavPress, 2001.

Haynes, Stephen R. *Noah's Curse: The Biblical Justification of American Slavery.* New York: Oxford University Press, 2002.

Hill, Robert A., and Barbara Bair, eds. *Marcus Garvey: Life and Lessons.* Berkeley: University of California Press, 1987.

Holifield, E. Brooks. *Theology in America: Christian Thought from the Age of the Puritans to the Civil War.* New Haven, Conn.: Yale University Press, 2003.

Hood, Robert E. *Begrimed and Black: Christian Traditions on Blacks and Blackness.* Minneapolis: Fortress, 1994.

Hopkins, Dwight N. *Down, Up, and Over: Slave Religion and Black Theology.* Minneapolis: Fortress, 2000.

Hopkins, Dwight N., and George C. L. Cummings, eds. *Cut Loose Your Stammering Tongue: Black Theology in the Slave Narrative.* 2nd ed. Louisville, Ky.: Westminster John Knox Press, 2003.

Johnson, Clifton H., ed. *God Struck Me Dead: Voices of Ex-Slaves.* Cleveland, Ohio: Pilgrim Press, 1993. (First published in 1969 as *God Struck Me Dead: Religious Conversion Experiences and Autobiographies of Ex-Slaves* by the United Church Press.)

Jordan, Winthrop D. *White Over Black: American Attitudes Toward the Negro, 1550-1812.* Chapel Hill: University of North Carolina Press, 1968.

Kelsey, George D. *Racism and the Christian Understanding of Man.* New York: Charles Scribner's Sons, 1965.

Killian, Charles, ed. *Bishop Daniel Alexander Payne: Sermons and Addresses, 1853-1891.* New York: Arno Press, 1972.

Kulikoff, Allan. *Tobacco and Slaves: The Development of Southern Cultures in the Chesapeake, 1680-1800.* Chapel Hill: University of North Carolina Press, 1986.

Marrant, John. *Narrative of the Lord's Wonderful Dealings with John Marrant, a Black.* In *Pioneers of the Black Atlantic: Five Slave Narratives from the Enlightenment, 1772-1815.* Edited by Henry Louis Gates Jr. and William L. Andrews. Washington, D.C.: Civitas, 1998.

Mays, Benjamin E. *The Negro's God As Reflected in His Literature.* New York: Antheneum, 1973. (First published in 1938 by Chapman and Grimes.)

———. *Born to Rebel: An Autobiography.* Athens: University of Georgia Press, 2003.

Mellon, James, ed. *Bullwhip Days: The Slaves Remember.* New York: Grove Press, 1988.

Morris, Elias Camp. *Sermons, Addresses and Reminiscences and Important Correspon-*

dence, with a Picture Gallery of Eminent Ministers and Scholars. Nashville: National
   Baptist Publishing Board, 1901.

Newman, Richard, ed. *Black Preacher to White America: The Collected Writings of Lemuel
   Haynes, 1774-1833*. Brooklyn: Carlson, 1990.

Noll, Mark A. *America's God: From Jonathan Edwards to Abraham Lincoln*. New York:
   Oxford University Press, 2002.

———. *The Princeton Theology, 1812-1921: Scripture, Science, and Theological Method
   from Archibald Alexander to Benjamin Warfield*. Grand Rapids: Baker Academic,
   2001.

———. *A History of Christianity in the United States and Canada*. Grand Rapids: Eerdmans, 1992.

O'Neale, Sondra. *Jupiter Hammon and the Biblical Beginnings of African-American Literature*. Metuchen, N.J.: American Library Association, 1993.

Paris, Arthur E. *Black Pentecostalism: Southern Religion in an Urban World*. Amherst:
   University of Massachusetts Press, 1982.

Payne, Daniel Alexander. *Recollections of Seventy Years*. Nashville: AME Sunday
   School Union, 1888.

Pelikan, Jaroslav. *The Christian Tradition: A History of Development of Doctrine, Volume 1: The Emergence of the Catholic Tradition, 100-600*. Chicago: University of
   Chicago Press, 1971.

———. *The Christian Tradition: A History of Development of Doctrine, Volume 4: Reformation of Church and Dogma, 1300-1700*. Chicago: University of Chicago Press, 1984.

Piper, John, and Justin Taylor, eds. *A God-Entranced Vision of All Things: The Legacy of
   Jonathan Edwards*. Wheaton, Ill.: Crossway Books, 2004.

Raboteau, Albert J. *Canaan Land: A Religious History of African Americans*. New York:
   Oxford University Press, 2001.

———. *Slave Religion: The "Invisible Institution" in the Antebellum South*. New York:
   Oxford University Press, 1978.

Saillant, John. *Black Puritan, Black Republican: The Life and Thought of Lemuel Haynes,
   1753-1833*. New York: Oxford University Press, 2003.

Saucey, Robert. *Scripture: Its Power, Authority, and Relevance*. Nashville: Word Publishing, 2001.

Scott, William R., and William G. Shade, eds. *Upon These Shores: Themes in the African-
   American Experience, 1600 to the Present*. New York: Routledge, 2000.

Sernett, Milton C. *African American Religious History: A Documentary Witness*.
   Durham, N.C.: Duke University Press, 1999.

Shields, John, ed. *The Collected Works of Phillis Wheatley*. New York: Oxford University
   Press, 1988.

Simpson, George E. "Black Pentecostalism in the United States." In *Native American*

Religion and Black Protestantism. Edited by Martin E. Marty. Modern American Protestantism and Its World. Vol 9. New York: K. G. Sauer, 1993.

Smith, Luther E. *Howard Thurman: The Mystic as Prophet.* Richmond, Ind.: Friends United Press, 1991.

Strong, Douglas M. *They Walked in the Spirit: Personal Faith and Social Action in America.* Louisville, Ky.: Westminster John Knox Press, 1997.

Thurman, Howard. *The Growing Edge.* Richmond, Ind.: Friends United Press, 1956.

———. *The Creative Encounter: An Interpretation of Religion and the Social Witness.* Richmond, Ind.: Friends United Press, 1972. (First published in 1954 by Harper & Brothers.)

———. *Jesus and the Disinherited.* Boston: Beacon, 1976. (First published in 1949 by Abingdon Press.)

———. *Disciplines of the Spirit.* Richmond, Ind.: Friends United Press, 1977. (First published in 1963 by Harper and Row.)

———. *Temptations of Jesus.* Richmond, Ind.: Friends United Press, 1978. (First published in 1962 by Lawton Kennedy.)

———. *With Head and Heart: The Autobiography of Howard Thurman.* Orlando: Harcourt Brace, 1979.

Tillich, Paul. *Systematic Theology, Volume One.* Chicago: University of Chicago, 1951.

Tise, Larry. *Proslavery: A History of the Defense of Slavery in America, 1701-1840.* Athens: University of Georgia Press, 1987.

Turner, Henry McNeal. *Respect Black: The Writings and Speeches of Henry McNeal Turner,* compiled and edited by Edwin S. Redkey. New York: Arno Press, 1971.

Washington, Joseph R., Jr. *Black and White Power Subreption.* Boston: Beacon, 1969.

Wells, David F., and John D. Woodbridge, eds. *The Evangelicals: What They Believe, Who They Are, Where They Are Changing.* Grand Rapids: Baker, 1977.

Woodson, Carter G., ed. *The Works of Francis Grimké.* Washington, D.C.: Associated Publishers, 1942.

Workers of the Writers' Program of the Work Projects Administration in the State of Virginia. *The Negro in Virginia.* Winston-Salem, N.C.: John F. Blair, 1994.

Wright, Kai, ed. *The African-American Archive: The History of the Black Experience Through Documents.* New York: Leventhal, 2001.

Subject Index

Scripture Index